Word Power Made Simple

PETER FUNK

NONFICTION

It Pays to Enrich Your Word Power
Word Memory Power in 30 Days
Coeditor, *Word Power*
Coeditor, *Super Word Power*
Reader's Digest feature "It Pays to Enrich Your Word Power"
Coauthor, Japanese edition, *It Pays to Enrich Your Word Power*
Coauthor, Canadian edition, *It Pays to Enrich Your Word Power*
Coauthor, *Guide Book for the New Christian*
High Spirits
Coauthor, computer software program *Power of Words*

FICTION

My Six Loves
Love and Consequences

MARY FUNK

EDITOR AND EDITORIAL CONSULTANT

Coauthor, Canadian edition, *It Pays to Enrich Your Word Power*
Coauthor, Japanese edition, *It Pays to Enrich Your Word Power*
Coauthor, computer software program *Power of Words*

WORD POWER
MADE SIMPLE

Peter Funk and Mary Funk

A MADE SIMPLE BOOK
DOUBLEDAY
NEW YORK LONDON TORONTO SYDNEY AUCKLAND

A MADE SIMPLE BOOK
PUBLISHED BY DOUBLEDAY
a division of Bantam Doubleday Dell Publishing Group, Inc.
666 Fifth Avenue, New York, New York 10103

MADE SIMPLE and DOUBLEDAY are trademarks of Doubleday,
a division of Bantam Doubleday Dell Publishing Group, Inc.

Library of Congress Cataloging-in-Publication Data
Funk, Peter.
  Word power made simple.
  Includes index.
  1. Vocabulary. I. Funk, Mary. II. Title.
PE1449.F773 1986   428.1   85-13117
ISBN 0-385-19618-0

5   7   9   10   8   6

Contents

Contents

1

First Things First—How to Make This Book Work for You

It has been proved again and again that if you merely add new words to your vocabulary, this simple act in itself will enrich your entire life.

Power Words

aborigine	marauder
abscond	mellifluous
acrimonious	modus operandi
allege	neophyte
antithesis	nostrum
apprehend	omnipotent
biodegradable	ostensible
boor	pandemonium
buoyant	partisan
curtail	perspicacious
debacle	picayune
deft	propitiate
demagogue	recourse
docile	retrogressive
eschew	scrupulous
fecund	subservient
fiasco	tryst
homage	ubiquitous
insipid	ulterior
judicious	voracious
languid	xenophobic
literal	zealot
loath	

The Good News About Words

"A rich vocabulary is one of the most invaluable possessions of the leaders in every profession, in every commercial enterprise, and in every department of active living." These words of Wilfred Funk, a pioneer in modern vocabulary development, have been proved to be true.

The more precisely you use your words, the more likely you are to get the results you want.

With a greater understanding of words, you can make better decisions and evaluations. Success in school and your career is more certain when you have the words you need.

Because the new facts and words you absorb translate into brain growth, your mind has the ca-pacity to expand throughout your entire life. Scientists have come to the momentous conclusion that you can actually become smarter as you grow older. Increasing your *word power* is one of the surest and most enjoyable ways of expanding your *brainpower.*

When you use *Word Power Made Simple,* you will learn how:
- to increase your active vocabulary;
- to pick up new words constantly from reading;
- to develop an effective style of writing and reading;
- to recognize good usage and to develop it in yourself;
- to find the enjoyment and pleasure of increasing your vocabulary through word study.

How to Get the Most Out of This Book

Word Power Made Simple is divided into fifteen specialized chapters on different areas of vocabulary, usage, roots, synonyms, and other important topics in the development of your word dynamics.

At the beginning of each chapter you will find thirty power words of a general nature plus fifteen additional power words (except in Chapter 1) that are more specifically related to the topic of that particular chapter. All forty-five fall into the category of general vocabulary. Power words are incisive ones you will want to know. They form the basis of *Word Power Made Simple.* You will find them valuable in your daily life, helping you to speak, write, read, and understand more effectively.

Each chapter takes up one or more areas of our vocabulary and language, ending with a **summary** and an entertaining and immensely helpful **Word-Power Test** on many of the **power words.** You will find the answers at the end of each section of the test.

Finally, there are three review quizzes. You will find out quickly the words about which you are uncertain and will want to review.

When you have finished *Word Power Made Simple,* you are going to discover a major improvement in your understanding of words. We are sure you will experience a whole new enjoyment of them.

Doors that have been closed will open for further study of the intriguing English language.

In computer jargon, we have tried to make this book "user friendly."

Now that you know the layout of the book, go over the list of power words, using the dictionary, before you take each test. If you don't have a dictionary at the moment, you can use the one at the end of the book. It is based on the Doubleday Dictionary.

Word-Power Test

When you finish the games in this test, and in all the others in the following chapters, write your answers and scores on a separate piece of paper.

In this test and all others, the answer may require a plural answer although we only list the singular form.

I Pick the target word that describes the people in this game from the following words:

partisan, zealot, demagogue, aborigine, neophyte, boor.

1. "I've never seen anyone so rude and ill-mannered," Jane said. He's a . . . . . .
2. If an experienced person is a professional, a beginner is a . . . . . .
3. Someone who has just arrived in a country is a newcomer. But the earliest known inhabitants of a place are . . . . . .
4. The man is a political agitator, a . . . . . . seeking power by playing on the emotions and prejudices of the people.
5. Sometimes the . . . . . . in their fanatic pursuit of a goal exhaust you.
6. George Washington warned the nation against people who were uncritical and strong supporters of a person, a group, or a particular faction. Such people are . . . . . .

ANSWERS: **1.** boor; **2.** neophyte; **3.** aborigines; **4.** demagogue; **5.** zealots; **6.** partisan.

II Which is the word opposite in meaning to the following power words? Match the two columns.

1. perspicacious		**a.** picky
2. acrimonious		**b.** clumsy
3. insipid		**c.** dull
4. voracious		**d.** kind
5. deft		**e.** exciting
6. languid		**f.** vigorous

ANSWERS: **1.** c; **2.** d; **3.** e; **4.** a; **5.** b; **6.** f.

III Match the power word with the appropriate answer.

1. debacle	**a.** appeal for help in trouble
2. curtail	**b.** disaster
3. abscond	**c.** leave suddenly and secretively
4. recourse	**d.** present everywhere
5. ubiquitous	**e.** shun
6. eschew	**f.** cut short

ANSWERS: **1.** b; **2.** f; **3.** c; **4.** a; **5.** d; **6.** e.

IV Pick the word or phrase closest in meaning to the power word.

1. antithesis   A: unfriendliness. B: agreement. C: direct opposite.
2. buoyant   A: flat. B: extremely deep. C: able to float.
3. loath   A: unconcerned. B: hesitant. C: unwilling.
4. pandemonium   A: relating to a Greek god. B: great fear. C: wild uproar.
5. picayune   A: generous. B: sharp. C: petty.
6. fecund   A: fruitful. B: barren. C: weak.
7. docile   A: angry. B: easily managed. C: stubborn.
8. xenophobia   fear of A: snakes. B: spiders. C: strangers.

ANSWERS: **1.** C; **2.** C; **3.** C; **4.** C; **5.** C; **6.** A; **7.** B; **8.** C.

V Fill in the blank with the correct power word chosen from the following words:

literal, apprehend, marauder, judicious, fiasco, biodegradable.

1. By making products out of . . . . . . materials, we could reduce environmental pollution.
2. He lost the notes for his speech, he showed up late, and he knocked over the podium. The evening was a . . . . . .
3. A . . . . . . judge listens to the various arguments and considers the facts carefully.
4. The enemy . . . . . . burned houses and plundered the town.
5. The young man was advised he could . . . . . . a criminal with a citizen's arrest.
6. The author made a . . . . . . translation of

the story following the exact words of the original.

ANSWERS: **1.** biodegradable; **2.** fiasco; **3.** judicious; **4.** marauders; **5.** apprehend; **6.** literal.

VI Pick the word or phrase that best fits the meaning of the power word in the sentence, from the three selections below it.

1. During the **tryst** she accused him of infidelity.
   a. rehearsal for a play
   b. meeting
   c. dance
2. The **ostensible** object of the visit was to welcome the new neighbors, but they just wanted to see their house.
   a. polite
   b. apparent
   c. planned
3. The board members were **scrupulous** in their decisions.
   a. devious
   b. painstakingly honest
   c. pleasing
4. The **subservient** people allowed the demagogue absolute freedom.
   a. submissive
   b. uneducated
   c. impoverished
5. The polititian had a **nostrum** for every problem in the county.
   a. excellent solution
   b. cure-all, quack remedy
   c. an allotment
6. The blackmailer's **modus operandi** was to demand more than they could pay.
   a. criticism
   b. schedule
   c. manner of working

ANSWERS: **1.** b; **2.** b; **3.** b; **4.** a; **5.** b; **6.** c.

VII Which are true? Which are false?

1. A *mellifluous* sound is described as having great variety. True or false?
2. When you *propitiate* someone's anger, you increase it. True or false?
3. If civilization is *retrogressive,* it is moving backward. True or false?
4. *Ulterior* motives are as clear as glass. True or false?
5. When the witness *alleged* the papers were stolen, she asserted this was true but had no proof. True or false?
6. She took control and ran the large company as if she were *omnipotent.* True or false?

ANSWERS: **1.** false; **2.** false; **3.** true; **4.** false; **5.** true; **6.** true.

Your Score
44–40 .... Word master
39–27 .... Very good
26–20 .... Fair

2

Dik shuh ner eez

"As sheer casual reading matter, I still find the English dictionary the most interesting book in our language."—Albert Jay Nock.

Power Words

abet	panorama
assuage	predatory
astute	remorse
auspicious	ribald
baroque	sinecure
cursory	statutory
definitive	subtle
denizen	taciturn
extricate	tenuous
ferret out	unctuous
innocuous	unique
latent	vacuous
mawkish	whimsical
nuance	windfall
opaque	wry

Special Words on Words

allude	extrapolate
ambiguous	glossary
anthology	graphic
archaic	lexicon
coherent	misnomer
colloquial	obsolete
compendium	paraphrase
etymology	

General Dictionaries

A list of dictionaries and reference books does not read like a best-selling novel. So bear with us in this chapter. The reason for it is that people ask us frequently to recommend a "good" dictionary. So this is what we have done in this chapter.

Dictionaries are a necessity for anyone even remotely interested in words and successful living. A dictionary is probably one of the most important books you will ever buy. In its vast collection of words, you will find a repository of the world's history, of science, life-styles, business. Virtually all of what we know about the world and its inhabitants is found in the words listed in the various general and specialized dictionaries.

Buy a dictionary if you don't have one. If you have an old one, give it to a flea market. Let someone else buy an unusable antique. What you don't want are antiquated definitions. And if you bring home one of the cheap varieties, you deserve to have knowledgeable friends raise an eyebrow when you pull it out. Having a poor dictionary is just about as bad as not having any dictionary. Get yourself a good one. The major dictionary publishers have paperback versions. And so, if price is a consideration, they've made it possible to have the best for a modest sum.

Here is a list of the reputable dictionaries. First, however, remember that the name Webster is a generic name (juh NER ik) and refers to a whole class or type and is not protected by a trademark. Anyone can use the word Webster. So, just because you see Webster on a dictionary does *not* mean it is well regarded. Get a "Webster's" from a reputable publisher.

1. Desk Dictionaries

• Webster's New World Dictionary of the American Language (William Collins + World Publishing Co., Inc.). A splendid, up-to-date dictionary with excellent etymologies. Used by the New York *Times* as the house desk dictionary.

• Webster's New Collegiate Dictionary (Merriam-Webster Inc.).

• The American Heritage Dictionary of the English Language (Houghton Mifflin Co., Inc.).

• Random House Dictionary of the English Language.

• Funk & Wagnalls Standard Dictionary. The most comprehensive and up-to-date paperback dictionary.

• Oxford American Dictionary (Oxford University Press). Concise meanings, and excellent pronunciation style.

• Doubleday publishes Webster Illustrated Contemporary Dictionary. Well-organized, easy-to-read, concise definitions. In addition, this dictionary has biographies of important people, grammar and usage, spelling, business law and wills, and much more. It is a miniencyclopedia.

• Collins English Dictionary is from England and is among the authors' favorites. The definitions and etymologies are first-rate. The only drawback is that the pronunciation relies on the International Phonetic Alphabet, useful only to orthographic experts.

• Harper & Row publishes various dictionaries.

To help you make a selection, we thought we might list some of the items we look for.

1. Check the publishing date. Our language is changing; an up-to-date dictionary is going to list the most recent additions.

2. Are the definitions full? Are there examples of usage when the word is somewhat more difficult?

3. Are the pronunciations relatively clear and simple?

4. What about origins? Not all dictionaries give etymology, but it is not only interesting, it may also help you to remember the word and to have a better understanding of it.

5. Are there usage notes? That is, some words may be confused with a look-alike or a sound-alike.

6. Are there idiomatic phrases for certain words such as "business is business" and the like?

7. Some dictionaries do a splendid job of listing and defining synonyms.

8. Some dictionaries have a wealth of information about language in the Introduction. Or they will have a section at the end giving instructions on how to write letters and address people, lists of weights and measures, and similar information.

2. Unabridged Dictionaries

Like language, most of us take dictionaries for granted. We not only relish the satisfaction of searching for and finding the meanings of troublesome words, but also the fun of browsing through the closely packed pages.

What about *pandiculation?* You and I probably *pandiculate* almost every day at some point. According to the Oxford English Dictionary, pandiculation is "An instinctive movement, consisting in the extension of the legs, the raising and stretching of the arms, and the throwing back of the head and trunk, accompanied by yawning; it occurs before and after sleeping. Sometimes loosely used for yawning." I'm glad to have a name for what I do naturally!

You don't hear *flibbertigibbet* being used today. A hundred years ago it was common parlance. It's

fun just to say the word, and its sound seems almost to fit its meaning: an irresponsible or silly person. Its original meaning of "gossip" is now **archaic.** Linguistically, **archaic** means no longer in common use. Words often have their heyday and then gradually fade out of the language.

You don't have to settle for just one dictionary. Many families have several. The **desk dictionaries** are fine as far as they go, but they are limited by size. Out of necessity, they leave out words, the definitions are shorter, and there are not many illustrations of usage.

And so we come to that most satisfying of all reference books, the **unabridged** dictionary. What a plethora of material! The largest American ones have more than 600,000 entries. The Oxford English Dictionary contains many more, as it includes the obsolete and the archaic.

Arranged in alphabetical order, the ones to consider are

• New Standard Dictionary of the English Language (Funk and Wagnalls);

• The Random House Dictionary of the English Language (Random House);

• The Oxford English Dictionary (Oxford University Press). This one deserves special mention. You can buy the dictionary either in sixteen volumes including four supplements to update it, or as two volumes read with the aid of a magnifying glass. The supplements would be additional. The OED, as it is known, is one of the great dictionaries of the world. It is expensive. But, for a word buff, worth every penny. When you are at your public library, scan it for a few moments. Among other fascinating items, you will find the date at which a word first appeared in English print (a feature also of Webster's New Collegiate Dictionary);

• Webster's New World Dictionary of the American Language (Collins + World);

• Webster's Third International Dictionary (Merriam-Webster Inc.).

Special Dictionaries

Synonyms, Antonyms, and Usage

• Webster's New Dictionary of Synonyms (Merriam-Webster Inc.). This book compares similar words carefully, giving antonyms as well as synonyms. Each synonym is used in an illustrative sentence.

• Roget's International Thesaurus (Harper & Row). An indispensable book for anyone writing—

GUIDE WORDS ————

are shown in large type at the top of each page and indicate the first and last entries on that page.

slippery

slip·per·y (slip′ər·ē) *adj.* **·per·i·er, ·per·i·est 1** Having a surface so smooth that bodies slip or slide easily on it. **2** That evades one's grasp; elusive. **3** Unreliable; tricky. **—slip′per·i·ness** *n.*

slippery elm 1 A species of small elm with mucilaginous inner bark. **2** Its wood or inner bark.

slip·shod (slip′shod′) *adj.* **1** Wearing shoes or slippers down at the heels. **2** Slovenly; sloppy. **3** Performed carelessly: *slipshod* work.

SYLLABICATION ————

is indicated by syllabic dots dividing main entry words.

slip·stream (slip′strēm′) *n.* *Aeron.* The stream of air driven backwards by the propeller of an aircraft.

slip-up (slip′up′) *n. Informal* A mistake; error.

slit (slit) *n.* A relatively straight cut or a long, narrow opening. **—v.t. slit, slit·ting 1** To make a long incision in; slash. **2** To cut lengthwise into strips. **3** To sever. [ME *slitten*] **—slit′ter** *n.*

slith·er (slith′ər) *v.i.* **1** To slide; slip, as on a loose surface. **2** To glide, as a snake. **—v.t. 3** To cause to slither. **—n.** A sinuous, gliding movement. [< OE *slidrian*] **—slith′er·y** *adj.*

MAIN ENTRY ————

is shown in boldface and consists of a word, phrase, abbreviation, prefix, suffix, or combining form.

sliv·er (sliv′ər) *n.* **1** A slender piece, as of wood, cut or torn off lengthwise; a splinter. **2** Corded textile fibers drawn into a fleecy strand. **—v.t. & v.i.** To cut or be split into long thin pieces. [< ME *sliven* to cleave] **—sliv′er·er** *n.*

slob (slob) *n.* **1** Mud; mire. **2** *Slang* A careless or unclean person. [< Ir. *slab*]

PRONUNCIATION ————

is shown in parenthesis in phonetic equivalent.

slob·ber (slob′ər) *v.t.* **1** To wet with liquids oozing from the mouth. **2** To shed or spill, as liquid food, in eating. **—v.i. 3** To drivel; slaver. **4** To talk or act gushingly. **—n. 1** Liquid spilled as from the mouth. **2** Gushing, sentimental talk. [ME *sloberen*] **—slob′ber·er** *n.* **—slob′ber·y** *adj.*

sloe (slō) *n.* **1** A small, plumlike, astringent fruit. **2** The shrub that bears it; the blackthorn. [< OE *slā*]

sloe gin A cordial with a gin base, flavored with sloes.

INFLECTED FORMS ————

are given when there is an irregularity of form. They consist of the past and present participles of verbs, the plural of nouns, and the comparative and superlative of adjectives and adverbs.

slog (slog) *v.t. & v.i.* **slogged, slog·ging 1** To slug, as a pugilist. **2** To plod (one's way). **—n.** A heavy blow. [?] **—slog′ger** *n.*

slo·gan (slō′gən) *n.* **1** A catchword or motto adopted by a political party, advertiser, etc. **2** A battle or rallying cry. [< Scot. Gael. *sluagh* army + *gairm* yell]

slo·gan·eer (slō′gə·nir′) *Informal n.* One who coins or uses slogans. **—v.i.** To coin or use slogans.

USAGE ————

information is included where necessary.

sloop (slōōp) *n.* A small sailboat with a single mast and at least one jib. [< Du. *sloep*]

HOMOGRAPHS ————

are words identical in spelling but having different meanings and origins and, sometimes, pronunciations. They are differentiated by superior figures.

slop¹ (slop) *v.* **slopped, slop·ping** *v.i.* **1** To splash or spill. **2** To walk or move through slush. **—v.t. 3** To cause (a liquid) to spill or splash. **4** To feed (a domestic animal) with slops. **—slop over 1** To overflow and splash. **2** *Slang* To show too much zeal, emotion, etc. **—n. 1** Slush or watery mud. **2** An unappetizing liquid or watery food. **3** *pl.* Refuse liquid. **4** *pl.* Waste food or swill. [< ME *sloppe* mud]

slop² (slop) **1** A loose outer garment, as a smock. **2** *pl.* Articles of clothing and other merchandise sold to sailors on shipboard. [ME *sloppe*]

Sloop

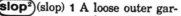

slug

an organization, or a place in a sequence. —*v.t.* **slot·ted, slot·ting** To cut a slot or slots in. [<OF *esclot* the hollow between the breasts]

sloth (slôth, slōth, sloth) *n.* **1** Disinclination to exertion; laziness. **2** Any of several slow-moving, arboreal mammals of South America. [<SLOW]

sloth·ful (slôth′fəl, slōth′-, sloth′-) *adj.* Inclined to or characterized by sloth. —**sloth′ful·ly** *adv.* —**sloth′ful·ness** *n.* —**Syn.** lazy, indolent, sluggish, shiftless.

slot machine A vending machine or gambling machine having a slot in which a coin is dropped to cause operation.

Three-toed sloth

slouch (slouch) *v.i.* **1** To have a downcast or drooping gait, look, or posture. **2** To hang or droop carelessly. —*n.* **1** A drooping movement or appearance caused by depression or carelessness. **2** An awkward or incompetent person. [?] —**slouch′y** *adj.* (·**i·er,** ·**i·est**) —**slouch′i·ly** *adv.* —**slouch′i·ness** *n.*

slough[1] (slou; slōō *esp. for def.* 2) *n.* **1** A place of deep mud or mire. **2** A stagnant swamp, backwater, etc. **3** A state of great despair or degradation. [<OE *slōh*] —**slough′y** *adj.*

slough[2] (sluf) *n.* **1** Dead tissue separated and thrown off from living tissue. **2** The skin of a serpent that has been or is about to be shed. —*v.t.* **1** To cast off; shed. **2** To discard; shed, as a habit or a growth. —*v.i.* **3** To be cast off. **4** To cast off a slough or tissue. [ME *slouh*] —**slough′y** *adj.*

Slo·vak (slō′väk, slō′vak) *n.* **1** One of a Slavic people of NW Hungary and parts of Moravia. **2** The language spoken by the Slovaks. —*adj.* Of or pertaining to the Slovaks or to their language. Also **Slo·vak′i·an.**

slov·en (sluv′ən) *n.* One who is habitually untidy, careless, or dirty. [ME *sloveyn*]

Slo·vene (slō′vēn, slō·vēn′) *n.* One of a group of s Slavs now living in NW Yugoslavia. —*adj.* Of or pertaining to the Slovenes or to their language. —**Slo·ve′ni·an** *(adj., n.)*

slov·en·ly (sluv′ən·lē) *adj.* ·**li·er,** ·**li·est** Untidy and careless in appearance, work, habits, etc. —*adv.* In a slovenly manner. —**slov′en·li·ness** *n.*

slow (slō) *adj.* **1** Taking a long time to move, perform, or occur. **2** Behind the standard time: said of a timepiece. **3** Not hasty: *slow* to anger. **4** Dull in comprehending: a *slow* student. **5** Uninteresting; tedious: a *slow* drama. **6** Denoting a condition of a racetrack that retards the horses′ speed. **7** Heating or burning slowly; low: a *slow* flame. **8** Not brisk; slack: Business is *slow*. —*v.t.* & *v.i.* To make or become slow or slower: often with *up* or *down*. —*adv.* In a slow manner. [<OE *slāw*] —**slow′ly** *adv.* —**slow′ness** *n.*

slow-mo·tion (slō′mō′shən) *adj.* **1** Moving or acting at less than normal speed. **2** Denoting a television or motion picture filmed at greater than standard speed so that the action appears slow in normal projection.

sludge (sluj) *n.* **1** Soft, water-soaked mud. **2** A slush of snow or broken or half-formed ice. **3** Muddy or pasty refuse, sediment, etc. [?] —**sludg′y** *adj.* (·**i·er,** ·**i·est**)

slue[1] (slōō) *v.* **slued, slu·ing** *v.t.* **1** To cause to swing, slide, or skid to the side. **2** To cause to twist or turn. —*v.i.* **3** To

DEFINITION

is the meaning. The order in which the different senses of the word are listed is based on frequency of use.

ILLUSTRATION

is to clarify the definition.

RUN-ON ENTRY

consists of words derived from the main entry by addition or replacement of a suffix. They are syllabified and stressed where needed.

ETYMOLOGY

is indicated in brackets following the definition. It gives the origin of the word.

PARTS OF SPEECH

follow the pronunciation. The labels, in italics, are abbreviated as follows: n. (noun), v. (verb transitive), v.i. (verb intransitive), adj. (adjective), adv. (adverb), prep. (preposition), conj. (conjunction), and interj. (interjection).

letters or otherwise. The antonyms and synonyms are carefully grouped according to subject matter.

• The Doubleday Roget's Thesaurus in Dictionary Form (Doubleday & Co., Inc.). The target words are listed from A to Z with synonyms and antonyms listed under each one. By far the quickest and easiest one to use.

Other Specialized Dictionaries and Vocabulary Builders, listed alphabetically:

• The Barnhart Dictionary of New English Words Since 1963 (Barnhart/Harper & Row, two volumes). An important and fascinating series. Covers all the technical, slang, jargon, and candidates for the general dictionaries. Buy it if you can.

• Bernstein's Reverse Dictionary (Quadrangle Books). If a word is on the tip of your tongue, but you can't pull it out, this book will help. An interesting approach.

• A Dictionary of Contemporary American Usage, by Bergen Evans and Cornelia Evans (Harper & Row). A helpful compendium of information, well written and authoritative.

• Harper's Dictionary of Contemporary Usage, by William Morris and Mary Morris (Harper & Row). A panel of experts in consensus, though not always 100 percent, guides you to using your words well. Often amusing reading as well as instructive. One of the best of its kind.

• It Pays to Increase Your Word Power, by Peter Funk (Bantam Books). A vigorous vocabulary builder with interesting and helpful information on words and language.

• Success with Words; A Guide to the American Language (Reader's Digest Association Press, Inc.). Up-to-date; easy to read; covers an amazing amount of information including regional dialects, black English, words from foreign countries adopted by Americans, as well as discussions on words and usage.

• Word Memory Power in 30 Days, by Peter Funk and Barry Tarshis (Dell). The book, easy to use and work with, combines memory techniques and expanded information on selected and important words.

• Word Power, by Peter Funk (Warner/Network for Learning). A forty-five-minute cassette on techniques to build a stronger vocabulary. You can use it in your car or at home.

• Word Origins and Their Romantic Stories, by Wilfred Funk (Harper & Row). One of the most enchanting books concerning the origins of words. Each one is a story. Good bedtime reading!

Now, What Was That Word Again?

Using a dictionary is basic, but what about remembering that word you've just looked up?

All of us, at any age, experience some difficulty in remembering the new words we encounter. But there are ways to get around this sometime problem.

First of all, if you find yourself without a dictionary at some point, try to work out the word's meaning in **context**. The Oxford American Dictionary describes **context** as "The words that come before and after a particular word or phrase that help to define its meaning."

In other words, try to get an inkling of what the sentence means and see if you can work out the meaning of the word from the meaning of the sentence. In any case, mark the word to look up later. If it's a newspaper, tear out the section and save it. Later:

1. Write down the word on a 3 × 5 card.
2. Give its pronunciation.
3. Note the word's origin, for sometimes this can be a help to the memory. Also, some origins are fascinating. We have fun with origins in another section of this book.
4. Write down the meaning. Sometimes there are more meanings than one you will want to know.
5. Write the sentence in which the word appears. But be alert, because sometimes writers misuse words. You may have to write your own or look in the unabridged dictionary for a usage example.
6. Keep the cards in alphabetical order.
7. Make a practice of looking at them frequently. Don't take too many at a time; it's better to take one word a day and overuse it so it sticks in your memory. Or put the card in your mirror or wherever you'll see it. Periodically review your words to see if you are using them. Our experience is, *Use* them or *lose* them.
8. This system works!

Points to Remember

1. A good, modern abridged (desk) dictionary is a must. Avoid, as if a virus, outdated, inauthentic dictionaries.

2. Read the introductory matter of dictionaries. You will learn a lot about language per se as well as the reference book you are about to use.

3. When you need more definitive information concerning a word, consult the unabridged dictionary.

4. If you have an opportunity, look over the list

of special books. You may want to buy some for your use. The list here is only a partial one, but it is a good starter. The money we spend on one dinner at a restaurant will buy any one of those books, and it will last you many years, rather than just one evening.

Word-Power Test

Before you try this series of quizzes, you will want to look up the words you are not certain of in the list at the beginning of this chapter.

I You may find this quiz particularly difficult, but it will let you find out just how well you do know the word. We give the dictionary definition of a word. Choose the power word you think fits.

1. Vividly effective and detailed
2. Of, like, or characteristic of a style of art, architecture, and music that flourished in sixteenth- and seventeenth-century Europe, characterized by elaborate and profuse ornamentation
3. Rapid and superficial; hasty; with no attention to detail
4. To search out by careful investigation
5. A shade of difference in tone or color or in anything perceptible to the mind
6. Pertaining to a legislative enactment (a law)

ANSWERS: **1.** graphic; **2.** baroque; **3.** cursory; **4.** ferret out; **5.** nuance; **6.** statutory.

II Find the word or phrase closest in meaning to the given word.

1. paraphrase   A: a restatement of the meaning of a passage, work, etc. B: roundabout way of saying something. C: afterthought.
2. extrapolate   A: to estimate or infer beyond facts. B: use too many words. C: examine page by page.
3. archaic   A: difficult to understand. B: about public records. C: belonging to a former period.
4. obsolete   A: slangy or informal. B: out of fashion. C: new.
5. glossary   A: list of technical words. B: frontispiece. C: table of contents.
6. lexicon   A: vocabulary specific to a subject or author. B: many-sided geometric figure. C: simplified spelling list.
7. compendium   A: long, heavy book. B: brief, comprehensive summary. C: comparison of two works.
8. anthology   A: research into the past. B: an analysis. C: collection of selected writings.

9. coherent   A: at the same time. B: logically consistent. C: harmonious.

ANSWERS: **1.** A; **2.** A; **3.** C; **4.** B; **5.** A; **6.** A; **7.** B; **8.** C; **9.** B.

III Pick the power word from the following list that fits the description:

wry, mawkish, whimsical, ribald, predatory, astute.

1. Helen Von Gipper, the legendary field-hockey coach, is a shrewd and sagacious judge of young athletes. Gipper is . . . . . .
2. Our cat is so laid-back and kindly, he refuses to catch mice or moles. I wish he were what most other cats are—that is, ...
3. Here I was, a young girl, walking down the street, minding my own business, when the construction workers began making those coarse, offensive, and indecent jokes. The humor was . . . . . .
4. Poor old Frank. Give him one beer and he gets all teary-eyed and foolishly sentimental when he thinks of the "good old days" at college. Frank is . . . . . .
5. We never knew what my aunt would do next— wearing her fanciest dress when she went shopping, sneakers to church, lemon *and* cream with her tea. She had many odd notions and fancies. She was what we call . . . . . .
6. Though he smiled, his lips and face twisted in a kind of grimace, so I knew he was displeased with my newest concoction: a peanut butter omelet. You might describe the expression on his face as . . . . . .

ANSWERS: **1.** astute; **2.** predatory; **3.** ribald; **4.** mawkish; **5.** whimsical; **6.** wry.

IV Answer *yes* or *no* to each question.

1. You propose to the love of your life and she gives you an *ambiguous* answer. Are you happy about that? Yes or no?
2. When you *extricate* yourself from a sticky situation, you are in even more trouble. Yes or no?
3. Do you believe that a speech by the President of the United States of America should be *colloquial?* Yes or no?
4. If offered, do you believe most people would accept a *sinecure?* Probably yes, probably no?
5. When Harry introduced me to his beautiful date, he confided she had a *vacuous* mind. Did he mean she was intelligent and her mind filled with information? Yes or no?

6. Are you absolutely positive that *etymology* is the study of words and not insects? Yes or no?

ANSWERS: **1.** no; **2.** no; **3.** no; **4.** yes; **5.** no; **6.** yes.

V Pick the sentence a, b, or c that corresponds to the numbered sentence.

1. The woman tried to *assuage* her distraught friend by strumming a familiar tune on her guitar.
   a. She tried to interest her in music.
   b. She thought some exciting tune might distract her friend.
   c. She tried to quiet her friend.

2. When they cast shadows on the rocks, the *denizens* of the deepest water make interesting subject material for photography.
   a. Old shipwrecks in deep water make unusual photographs.
   b. Old shoes, tires, and fishing rods lost in deep water are excellent material for modern photography.
   c. Creatures in the depths of the ocean, photographed skillfully, will make fine pictures.

3. Though the man seemed *innocuous* as he wandered down the street, he proved not to be.
   a. He seemed dreamy.
   b. He seemed lost.
   c. He seemed harmless.

4. No one thought the Queen had enough *latent* power to quell the revolt.
   a. Her authority seemed questionable.
   b. Most of the Army had deserted to the revolutionaries.
   c. The Navy seemed insufficient.

5. One sparkling morning, we saw a mist from the river winding through the valley, creating an unforgettable *panorama* from our window high on the mountainside.
   a. It gave the final evidence of pollution.
   b. The mist was filled with multicolored reflections from the sun.
   c. The extensive view was memorable.

6. Their *remorse* for their part in the crime remained.
   a. They managed to keep the money.
   b. They were constantly nagged by their consciences.
   c. They concealed the evidence so well no one would ever find it.

ANSWERS: **1.** c; **2.** c; **3.** c; **4.** a; **5.** c; **6.** b.

VI Match the power word with the appropriate answer.

1. unique	**a.** conclusive; final
2. tenuous	**b.** wrongly applied name
3. definitive	**c.** having no equal
4. windfall	**d.** unexpected piece of good luck
5. misnomer	**e.** refer to indirectly
6. allude	**f.** thin; insubstantial

ANSWERS: **1.** c; **2.** f; **3.** a; **4.** d; **5.** b; **6.** e.

VII Fill the blank spaces in the sentence with the correct words from the following selection:

subtle, taciturn, opaque, abetting, auspicious, unctuous.

1. Tommy, the computer whiz kid, didn't realize he was . . . . his friend Joe in a crime when they broke into the research company's data bank.

2. Frances felt at last she'd win the beauty contest, since all the . . . . . . signs of success were there.

3. The cavernous room was dark and gloomy, for the high, ... windows kept out the light.

4. (Both blank spaces contain the same word, which has several meanings.) We hid in the dark corner. When she walked by, we could just barely catch the faint, ... fragrance of her perfume. "Ah! I recognize the perfume and who the person is who wears it," my detective friend said, his . . . . mind putting the facts together; "I know now who committed the murder."

5. "So maybe your dog does talk," the theatrical agent said. "The trouble is, he only says a few words at a time. He's too . . . . . . We can't use him."

6. The . . . . . . ambassador, bowing and smiling repeatedly, assured the President in soothing, persuasive words that his country had only peaceful intentions.

ANSWERS: **1.** abetting; **2.** auspicious; **3.** opaque; **4.** subtle, subtle (each blank in this sentence uses the same word, using a subtle difference in meaning); **5.** taciturn; **6.** unctuous.

Your Score
45–40 correct . . . . . . Word master
39–27 correct . . . . . . Word craftsman
26–20 correct . . . . . . Word novice

3

So You Want People to Hear You!

Like Eliza Doolittle, in George Bernard Shaw's play *Pygmalion*, you might improve your life by improving your speech habits.

Power Words

acumen	mendacious
adamant	mode
banal	onerous
blatant	parable
cajole	promulgate
concise	querulous
dour	sagacious
erudite	thwart
expiate	uncouth
fatuous	ungainly
flamboyant	utilitarian
gingerly	vagary
ineffable	valid
jaunty	vapid
levity	vertigo

Special Words Concerning "How We Use Words"

captious	plausible
delineate	prolix
discursive	remonstrate
ephemeral	strident
lampoon	tacit
nebulous	truncate
obdurate	tumid

Remember Eliza Doolittle, in the musical *My Fair Lady?* She was based on George Bernard Shaw's *Pygmalion.* At first she spoke with a cockney accent using the street vernacular. Her mentor, Professor Higgins, regarded her language as vulgar. He knew he would never get this pretty girl out of her environment unless she learned to speak properly. The professor vowed that by altering her speech habits he would change her life.

After a period of relentless work, he proved his point when he introduced her at a fashionable party. The magical moment swept over her. Everyone thought she belonged to royalty because of the way she used and pronounced her words. Though the play may be only a story, it is based on a deep linguistic truth.

As people tend to judge us by our clothes, they will also make certain decisions about us based on the way we speak and write.

For example, to go to work in an office in a T-shirt, cut-off jeans, and bare feet is certainly the exception, rather than the rule. Nor it is normal to go to a very casual party dressed in a three-piece suit or a formal dress. We try to fit our clothes to the circumstances. We treat our language usage in much the same way.

Over the past five hundred years or so, English has more or less settled into certain levels of usage in the following descending order: (1) standard, or formal; (2) informal, or colloquial (*col-*, an alteration of *con-*, "with," and *loquor*, "to speak"); (3) slang; (4) jargon and cant (the slang and technical vocabulary or shoptalk of a particular group such as lawyers, doctors, astronauts, thieves et al.); (5) nonstandard or substandard (words and phrases such as "ain't" and "can't hardly ever").

These levels frequently overlap, of course, because our language is not fixed by some authority. It is the result of a worldwide unofficial consensus about the way language should be used. The public thinks of a dictionary as an arbiter of language. It is not. It merely records the way people speak now.

Levels, however, are a helpful guide through the thickets of usage—of when and where. The following are a few thoughts about these various levels of usage, as **Standard English, colloquial, substandard,** and language that tends to be **pompous.**

Standard Language (Formal)

This is language dressed up in its Sunday best. It's been defined as the "prestige English." When do we use it? Tonight listen to a TV or radio newscast. Chances are that most of it will be delivered in **Standard English.** Business letters, reports, the majority of speeches, magazine articles, textbooks, and the like utilize **Standard English.** And most of the time, **Standard English** is clearer, and more explicit and descriptive, than slang or jargon and, therefore, especially important to us. The vast majority of words used to communicate our thoughts and feelings belong to this level.

The following write-up, by Pamela Fiori, of a hotel along the Amalfi coast in Italy appeared in *Travel and Leisure*. It's an example of **Standard English.**

"All the guests at the San Pietro seemed to be on honeymoons, whether first, second or 25th. The crowd—primarily Italian, British, German and American—was sophisticated and decidedly un-snobbish. There were even a few celebrities on view. A famous producer, his wife and friends stopped by for dinner while their chartered yacht lay anchored in the harbor. Two well-known actors arrived the day we left. Another star was there but, for some reason, stayed in her room most of the time. Nobody asked for autographs—probably too busy having their own good time."

Colloquial Usage

Here is our everyday, natural speech we wake up with and end the day with. We use it to write personal letters, to talk to ourselves or to others, and conduct our mundane affairs. We use **colloquial** language 90 percent of the time. It is a more relaxed and informal English.

Bergen and Cornelia Evans, in A Dictionary of Contemporary American Usage, write: "It used to be said that colloquial English was like a good business suit and literary English like a formal dress. The analogy still holds. But one should remember that times have changed, that a good business suit is seldom out of place, and that formal dress, where it is not required—at a picnic, for example—may be ridiculous."

Let's take another look at that honeymoon Shangri-la from the viewpoint of a friend telling you about the Hotel San Pietro.

"Hey, Jane. Bob and I just got back from a fabulous honeymoon at a place in Italy. It's called San Pietro. It's loaded with atmosphere. And everyone else seemed to be on a honeymoon also. I guess some could have been on their 25th! People from all over—Italy, England, Germany, even some of us from America. And no one was at all snobby. There were some famous people there too. A producer had this huge yacht, and he and his friends ate dinner at the hotel. And then there were some movie stars. But, you know, no one asked for auto-

graphs. I guess we were all too busy doing our own thing."

If you were writing a letter to the same friend, you could certainly express your thoughts in an equally informal manner.

Such words as *great* for something impressive, *nice* for whatever is pleasant, *funny* when you mean strange, *dumb* for stupid, or fillers such as *kind of, sort of* and such contractions as *isn't, aren't* and the like are **colloquial,** and all right, up to a point.

The snare of informal language, however, is that we can become lazy with our vocabulary, opting for what seems to be the easy word, rather than the more accurate one. This can create something of a ripple effect. Though we may not realize it, our thoughts become more nebulous. We can't really describe clearly what we think and feel, and we tend to become discursive.

A woman with marital difficulties said: "I'm going from pillar to post. I'm like a bouncing ball." What did she mean exactly? We have a sense of the way she *feels* but nothing that describes the reality of her situation. And she goes around and around the same problem year after year, frustrated and complaining. One of her problems is that, because she can't describe what is happening to her verbally, she doesn't know how to resolve her situation.

Pomposity

What a descriptive word! Doesn't it sound as though it's about to blow off the page? Pompous writing or speaking is a misunderstood concept of formal English, and its style is apt to be turgid. It's a way of trying to impress people, or simply to fool them with high-sounding words. But the writer ends up looking foolish. It's just another form of substandard expression, and you will find too much of it in bureaucratic-type writing. Dr. Bunk might expound in the following way:

"The luxurious ambience of this exotic setting, which we chanced upon during our desultory peregrination south along the Amalfi Coast, is found in the Hotel San Pietro, a charming edifice. All the guests seemed to be on a nuptial holiday, whether the first or the 25th. The place had a number of luminaries who were not at all condescending. Among the distingué guests was a producer with his entourage, who came in from their palatial yacht and dined at the hotel . . ." and so forth!

Substandard Usage

And finally there is the cellar-floor level, of sub-standard and taboo words. Most of us know them, but we don't use them, because we don't want to appear illiterate or vulgar. People who rely on such words regularly usually have a limited vocabulary or are simply using them for shock value.

If one of Eliza Doolittle's American peers came back from a visit to San Pietro—if they let him in there in the first place—perhaps he'd say something like this: "Hey man! Those guys at Saint Pizza's do things right. People from all over the place. A lot of them on their honeymoon. We had a **bleeping** good time, I'll tell you that. Some of them thought they were **bleeping** famous, but they didn't bother us. Some guy had this big **bleeping** yacht out there and came in with his buddies to eat. Couple of Hollywood broads. One didn't come out while we were there. Scared I'd probably **bleep** her. **Bleep**, man, you should've been with us." Something like that, with whatever slang is in season.

The bleeped-out words and the informal phrases and words aren't "bad." There are no "bad" words as such. All words are born equal. But, for various reasons, they are out of mainstream usage. Most of the time, they have limited meanings and give an ambiguous and faulty picture of a situation. And they mark the speaker as being ignorant.

Slang

Slang did not originate with Americans—it's always been a part of language. Americans, however, seem to have a genius for looking at things and situations in a new way, often coming up with a colorful, vivid, or witty description we call **slang**.

Think of the expressions that have become a part of the daily fabric of language just within the past few years: *hang-up, to hack it, greenmail, bottom line, off the wall, kinky, to blow your mind, gut reaction, grass, to flip out.* Some of these may last. Others will fade away. But all have a sense of energy and paint word pictures.

"American slang is one of the success stories of the English language. There are probably some 35,000 expressions that are, or once were, American slang. Along with baseball, apple pie, supermarkets and jeans, our slang seems to symbolize America, and some of its most interesting and popular terms have spread the globe. Yet, many Americans aren't sure whether, or when, slang can be used as an acceptable part of their speech, whether they will be criticized for using it, or whether it might not indeed threaten the language and its clarity." (*Success with Words,* Reader's Digest Association, Inc., 1983)

By all means, use slang. It's virtually impossible to keep from doing so. In informal situations, slang can add flavor to your conversation and writing. But don't overuse it, and be chary in selection.

A lot of slang, however, is faddish and short-lived. It can also be dull, overworked, and trite. The words are not always the most picturesque or descriptive. Too often, they are an inferior substitute for a more penetrating observation. And nothing dates us faster, or stamps us as being more unoriginal, than our overuse of outmoded slang. It's hard to believe that *twenty-three skiddoo, heavy, to blow a fuse,* and to have *the screaming meemies* were once "in" slang.

Another aspect of slang is that it is a proving ground for new words. New words enter our general language constantly. Usage and popular opinion act as a filter, retaining only the most useful. Slang "is created by the converging of 'in-groups' and their words with the general public and its Standard Vocabulary." *(Success with Words)*

It's amusing to learn that the famous eighteenth-century English lexicographer Samuel Johnson railed at such "slang" as *touchy, budge,* and *fun.* Did you know that *blizzard, good-by,* and *movie* were once considered slang? Most dictionaries place *OK* under an informal label, while a few consider it **standard usage.**

Jargon

Most linguists consider **jargon** and **cant** nearly one and the same today, though **cant** also carries an additional meaning of hypocrisy and pretense. At one time, **jargon** was thought of as shoptalk—the specialized language of many professions, as lawyers, doctors, artists, and so forth. Men and women in various occupations use vocabularies familiar to themselves but meaningless to the uninitiated. It is a specialized vocabulary.

The following are a few examples of what we mean by jargon:

JARGON	TRANSLATED
Medical	
contusion	bruise
postpartum	after childbirth

JARGON	TRANSLATED
Music	
bluegrass	the true, old-time country music
gig	playing or recording engagement
Business	
bottom line	final figures on a profit-and-loss statement
head hunter	employment agency for top executives
CEO	chief executive officer (the top honcho!)

Regional Words (Dialects)

People in different geographical locations often have different and picturesque words and expressions to describe the same object. Such words and phrases are **dialects.** Here are a few examples from different dialects around the country:

• Hudson Valley Dialect. To *belly whop* is to flop on a sled and coast down a hill in the winter. A *stoop* is a small porch, or a flight of steps leading to the main door of a house.
• Upper Midwestern Dialect. A *parking* is a strip of grass between the sidewalk and the street.
• Pacific Northwest. A *no-see-um* is a tiny, stinging gnat. A *potlatch* is a festive celebration.
• Pacific Southwest. A *lanai* is a patio or covered walk, while a *crowbait* is a worthless horse or some other animal.

Points to Remember

The proof has been in for a long while. No matter what work you do, whether as a homemaker or an executive, on the assembly line or as a clerk, the way you speak and use your words is going to have a definite effect on many aspects of your life. We may not agree with the fairness of it, but, most of the time, people will rate us by the way we dress and sound.

Word-Power Test

I   Match the power word with the appropriate answer. Two additional possible answers are given.

1. levity
2. fatuous
3. adamant
4. promulgate
5. truncate
6. jaunty
7. denigrate
8. parable
9. discursive

a. complacently stupid
b. immovable and unyielding
c. lightness and humor
d. sprightly and lively
e. announce officially
f. cut the top or end from
g. curve composed of points in a plane
h. slander, defame
i. haughty
j. wandering from one subject to another
k. short story based on familiar things to convey a moral lesson

ANSWERS: **1.** c; **2.** a; **3.** b; **4.** e; **5.** f; **6.** d; **7.** h; **8.** k; **9.** j.

II   Find the word or phrase closest in meaning to the power word.

1. acumen   A: quickness of insight. B: shrewdness. C: force.
2. dour   A: bitter. B: sly. C: gloomy.
3. mode   A: manner or way. B: addiction. C: shape.
4. sagacious   A: muddled. B: ancient. C: intelligent.
5. vagary   A: puzzle. B: slowness. C: wild fancy.
6. nebulous   A: indifferent. B: opaque. C: indistinct.
7. prolix   A: circuitous. B: wordy. C: efficient.
8. ephemeral   living for A: one day only. B: eternity. C: two weeks.
9. gingerly   A: casually. B: sharply. C: cautious.
10. vertigo   A: paleness. B: fear of falling. C: dizziness.
11. tumid   A: hot. B: swollen or pompous. C: fearful.

ANSWERS: **1.** A; **2.** C; **3.** A; **4.** C; **5.** C; **6.** C; **7.** B; **8.** A; **9.** C; **10.** C; **11.** B.

III   Pick the word that comes closest to describing the following situations:

1. This is the most trite, the most commonplace, uninteresting movie I've ever seen. You could say it is . . . .
2. Finally, she interrupted the long-winded explanation and repeated the instructions in a much briefer, compact way. In short she was . . . .
3. The student looked sadly at his teacher. "I've got spring fever," he said, "and I find that I characterize homework as difficult, laborious and

a burdensome responsibility." "You mean you find it . . . . ," the teacher said.

4. Have you ever tried a sport and felt awkward or clumsy? Boiling it down to one word, you felt . . . .

5. The map was drawn in outline and traced our path accurately. It also portrayed some scenes pictorially with a verbal description. It . . . . just where and how we should go.

6. I used to cringe when the proofing editor screamed across the room in a loud, harsh voice, "You've made another spelling mistake." She had a . . . . voice.

ANSWERS: **1.** banal; **2.** concise; **3.** onerous; **4.** ungainly; **5.** delineate; **6.** strident.

IV Choose the word or phrase that best describes the meaning of the power word in the sentence, from one of the three selections below it.

1. She caught him in an *obtrusively obvious* or *glaring* lie.
   A. unfortunate
   B. blatant
   C. humorous

2. She tried to *wheedle and coax* her way past the customs officer.
   A. humor
   B. cajole
   C. enamor

3. "The beauty is too overwhelming for me to express in words," the writer wrote. "It's indescribable."
   A. fruitless
   B. translucent
   C. ineffable

4. In his autobiography, *Iacocca,* the businessman reports how some of his plans were *obstructed* or *frustrated* by other executives.
   A. menaced
   B. thwarted
   C. outwitted

5. What at first had seemed to be a bright and funny show turned out to have lost its sparkle and become *flat.*
   A. vulgar
   B. vapid
   C. silly

6. The policemen smiled at the woman's humorous and *believable* story.
   A. dependable
   B. plausible
   C. understandable

ANSWERS: **1.** B; **2.** B; **3.** C; **4.** B; **5.** B; **6.** B.

V What is the *antonym* (the opposite) of the italicized word in each of the following sentences? Pick a power word from the ones given below:

erudite, tacit, utilitarian, valid, querulous, captious, remonstrate.

1. An *ignorant* person is not necessarily an illiterate one.

2. The argument seemed *unsound;* therefore we stopped further discussion.

3. The actor was a delightful, *easygoing,* laid-back character.

4. The inventor's associates found him to be an *impractical,* spacey sort of fellow.

5. The young mother was *appreciative* of the meals her friends brought her after the baby arrived.

6. Even though she is blamed for mistakes she doesn't make, she *accepts* the reprimands quietly.

7. The company gave him *explicit* orders as to how to proceed with the program.

ANSWERS: **1.** erudite; **2.** valid; **3.** querulous; **4.** utilitarian; **5.** captious; **6.** remonstrates; **7.** tacit.

VI Fill in the blank with the correct power word from the words listed immediately below:

uncouth, mendacious, expiate, lampoon, obdurate, flamboyant.

1. Dressed in a . . . . , shiny, ornate, silver and sequined suit, the rock star acknowledged the applause.

2. "She is a . . . . . . witness," the lawyer said to the jury. She is a compulsive liar.

3. Slurping his soup noisily and using coarse language, the . . . . . . man embarrassed everyone at the table.

4. The soldiers tried to . . . . their mistaken attack by rebuilding the destroyed village.

5. The savagely witty . . . . . . poked cruel fun at the President.

6. She was the most . . . . person we'd ever known, persisting in her foolish ideas, absolutely refusing to listen or to change in any way.

ANSWERS: **1.** flamboyant; **2.** mendacious; **3.** uncouth; **4.** expiate; **5.** lampoon; **6.** obdurate.

Your Score
45–40 . . . . Word master
39–27 . . . . Very good
26–20 . . . . Fair

4

Synonyms Are Close Together; Antonyms Are Miles Apart

Be glad you speak English. Not only is it among the most efficient languages—saying more with fewer words—but it is blessed with an incredibly vast repository of words.

Power Words

abhor	engender
abject	esoteric
affable	forthright
ameliorate	fractious
beguile	heinous
candor	infallibility
chary	infraction
chide	inure
conducive	mercenary
dotage	niggardly
duress	overt
dynamic	scion
emergent	temporal
encomium	

*Special Words Having to Do with
Synonyms and Antonyms*

gourmand / gourmet
desecrate / profane
celibate / promiscuous
consensus / disagreement
diatribe / tirade
ominous / auspicious
tentative / wary
distraught / equanimity
loquacious / reticent

An advantage you have with English as compared with other languages lies in its **synonyms.** With them, you can express just about any shade of feeling, or describe almost anything in minute detail.

Let's take a look at the definition of a **synonym.** According to the Oxford American Dictionary, it is a word or phrase with a meaning similar to that of another in the same language.

Not *exactly* the same meaning. Only close to it.

If you recall, in Chapter 2, under **Special Dictionaries,** we discussed the "thesaurus," a reference book listing synonyms and antonyms. As writers, we refer to such books frequently. We do this not just to select another word, but, rather, to see if the word we are thinking of is truly the one we want.

For example, one day we came across the word **decry** in a magazine article in which a critic discussed a particular artist: "This new painter who suddenly is so popular is **decrying** everything that tradition in art has to offer." We looked up the definition, finding that to **decry** implies open or public condemnation or censure with the intent to discredit or run down something or someone.

Wondering about its synonyms, we checked out **depreciate, disparage, derogate, detract, belittle,** and **minimize.**

You've probably heard of one or more of these, but do you really know what they mean? Can you discriminate between them so as to use them with reasonable accuracy?

Depreciate (deh PREE she ate) means to represent a thing or a person as being of less worth than is usually associated with him, her, or it. "The painter **depreciates** tradition because he's had no real training in the fundamentals of art."

Disparage (dis PAR [the *a* as in fat] ij) is to speak contemptuously of, as if the thing or person has no worth at all. "The painter retaliated by **disparaging** most critics as artists who couldn't make it."

Derogate (DER uh gate) has a similar sense of devaluating the worth of something by taking the essence of it away, or detracting from it: "The artist's thoughtless comment shouldn't **derogate** from the importance of art critics." Also **derogate** gives us the better-known and more often used adjective **derogatory:** "The critic felt that the artist's **derogatory** comment was an insulting put-down." Actually, **detract** and **derogate** are close synonyms and can be used interchangeably. Our advice is to use **detract** most of the time because it can be used with either a personal or an impersonal subject.

Both **belittle** and **minimize** imply criticism designed to diminish the worth of something. In *Modern Guide to Synonyms,* S. I. Hayakawa discusses these two words, suggesting that **belittle** is the more general and informal of these. It may indicate a fault-finding attitude: "The artist **belittled** the critic at every opportunity." Or the word may imply an attitude that cannot tolerate excellence or effort in another: "The critic **belittled** the energy it took to create such an enormous piece of artwork."

Finally, **minimize** is a more formal substitute for **belittle.** It refers specifically to the attempt to set a lower value on something than it commonly carries or deserves: "The artist **minimized** the role of the critic." Yet, **minimize** does not necessarily carry a spiteful or faultfinding tone, but may express a reasoned assessment: "Other artists and critics **minimized** the effect this squabble would have on the public."

Discussing this cluster of words gives some indication of the infinite garden of meanings we have to pick from. The more familiar you are with one key word, the more interesting it is to see what those close to it look like. What about the differences between **boisterous** and **blustering?** Or in what way does **imperfection** differ from **deficiency?**

Look for just the right word. You will find that by using synonyms wisely, you add variety, interest, and often spice to your writing and speaking. But the most important service synonyms offer is that of helping you to become more exact in expressing yourself. You can choose the words that distinctly meet your meaning and convey it distinctively. As you and I know all too well, we cannot always come up with the word we want. A book of synonyms can be extremely useful.

To repeat and expand on Chapter 2, Peter Mark Roget (row ZHAY) summarized our dilemma a hundred years or so ago: "For words like spirits from the vasty deep . . . come not when we call . . . Appropriate terms, notwithstanding our utmost efforts, cannot be conjured up at will."

There are various books of synonyms which are based on Peter Mark Roget's (1779–1869) pioneering effort. He felt a need to classify words to help him express his thoughts as well as clarifying confused or vague ideas. When he retired as secretary of the Royal Society of London for the Advancement of Science, at the age of seventy, he created his famous work, the Thesaurus of English Words and Phrases. A **thesaurus** is defined as a book containing ·sets of words grouped according to their meanings. Some of the words so gathered together are truly synonymous, though many are more like

the various degrees of cousins in a family—connected, but not closely.

Today there are three types of thesauruses: the kind developed by Roget, listing words that fall into categories or topics; those arranged alphabetically, as a dictionary; and the alphabetical dictionary that describes and compares the various synonyms.

How would you use a thesaurus? Let's assume you have traveled to New Zealand for a vacation and on one of the tours you've seen some sculptures by the native people, the Maori. When you get back home, you write a postcard to a friend trying to describe the artwork. You want a word that expresses the thought of something that is unembellished, devoid of anything elaborate. You think of the word **plain,** but that doesn't convey the strong impression the works made on you. The word you want refuses to appear.

You go to the thesaurus and look up **plain** to see what words are grouped around it. You find: easy, simple, slight, etc. Since those don't fit, you go to the next grouping: clear, understandable, obvious, etc. You still haven't found what you want. And so you move on, finding: common, unaffected, down-to-earth, etc. Better, but still off the mark, and you move on: unadorned, restrained, severe, **stark.** You stop there. You think **stark** may be the word.

You turn to the dictionary and find one of the following meanings: devoid of any elaboration; blunt; unadorned; stiff or rigid. To make sure you want this word, you check out your book of synonyms and find that **stark** is lumped together with: stiff, rigid, inflexible, tense, wooden. Under **stark** you read that it "usually suggests a stiffness that is associated with loss of life, warmth, power, vitality, fluidity and therefore often also connotes desolation, or barrenness."

All in all, **stark** seems to be the word that comes closest to your experience and so you use it. (This explanation takes longer than the actual process.)

As you can see, the other possible words do not quite communicate your impression. They have their own boundaries of meaning and feeling.

For the fun of it, see how many synonyms you can think of for the following three words—an adjective, a noun, and a verb. But remember that a synonym is **not** an exact replica of the target word. Some are closer in meaning than others.

Give yourself 5 points for each synonym. There

are 85-plus possibilities. If you get 200 or more points, you are in the upper echelon of wordsmiths. Though it's not easy to think of words, it's a superb way to **expand** (you get a "freebie" on one of the synonyms for **extend**) your vocabulary. You may come up with some we haven't listed.

> *indisputable*
> *happy*
> *extend*

ANSWERS: *indisputable* undeniable, undoubted, incontestable, indubitable, irrefutable, unquestionable, unassailable, impregnable, incontrovertible, positive, unmistakable, certain, sure, infallible, assured, definite, unequivocal.

happy joyous, joyful, merry, mirthful, glad, delighted, delightful, cheerful, cheering, gay, contented, satisfied, prosperous, rapturous, felicitous, cheery, blithe, blithesome, jolly, blessed, blissful, rejoiced, rejoicing, jovial, jocund, glad, propitious, favorable, pleased, gratified, pleasing, fortunate, peaceful, comfortable, light, bright, buoyant, vivacious, sunny, dexterous, smiling, successful, sprightly, lucky, lively, animated, spirited, exhilarated, exhilarating, laughing, satiated, elated, exultant, satisfied, fortunate.

extend reach, stretch, lengthen, enlarge, increase, protract, amplify, augment, add, expand, dilate, spread, elongate, draw out, magnify, inflate, distend, prolong, run, go, range, reach out, stick out, put forth, drag out.

Some Excerpts from Books of Synonyms. We thought it might be helpful to see three selections from three types and the different ways in which they are organized, each involving the word **color.**

Roget's International Thesaurus, Harper & Row, Inc. Roget made up eight classifications of words. **Class One:** Abstract Relations; **Class Two:** Space; **Class Three:** Physics; **Class Four:** Matter; **Class Five:** Sensation; **Class Six:** Intellect; **Class Seven:** Volition; **Class Eight:** Affections. If we take the word *color,* in **Class Three,** Physics, we get the following breakdown: NOUNS 1. *color, hue; tint, tinct* (poetic), *tincture* (poetic), *tinge, shade; tone, cast; dye, stain; coloring, coloration; complexion, schoolgirl complexion; under-color, color; Technicolor; colorama.* 2. *warmth, warmth of color, warm color; blush, flush, glow,* and so forth.

The list goes on and on, paragraph after paragraph, through all the nouns, verbs, adjectives, ending finally with: soft-colored, *soft,* softened, *subdued,* mellow, delicate, tender, sweet.

The Doubleday Roget's Thesaurus in Dictionary Form, Doubleday & Company, Inc. You recall, in Chapter 2 we mentioned that this thesaurus lists the target words alphabetically. It's a quick way to get a fix on a word.

We find *color* under the C's, just as we would in an ordinary dictionary: *color* (noun): 1. hue, tone, cast, tint, coloration, coloring. 2. pigment, dye, paint, coloring, stain. 3. semblance, appearance, show, cast, look, aspect, effect, intent. 4. animation, vividness, eclat, brilliance, richness, liveliness. (verb) 1. paint, dye, stain, tint, tinge. 2. misrepresent, exaggerate, distort, prejudice, slant, cast, tilt, falsify, embroider, embellish. 3. blush, flush, mantle, redden, brighten, ripen.

Webster's New Dictionary of Synonyms, Merriam-Webster, Inc. We look up *color* and find along with this word a listing for hue, shade, tinge, tone. "They mean a property or attribute of a visible thing that is recognizable only when rays of light fall upon the thing and that is distinct from properties (as shape or size) apparent in dusk." The article then goes on to discuss each word closely, giving numerous examples. You will know thoroughly what each means when you finish.

Antonyms—Those Far-Apart Words

A discussion of **synonyms** is not complete unless we also consider their opposite, **antonyms.**

You live in an era of **antonyms:**

• The free world is *democratic.* The Communist world is *despotic.*

• Many countries are economically *chaotic.* Others have a more *orderly* economic situation.

• Some nations have *tolerant* sexual mores. Other nations, such as the Islamic ones, have *Draconian* sexual standards.

• There are racially *biased* countries, while others practice racial *fairness.*

An **antonym** is thought of as a word that differs in some way or degree from another word—either completely or at least partially. There are various terms for the degrees of difference. For example, according to Webster's New Dictionary of Synonyms:

Contradictory terms are so opposed to each other that they are mutually exclusive. If either is true, the other must be false; if either is false, the other must be true. For example, a thing is either **perfect** or **imperfect.** You may **agree** with the opinion of someone else, or you may **disagree.** It is unimportant whether the disagreement is radical or superficial or the difference concerns a major or a very minor point; you cannot be said to agree.

Contrary terms are diametric opposites. But they must be or must apply to things of the same fundamental kind. Thus, **white** and **black** represent the extremes in color. **Equanimity** and **perturbation** are at opposite ends of meaning.

Relative terms are pairs of words that cannot be used without suggesting the other; as, *parent* and *child*, or *husband* and *wife*.

Contrasted terms never fully clash, but show a difference in only a part of their meaning; as, **loquacious** and **reticent, curious** and **blasé, wary** and **thoughtless.** These words are not diametrically opposite, though they suggest a strong difference.

Just for the sake of interest, for your own greater enjoyment of language, look up these various words in your dictionary and see the shades of difference. We find this part of language tremendously exciting. We take a 3 × 5 card, or even a larger one, and write down the **synonyms** *and* the **antonyms,** giving their meanings. This is a terrific way to build your vocabulary, and the most interesting. When you truly understand a word as compared or contrasted with another, then you really understand that word, and you will never again misuse it. This is the beauty of using language well.

Here are a few examples from writers who have used antonyms in various degrees.

1. "Man, unlike any other thing, *organic* or *inorganic,* in the universe, grows beyond his work, walks up the stairs of his concepts, emerges ahead of his accomplishments." (John Steinbeck)

2. "The greatness of art is not to find what is *common,* but what is *unique.*" (Isaac Bashevis Singer)

3. "Catholics and Communists have committed great crimes, but at least they have not stood aside, like an established society, and been indifferent. I would rather have *blood* on my hands, than *water* like Pontius Pilate." (Graham Greene)

Points to Remember

1. By being aware of synonyms, we can express ourselves more carefully and accurately.

2. Antonyms help us to understand the true meaning of a word.

3. If you want to make sure you know and remember a word, write down its *synonyms* and *antonyms* on a card.

Word-Power Test

I Pair off the ANTONYMS *or* SYNONYMS in the following list of words:

1. gourmand	**a.** reticent
2. desecrate	**b.** wary
3. celibate	**c.** equanimity
4. consensus	**d.** profane
5. diatribe	**e.** favorable
6. ominous	**f.** disagreement
7. tentative	**g.** gourmet
8. distraught	**h.** tirade
9. loquacious	**i.** promiscuous

ANSWERS: **1.** g; **2.** d; **3.** i; **4.** f; **5.** h; **6.** e; **7.** b; **8.** c; **9.** a.

II Answer yes or no to each question.

1. The *candor* in her comments hurt some and pleased others. Her honesty offended some and was enjoyed by others. Yes or no?

2. The teacher did not recommend the *esoteric* book to his younger students. The book was too profound. Yes or no?

3. We must not trust the *infallibility* of people in office. People find politicians are never wrong. Yes or no?

4. Though they had plenty of money, the *mercenary* couple sold their faithful old dog. They were motivated by money. Yes or no?

5. The minister said his congregation spent too much time on *temporal* affairs. He thought they needed to think more about God. Yes or no?

ANSWERS: **1.** yes; **2.** no; **3.** no; **4.** yes; **5.** yes.

III Pick the phrase or sentence in a, b, or c that best explains the given sentence.

1. She *abhorred* the room's color combinations of pink, gold, black, purple, and orange.
   a. Did she regard them with loathing and horror?
   b. Did she find them outrageously humorous?
   c. She looked at them with a kind of admiring awe.

2. "I can assure you," the doctor said, "he is not in his *dotage.*"
   a. Did the doctor state the man was not senile as a result of old age?
   b. The doctor felt the man was not creative.
   c. The doctor asserted the man had left wherever he had been staying.

3. He accepted his *encomium* with gratitude.

a. He accepted his tip gratefully.

b. He accepted his praise with thankfulness.

c. He was happy to get back his book.

4. The *fractious* youngster talked back to his parents, punched his friend, took off his clothes, and ran out to the sidewalk.

a. The youngster was mischievous.

b. The youngster was broken up over something that distressed him.

c. The youngster was unruly.

5. The lawyer looked at the *scion* carefully and decided to tell him everything.

a. The lawyer felt that the descendent should know all the details of his family.

b. The lawyer decided the wealthy person was worth cultivating.

c. The lawyer felt the ruler was entitled to know all.

ANSWERS: **1.** a; **2.** a; **3.** b; **4.** c; **5.** a.

IV Select the word or phrase closest to the given word.

1. affable   A: comical. B: happy. C: friendly.

2. chary   A: burned. B. puzzled. C: cautious.

3. conducive   A: restrained. B: helpful. C: permissive.

4. dynamic   A: violently angry. B: forceful or energetic. C: having to do with electricity.

5. forthright   A: erect. B: hurrying. C: straightforward.

6. heinous   A: laughing incessantly. B: unforgettable. C: extremely wicked.

7. inure   A: become used to something. B: familiar with. C: intrigued.

8. overt   A: open to view. B: turned upside down. C: turned up.

ANSWERS: **1.** C; **2.** C; **3.** B; **4.** B; **5.** C; **6.** C; **7.** A; **8.** A.

V Pick the sentence from a, b, or c that matches the numbered sentence closely.

1. John is in his office *ameliorating* a tense situation with Amanda's partners.

a. John is negotiating with her partners.

b. John is improving the situation.

c. John is keeping the status quo with Amanda's partners.

2. The professor *chided* Oswald for eating messy sugar doughnuts and ice cream during lectures.

a. The professor complained about Oswald's eccentricity.

b. The professor scolded the student.

c. The professor grumbled about his student's behavior.

3. The couple was *beguiled* by the brochure of the cruise.

a. The couple was confused.

b. The couple was suspicious of the brochure.

c. The couple was deceived and charmed by the brochure.

4. "I signed under *duress*," the defendant claimed.

a. The defendant was compelled by force or fear to sign.

b. The defendant signed after being carefully advised.

c. The defendant signed only because he was confused and upset.

5. The Third World *emergent* nations are in financial stress.

a. They are relatively new nations.

b. They are nations that need help immediately.

c. They are nations that still have ties to older, more established countries.

6. The promotion of the baboon in a white tie and tails *engendered* publicity.

a. The stunt produced the publicity.

b. The promotion hindered publicity.

c. It brought about the wrong kind of publicity.

7. "There have been two *infractions* of the bed-check rules," the coach said.

a. The coach has added two new rules.

b. The coach has removed two rules.

c. The coach said two rules have been broken.

8. "The landlord is certainly a *niggardly* person," Amy observed. "He won't run hot water more than two hours a day."

a. The landlord is stingy.

b. The landlord is careful.

c. The landlord is mean and calculating.

9. The old couple lived in *abject* poverty for two years.

a. They lived in wretched poverty.

b. They lived on the verge of poverty.

c. They lived in poverty they had brought on themselves.

ANSWERS: **1.** b; **2.** b; **3.** c; **4.** a; **5.** a; **6.** a; **7.** c; **8.** a; **9.** a.

Your Score

36–32 .... Word master

31–22 .... Very good

21–15 .... Fair

5

You, Too, Can Be a Word Mechanic!— Getting to the Roots

A word can be taken apart and tinkered with just as if it were a piece of machinery.

Power Words

abrogate	omniscient
accretion	parsimonious
anathema	pensive
anthropomorphic	posthumous
congruent	proscribe
contiguous	psychotic
convert	refractory
expedient	resilient
extemporize	reverberate
holocaust	sensuous
impeccable	temerity
lethargic	torpid
magnanimity	totalitarian
memorabilia	totem
moribund	vestige
noxious	

Special Words Having to Do with Roots of Words

autonomous	regimen
despicable	regressive
exculpate	respite
homogeneous	specious
introspective	spectrum
prospectus	speculate
regalia	undulate
regime	

You don't need a screwdriver and pliers to separate words into separate parts. They already come with a built-in divider. Most words, like stories, have a beginning, a middle, and an end.

The beginning is the **prefix,** the **root** is often the middle, and the end is called the **suffix.** The prefix and the suffix are also known as **affixes.**

First let's get the definitions out of the way.

A **prefix** is an addition of one or more letters at the beginning of a word that alters or modifies its meaning. Suppose we take the word *change.* We know it means "to make or become different." When

we add the prefix **ex,** "out, or outside, of," the word is altered to now mean "to give or to receive one thing in place of another."

A **suffix** is a letter or a combination of letters added to the end of a word. From it you can tell whether the word is a noun, adjective, verb, or adverb. For example, **ment** is a noun-forming **suffix** meaning "a result, or product." Add it to the verb *improve* and we get the noun *improvement.*

Because the **root** is the original word, to which **prefixes** and **suffixes** are gradually added during its history, let's spend time in this chapter taking a look at **roots** and what they mean to our language. We'll talk about **prefixes** and **suffixes** in the next chapter.

Words Grow from Roots. Words, like people, have families. And like people, they marry and create offspring of their own. For example, among the following words, the founding ancestor is the Latin verb *specere*, "to look at": **introspective, auspices, spectacular, respite, especial, conspicuous, speculate, aspect, retrospect, spectrum, despicable, specify, introspective.** And there are many other words as well.

In each of these, you can find the root *spec-* in *specere* in one form or another, and you could make a stab at understanding the word if you knew the meaning of the Latin.

introspective   looking within oneself.

auspices   a helpful influence, literally "looking to the birds" for help, an ancient Roman soothsaying procedure.

spectacular   sensational to see.

respite   rest; and in a sense, a looking back.

especial   "seeing something" very special.

conspicuous   prominent, because it can be seen all around.

speculate   from Latin *speculari,* to spy out.

aspect   appearance, from Latin *aspicere,* to behold.

retrospect   recollection, from Latin *retrospicere,* to look back.

spectrum   a rainbow of colors, from Latin *spectrum,* appearance.

despicable literally, able to be looked down upon.

specify when you **specify** certain items, you make them so clear that people can "see" them.

For your own interest, you might want to underline the root in each of the previous words. Then you will be able to see more clearly the **affixes** (the **prefixes** and **suffixes**).

Roots are really the building blocks of your vocabulary. They form the essence of the word, and the **affixes** cluster around them. When you come across a word that initially looks unfamiliar to you and then you recognize the **root,** you are on the way to ferreting out its meaning. By the way, *ferret* comes from the small, weasel-like animal that can wriggle in and out of small holes to hunt rabbits, rats, and the like. And so when you "ferret out a meaning," you are forcing it out of hiding; you are searching for it.

We plan to give you thirty-five of the most commonly occurring **roots**—twenty-five Latin and ten Greek—and a few examples of the words in which they appear. With this collection you have the potential of recognizing, understanding, and even memorizing thousands of words new to you.

At first this may seem like a lot of **roots** to plant in your mind. Don't worry if they seem like "Greek" to you at first. Return to this chapter from time to time to refresh your memory. Write down on a 3 × 5 card the ones in this chapter that you find give you the most trouble.

As a bonus we will give you a list of medical roots so you can understand your doctor.

Caution! Not every **root, prefix,** or **suffix** always ends up looking exactly the same as the original. As I've written in *Word Memory Power in 30 Days*, don't get thrown off by the change when a **prefix** such as *ad-* changes to *ap-* or *at-*. The change depends on the letter that follows in the rest of the word. The same situation prevails for **roots.** We give the changed forms in parentheses following the root word.

LATIN ROOTS

CADO (cas, cis, cad, cid) "fall, cut, kill": cascade, incision, decadent, occident, decide, excise, homicide.

CAPIO (cap, capt, cip, cept) "take, hold, seize": captivate, anticipate, receptacle, participant, inception, deception.

CEDO (ced, cess, ceed) "move, go, yield, withdraw": recede, recession, proceed, accessory, antecedent, concede, recess.

CERNO (cern, cret, creet, cert) "pick out, see as being different, separate": discern, secret, certitude, secretive, discreet.

CLAUDO (claus, clud, clus, clois) "shut, close": claustrophobia, conclude, seclusion, cloister.

CURRO (cur, curs, cour) "run, go": concur, precursor, recourse, curriculum, cursive, excursion, recurrence,

DICO (dict, dex) "say": dictum, index, abdicate, malediction, edict, valedictory.

DUCO (duc, duct) "lead, take, bring": induce, abduct, conduce, seduce, production.

FACIO (fac, fic, fact, fect, fy) "do, make": facsimile, fortification, factotum, perfect, magnify, confection, efficient, facile, suffice.

GENERO (gen) "give birth to": degenerate people have fallen from their position at "birth"; geniuses are born that way, and generous people "give" to others. "Genesis," the first book of the Bible, tells us of the birth of the world.

JACIO (jac, ject) "throw, cast": adjacent, interjection, projectile, rejection, ejaculate.

LIGO (lig, ligat, ly, leag, loy, legat) "to bind": obligation, ligatures, ally, league, alloy, allegation.

LOQUOR (loqu) "say, speak, talk": loquacious, soliloquy, grandiloquence, colloquial, colloquy, elocution, ventriloquist.

MAGNUS "great, large": magnifying glass, magnanimous.

MANUS (manu, mani, man) "hand": manuscript, manifest, emancipate, manacle, manipulate, manner.

MITTO (mit, mis) "send, let go": remit, admissible, emissary, dismissal, missive.

PLICO (plicat, plicit, ply, plic, plex) "fold, twist, bend": complicate, implicit, comply, application, complex, inexplicable.

RUMPO (rupt) "break, burst": ruptured, abrupt, disrupted, corruption, eruption.

SALIO (sali, sult, sail, [x]ult, sault, sil) "leap, jump": A salient fact "jumps" out at you; assail, exult, desultory, resilient, result.

SCRIBO (scrip, script) "write": prescribe, postscript, proscribe, scripture, scribble, conscript, description, inscription.

SEQUOR (sequ, secut, [x]ecut) "follow": sequel, persecute, non sequitur, consequence, executive, subsequent, sequence.

SPECIO (spec, spic, spect, speculat) is described at length, with its words, a few paragraphs earlier in this book.

TENDO (tend, tens, tent) "stretch, strain, thin, weak": portend, tension, pretentious, tendon, tenet, pertain, sustain, tenements.

VENIO (ven, vent) "come": revenue, convention, convene, advent, convent, eventual, circumvent.

VIDEO (vid, vis) "see, look, provide": provident, television, evident, provide, revise (literally, look at again), invidious, vista, visualize.

Here's a quick quiz to help you get into the habit of recognizing **roots**. Find and underline the root in each of the following words.

1. suspicion
2. retention
3. missive
4. magnitude
5. conjecture
6. petrify
7. attentive
8. forceps
9. cascade
10. tenet

ANSWERS: **1.** spic; **2.** tent; **3.** miss; **4.** magn; **5.** ject; **6.** petri *and* fy; **7.** tent; **8.** ceps; **9.** cas; **10.** ten.

GREEK ROOTS

ARCH (pronounced ARCH or ARK) "ruler, main, chief, principal": anarchy, literally, "without a ruler"; archenemy, archangel, monarch, oligarchy, patriarch.

CHRONOS (chrono, chron) "time": synchronize, chronic, chronicle, chronometer.

GLOSSA (gloss, glot) "tongue, language": glossary, glossolalia (speaking unintelligible words as if from a deep religious experience), epiglottis.

GRAPHO (graph, gram) "write, draw": graph, grammar, graphite, graphic, anagram, epigraph.

KOSMEO (cosm) "to order, arrange"; KOSMOS means world or universe because it is perfectly *arranged:* cosmopolitan, microcosm.

ONYMA (onym) "name": synonym, antonym, pseudonym.

PHILOS (phil) "loving": philately (stamp collecting), philharmonic (loving music).

PHONE (phone, phon) "sound": telephone, megaphone, microphone, phonetics.

POLY, "many": polysyllabic, polytechnic, polymath (person knowing many subjects).

THERM, "heat": thermostat, thermometer, thermodynamics.

In this quick quiz, search out the Greek **roots,** underlining them.

1. epigram
2. anonymous
3. philanthropy
4. archbishop
5. anachronism
6. thermonuclear
7. epiglottis
8. macrocosmic
9. euphonious
10. polyunsaturated

ANSWERS: **1.** gram; **2.** onym; **3.** phil; **4.** arch; **5.** chron; **6.** therm; **7.** glot; **8.** cosm; **9.** phon; **10.** poly.

Points to Remember

Latin and Greek roots form the basis of at least 60 percent of our words. By learning them, you can more easily understand new words, as well as recall older ones. Roots help also in memorizing the ones you want to remember.

Word-Power Test

I Here are the dictionary definitions of five of the power words. Choose the one you think fits the description.

1. concealed; secret
2. having infinite knowledge, knowing everything
3. hard to control; stubborn, obstinate
4. looking within oneself, examining one's own mental and emotional processes
5. going back, moving backward

ANSWERS: **1.** covert; **2.** omniscient; **3.** refractory; **4.** introspective; **5.** regressive.

II Pick the word definition that best fits the meaning of the power word in the sentence.

1. Do you think they will *abrogate* the treaty?
   a. annul or cancel
   b. extend or postpone
   c. make different
2. Unexpectedly and to his horror, he found himself before a huge audience and began to *extemporize.*
   a. be unable to talk
   b. improvise
   c. make apologies
3. Popular sentiments told them this kind of film was not *moribund.*
   a. depressing
   b. gruesome
   c. dying
4. She explained to her curious friends that she lived under a *totalitarian* government.
   a. a government controlled by one party, with no rival parties permitted

b. a type of government that is designed totally for the people

c. a government with the authority residing in the people

5. Of any sales presentation I ever heard, this had to be the most *specious.*

a. apparently good and sound at first sight, but actually not

b. covering a broad area of interest, yet very much to the point

c. easygoing, relaxed, and friendly

6. Iago, in Shakespeare's *Othello,* was a *despicable* man.

a. contemptible

b. ugly and lewd in every way

c. dishonest

ANSWERS: **1.** a; **2.** b; **3.** c; **4.** a; **5.** a; **6.** a.

III Which words are opposite in meaning to the numbered words?

1. anathema		a. unresponsive
2. proscribe		b. alert
3. resilient		c. exhaustion
4. torpid		d. blessing
5. respite		e. smooth
6. undulate		f. permit

ANSWERS: **1.** d; **2.** f; **3.** a; **4.** b; **5.** c; **6.** e.

IV In the following sentences, which is closest to the given sentence, a, b, or c?

1. Which piece of coral is the result of *accretion?*

a. Gradually, over a period of time, the Great Barrier Reef, in Australia, grew by *accretion.*

b. Ecologists worry that the Great Barrier Reef is slowly disintegrating by *accretion.*

c. When coral is taken out of the water it hardens because of *accretion.*

2. The *holocaust* destroyed the city.

a. A raging fire utterly devoured the city.

b. A hurricane and tidal wave leveled the city.

c. A plague killed most of the inhabitants, destroying the city.

3. The statuettes were *vestiges* of ancient Greece.

a. In ancient times, images of virgin priestesses were worshiped.

b. They were traces of the past.

c. Grecians used art objects for barter in the marketplace.

4. *Memorabilia* became an obsession in Peg's life.

a. Peg collected anything and everything that reminded her of the past.

b. She worried when she forgot the smallest item.

c. She wrote in her appointment book to the point of fanaticism.

5. They tried to get Jim's explanation, even though it would not *exculpate* him.

a. They would not let him leave the country even if he explained his actions.

b. He could not get a divorce under the present law.

c. His explanation would not free him from blame.

6. They passed the legislation as an *expedient* to get the budget accepted.

a. The legislation was meant to encourage the finance committee.

b. It was useful to get the budget passed, though not a perfect solution.

c. The legislation was a favor to the public.

7. The bear became a *totem* to a North American tribe of Indians.

a. It caused them to be fearful.

b. It became a burden to feed.

c. They felt it to be a kindred spirit and emblem.

8. Sometimes, the previously unrecognized artist will receive many *posthumous* awards.

a. The awards are late.

b. The awards come after death.

c. Suddenly people rush to present awards.

ANSWERS: **1.** a; **2.** a; **3.** b; **4.** a; **5.** c; **6.** b; **7.** c; **8.** b.

V Have you ever heard people slip up on these words? It's easy to do if you are not sure. Which is right, A or B?

1. noxious   A: smelly and filthy. B: causing injury.

2. contiguous   A: adjoining. B: infectious.

3. congruent   A: side by side. B: conforming, agreeing.

4. temerity   A: boldness. B: fearfulness.

5. regimen   A: system of exercise or diet. B: leaders in a government.

6. regime   A: system of government. B: system of exercise.

7. prospectus   A: a description of a proposed business undertaking. B: a mental attitude.

8. speculate   A: to weigh mentally. B: take for granted.

9. homogeneous   A: similar in character. B: different in nature.

10. spectrum   A: mirror used as reflector. B: continuous band of diffracted sunlight.
11. reverberate   A: to pray. B: reecho.
12. impeccable   A: not liable to commit sin. B: extremely attentive to detail.
13. regalia   A: burst of laughter. B: insignia of royalty.
14. autonomous   A: existing independently. B: movable, not fixed.

ANSWERS: **1.** B; **2.** A; **3.** B; **4.** A; **5.** A; **6.** A; **7.** A; **8.** A; **9.** A; **10.** B; **11.** B; **12.** A; **13.** B; **14.** A.

VI   The following people are best described by one of the words or phrases following the sentence. Pick the right one.

1. The man was foolishly *anthropomorphic.*
   a. He treated animals as if they were people.
   b. He acted like a caveman.
   c. He worshiped ancient heros.
2. The strange day made her feel *lethargic.*
   a. peppy
   b. abnormally drowsy
   c. sad
3. A *pensive* child changed my life.
   a. thoughtful
   b. begging
   c. school
4. She walked into the shop in a *sensuous* way, inviting attention.
   a. in a ridiculous or foolish way
   b. in a very showy way
   c. appealing to the senses
5. It was difficult to tell whether the mugger was *psychotic* or not.
   a. causing danger
   b. trying to deceive people
   c. suffering from a severe mental disorder
6. Jack was so *parsimonious* he would not treat his own grandchildren to a ten-cent candy.
   a. grouchy
   b. stingy
   c. health-conscious

ANSWERS: **1.** a; **2.** b; **3.** a; **4.** c; **5.** c; **6.** b.

Your Score
45–40 . . . . Word master
39–27 . . . . Very good
26–20 . . . . Fair

First Review Quiz

Congratulations! You have completed five chapters. Some of the words you knew already, some you were somewhat unsure of, while some were new. To help you reinforce your memory, some of the words will appear in the following quiz.

1. antithesis   A: unfriendliness. B: opposite. C: summary.
2. demagogue   A: one advocating violence. B: one agitating politically. C: dictatorial one.
3. biodegradable   A: capable of decomposing. B: chemically systematized. C: polluting.
4. modus operandi   A: prestige. B: way of working. C: international agreement.
5. omnipotent   A: threatening. B: arrogant. C: all-powerful.
6. voracious   A: truthful. B: lively. C: ravenous.
7. xenophobic   A: militantly fanatic. B: hating religion. C: fearful of strangers.
8. allege   A: to declare without proof. B: offer a suggestion. C: promise solemnly.
9. etymology   A: the study of the derivations of words. B: the study of the meanings of words. C: the study of insects.
10. innocuous   A: devious. B: harmless. C: audible.
11. opaque   A: transparent. B: not transparent. C: translucent.
12. panorama   A: three-dimensional image. B: excitement. C: extensive view.
13. windfall   A: row of bushes and trees. B: calm. C: good fortune.
14. ambiguous   A: long-winded. B: able to use either hand with equal ease. C: not clear.
15. allude   A: to trick. B: intimate. C: sidestep.
16. extrapolate   A: add up. B: summarize. C: estimate.
17. promulgate   A: to force upon others. B: announce. C: start a rumor.
18. remonstrate   A: condemn. B: show clearly. C: protest.
19. acumen   A: accuracy. B: shrewdness. C: force.
20. fatuous   A: foolish. B: uneducated. C: obsessed.
21. delineate   A: do away with. B: quiet down. C: give detailed instructions.
22. tumid   A: moist. B: warm. C: swollen.
23. truncate   A: to confine. B: cut off. C: extend.
24. cajole   A: to soothe. B: trick. C: coax.
25. diatribe   A: slander. B: tirade. C: crisis.
26. loquacious   A: good at languages. B: smoothly pleasant. C: talkative.
27. encomium   A: speech. B: apology. C: high praise.

28. conducive   A: permissive. B: helpful. C: pleasing.
29. affable   A: comical. B: affected. C: ingratiating.
30. ameliorate   A: to appease. B: make better. C: humiliate.
31. chide   A: to scold. B: to discredit. C: fret.
32. beguile   A: to envy. B; charm. C: lament.
33. extemporize   A: to make up on the spur of the moment. B: honor. C: talk on and on.
34. specious   A: roomy. B: nonessential. C: seemingly true.
35. moribund   A: dying. B: unwilling to work. C: depressed.
36. congruent   A: coinciding. B: lacking. C: contrary.
37. magnanimity   A: nobility of spirit. B: exaggeration. C: enormous size.

38. anthropomorphic   reflecting a feeling that animals A: are threatening. B: have human characteristics. C: are good luck.
39. anathema   A: desertion of principles. B: compelling necessity. C: something detested.
40. temerity   A: fear. B: recklessness. C: diffidence.

ANSWERS: **1.** B; **2.** B; **3.** A; **4.** B; **5.** C; **6.** C; **7.** C; **8.** A; **9.** A; **10.** B; **11.** B; **12.** C; **13.** C; **14.** C; **15.** B; **16.** C; **17.** B; **18.** C; **19.** B; **20.** A; **21.** C; **22.** C; **23.** B; **24.** C; **25.** B; **26.** C; **27.** C; **28.** B; **29.** C; **30.** B; **31.** A; **32.** B; **33.** A; **34.** C; **35.** A; **36.** A; **37.** A; **38.** B; **39.** C; **40.** B.

Your Rating

40–35 . . . . Excellent
34–25 . . . . Good
24–18 . . . . Fair

6

The First and Last of Things—Prefixes and Suffixes

A teacher with a sense of humor asked her class to use three words in a sentence, each word beginning with the prefix **de-**. The words were **detail, deduct,** and **defense.** After the young people struggled for a while, she wrote on the blackboard: **"De tail of de duck** went over **de fence."**

Power Words

abortive	epitaph
adulation	euthanasia
affluent	finesse
antediluvian	fortuitous
antipathy	immanent
bathos	indict
centrifugal	indigent
centripetal	lethal
contraband	lugubrious
debilitating	malleable
deduction	matriculate
disconcert	opportune
dissident	pagan
eclipse	protagonist
epigram	staccato

*Special Words Having to Do
with Prefixes and Suffixes*

Prefixes	**Suffixes**
acclimate	aphorism
circumvent	credible
commodious	deleterious
depreciate	incommensurate
dissonance	magnanimity
epithet	nihilism
extenuate	paternalism
	sententious

"Good heavens! For more than forty years I have been speaking prose without knowing it," said a character in Moliere's play *Le Bourgeois Gentilhomme.*

And we can say without depreciating ourselves that without always being conscious of it, we've been using **prefixes** and **suffixes** all our lives. They are so much a part of our daily language of speaking, reading, and writing that we're scarcely aware of them.

Yet they are the elements that give a word its final meaning, as well as determining whether it is singular or plural, in the present or past tense, or a noun, verb, adjective, or adverb. They are linguistic fragments that modify the meaning or a function of a word.

For example, take the word **fix.** We know that one of the meanings is "to fashion, or attach firmly." I don't mail a letter until I **fix** a stamp onto it. Now add the element **pre-,** meaning "before," and our word now means "fix or attach before."

The Latin prefix *ab-* means from. Therefore we can see easily that the meaning of **abnormal** is away from whatever is normal.

In the previous chapter, one of the root words came from the Latin word *specere* (to look), and we learned that **respite** means rest, and in a sense, "a looking back." As you can see, the prefix is *re-*, which can have either one of two meanings: "back," as in **repay,** and "again, new, or over again," as in **reappear** or **retell.**

One of the most common prefixes is the Latin *de-*, with several meanings, all closely allied:

- away from, off, as in **detach**
- down, as in **decline**
- entirely, as in **defunct**
- undo, or reverse the action of, as in **defrost.**

Your Extended Family

When you or your relatives marry, the original family extends and grows and new members are added. The same is true with words. When you "marry" a **root** word to a **prefix,** your family of new words expands.

A common root is from the Latin verb *venire,* "to come." It usually appears in English words as **ven** or **vent.** Let's add various prefixes and see what happens.

- Add *inter-,* "between, among," and we get **intervene.**

• Add *circum-,* "around," which gives us **circumvent,** "to evade" or "to find a way *around.*"

• Add *pre-,* "before, beforehand," and the word **prevent** is formed, literally something that comes before or ahead that serves to check, hinder, or stop.

Can you think of other words that come from this root? Fill in the blank spaces following the prefix. Each space represents a letter. The meaning is given immediately following the word. The meaning of the prefix is in parentheses.

1. super . . . . —to follow closely upon something as an extraneous or additional circumstance. (*Super-* means "over and above.")
2. co . . . . . . —a formal and binding agreement entered into by two or more persons or parties; a compact. (*Co-* is another form of the prefix *com-,* meaning "with or together.")
3. ad . . . . —a coming or arrival. (*Ad-* is the prefix "to, toward, near.")
4. contra . . . . —to act against, or to infringe upon, as a law. Also, to argue or disagree with. (*Contra-* means "against.")
5. con . . . . . . —a formal professional or political meeting. Also, rule or custom; something not natural, spontaneous, or unusual. (As in #2, *con-* means "with or together.")
6. e . . . . . . —taking place after a period of time or as a result of a succession of events; subsequent. (The prefix *e-,* another form of *ex-,* means "out, out of, from, without.")

ANSWERS: **1.** supervene; **2.** covenant; **3.** advent; **4.** contravene; **5.** convention (conventional also comes from the root and prefix); **6.** eventual.

The Most Common Prefixes

Glancing at the following list, your first reaction might be: "They're telling me more than I want to know." But don't worry. It's not as bad as it seems. Some are easy to remember. Some you know already. Others you will get used to gradually. We suggest you mark this chapter and come back to it from time to time.

You will discover, to your interest and enjoyment, that it is one of the surest ways to increase your word power. And in the long run it will save you time, for these prefixes and, later in the chapter, the suffixes will help you to not only understand a word more quickly, but also to remember it.

Three important pieces of information are needed before we begin.

1. Many prefixes keep their original spellings despite being attached to various roots.
2. *But* some prefixes disguise themselves. That is, they do not always appear in the same form as the original element. Sometimes they assimilate the first letter of the root to which they are attached. For example, *ad-* becomes *ab-* in the word *ab*breviate. The changes, however, are not always so obviously logical, and prefixes change for historical and other linguistic reasons. The following list covers the majority of alterations. We have put each alteration in parentheses, followed by a word as an illustration.
3. Other prefixes look enough alike to be confusing when seen attached to a root—such prefixes as *hyper-* and *hypo-,* and *ante-* and *anti-.*

To make it easier, therefore, we have three lists of prefixes.

One more thought; some prefixes carry more than one meaning, though in most cases these meanings are related.

The Most Common Prefixes
Group One (Unchanged Forms)

A   "at, in, to" **a**bove, **a**sleep

AMBI   "both, on both sides, around" **ambi**dextrous

AUTO   "self" **auto**biography

BE   "around; completely, off, or away" **be**smudge, **be**set, **be**head

CIRCUM   "around; on all sides" **circum**ference, **circum**vent

COUNTER   "in opposition to, or contrary; in exchange or retaliation, corresponding" **counter**clockwise, **counter**attack, **counter**part

DE   "away or off, down, completely, the reversing of or ridding of the action or condition expressed by the main element" **de**capitate, **de**cline, **de**hydrate, **de**centralization

DIA   "through, across, between" **dia**meter

EX   "out, remove from, former (used with a hyphen)" **ex**cerpt, **ex**tinguish, **ex**-president

HEMI   "half" **hemi**sphere

HOMO   "same" **homo**genize

NEO   "new" **neo**phyte

NON   "not" **non**intervention, **non**fiction

MIS   "bad, badly, wrongly, unfavorably, dishonestly" **mis**take, **mis**judge, **mis**carriage

OUT   (combining form) "external, going forth, expressing results, beyond" **out**lying, **out**reach, **out**come, **out**do

OVER   "beyond, excessive" **over**flow, **over**kill, **over**eat

PARA "beside, near, beyond" **para**llel, **para**medic

POLY "many, several" **poly**graph (lie detector), **poly**unsaturated

POST "after, behind" **post**humous, **post**script

SEMI "partly, not fully, half" **semi**final, **semi**circle

SUPER "above in position, superior to, excessive" **super**structure, **super**lative, **super**fluous

TRANS "across, through, into another state or place" **trans**atlantic, **trans**action, **trans**fix

ULTRA "going beyond the limits or range, excessive" **ultra**sonic, **ultra**violet, **ultra**conservative

UN "not" **un**intelligible, **un**pretentious

UNI "one" **uni**sex, **uni**lateral

Group Two (Changed Forms)

AB "from, away from, off" **ab**hor, (a-) **a**vert

AD "to, toward" **ad**minister (*ad-* tends to assimilate the letter following, dropping the "d," as in **ap**pear, **at**tend, **an**nex, **ar**rive, etc.)

AN "not, without" **an**onymous, (a-) **a**trophy

BI "two, twice" **bi**gamy, (bin-) **bin**oculars

CATA "down, wholly, against" **cata**ract, (cath-) **cath**edral, (cat-) **cat**echism

COM "with, together, thoroughly" **com**passion, (co-) **co**equal, (con-) **con**duct, (col-) **col**lusion, (cor-) **cor**respondence

DIS "apart or away, reverse of, a lessening, not" **dis**miss, **dis**arm, **dis**able, **dis**enchant, (di-) **di**lapidated, (dif-) **dif**ference

MAL "bad, wrong, evil, ill" **mal**practice, (male-) **male**volent

META "altered, beyond or transcending" **meta**morphosis, **meta**physics, (meth-) **meth**odical

OB "against, toward" **ob**literate, **ob**verse, (o-) **o**mit, (oc-) **oc**cult, (of-) **of**ficiate, (op-) **op**ponent

SUB "under, almost, up" **sub**marine, **sub**ordinate, **sub**tropical, (subter-) **subter**fuge, (suc-) **suc**cumb, (suf-) **suf**fer, (sug-) **sug**gest, (sum-) **sum**mon, (sup-) **sup**press, (sus-) **sus**pend

SYN "with, together" **syn**thesis, (sym-) **sym**metrical, (syl-) **syl**lable, (sys-) **sys**tem

Group Three (Forms Somewhat Alike in Spelling or Sound)

ANTE "before" **ante**date, **ante**cedent

ANTI "against, opposed to" **anti**biotic, **anti**freeze

CONTRA "against, opposite, contrary" **contra**ceptive

COUNTER "in opposition, contrary" **counter**clockwise, **counter**productive

FOR "away, off, past" **for**sake, **for**go

FORE "ahead, before" **fore**bode (to have a sense of something about to happen)

EN "to cover or surround with, in or on, cause to be or make" **en**circle, **en**shrine, **en**danger, (em-) **em**power

IN "in, toward" **in**ject, **in**come, (il-) **il**lumine, (im-) **im**itate, (ir-) **ir**rigate

IN "not, without" **in**sufferable, **in**correct, (il-) **il**literate, (im-) **im**modest, (ir-) **ir**resistible

INTER "between, among, with each other" **inter**lude, **inter**rupt

INTRA "inside, within" **intra**venous, **intra**mural

INTRO "in, into" **intro**duce, **intro**vert

HYPER "over, above, excessive" **hyper**tension, **hyper**active, **hyper**thermia (a high fever)

HYPO "under, beneath, less than" **hypo**dermic (under the skin), **hypo**thermia (subnormal body temperature)

PER "through, completely (as an intensive)" **per**vade, **per**suade, **per**turb

PRE "before, earlier" **pre**face, **pre**school, **pre**clude

PRO "forward, in place of, in favor of" **pro**ject, **pro**mulgate, **pro**noun, **pro**fess, (pur-) **pur**suit, **pur**port

Time Out for a Quick Quiz

Which one of the following words is correct, a or b?

1. a) proturb_____ b) perturb _____
2. a) symmetry _____ b) synmetry _____
3. a) convolution ____ b) comvolution _____
4. a) antedate _____ b) antidate _____
5. a) intervenous ____ b) intravenous _____

ANSWERS: **1.** b; **2.** a; **3.** a; **4.** a; **5.** b.

Give the negative forms of the following words.

1. inherit
2. reliable
3. finite
4. fuse
5. organic

ANSWERS: **1.** disinherit; **2.** unreliable; **3.** infinite; **4.** defuse; **5.** inorganic.

Suffixes

A **suffix** plays two roles.

1. Functional shift changes a word from one part of speech to another. For example, by changing the ending of the noun **apology** from *-y* to *-ize,* we now have the verb **apologize.** Take the adjective **jealous** and add *-ly* and we get the adverb **jealously.**

2. Derivational suffixes actually change the meaning of a word. The element *-ic* added to **alcohol**

gives us **alcoholic,** a different word. What about appending *-hood* to the word **mother?** Combine **work** with **out.** We have a word with a different meaning entirely.

In thinking about how an ending changes a word from one part of speech to another, we wish we could say that it is always neat and clear, and that a particular suffix always signifies a particular part of speech. Unfortunately, this is not true. For example, you find the ending *-le* on a verb such as ming**le,** or with an *adjective* such as "litt**le.**" And just to complicate matters further, the same suffix may have differing spellings: "depend**ent**" and "signifi-c**ant.**"

With that caveat in mind, however, let's review some of the more common endings having to do with **functional shift.** After that, we can take a look at a few of the **derivational suffixes.**

Suffixes and Nouns (Functional Shift)

To refresh our memories, a **noun** is a word used as the name of a thing, quality, or action either existing or conceived by the mind.

Here are some of the more common suffixes that mark a word as being a noun:

ACY: "quality, state, office, etc." prim**acy,** democ-r**acy**

-ANCE, -ANCY, -ENCE, -ENCY: "state, or condition." forbear**ance,** hesit**ancy,** emerg**ence,** emer-g**ency**

-ATE: 1. "suggesting office, function or state." magistr**ate;** 2. "result or action" mand**ate**

-DOM: "state, or condition of" free**dom,** wis**dom**

-ER: 1. "who or what does, or is connected with" buy**er;** 2. "person concerned with or practicing a trade or profession" doct**or;** 3. "person, thing, or place related to or characterized by" New York**er**

-ERY: 1. "business, place of business, or where something is done" brew**ery;** 2. "place, residence of" nunn**ery;** 3. "a collection of goods, etc." pot-t**ery;** 4. "the qualities or practices of" snobb**ery;** 5. "art, trade, or profession" poet**ry** (this is a variant of *-ery*); 6. "condition of" slav**ery**

-HOOD: "state or condition of" child**hood,** state-**hood**

-ISM: 1. "act or process" ostrac**ism;** 2. "condition of" skeptic**ism;** 3. "characteristic behavior" hero-**ism;** 4. "beliefs" Buddh**ism,** Juda**ism,** commun**ism**

-ITUDE: "forms abstract nouns from adjective" mult**itude,** serv**itude**

-ITY: "nature, condition, state of" magnanim**ity**

-IVE: "having the nature or character of" disrup-**tive,** na**tive**

-MENT: "result or product of" nutri**ment,** testa-**ment,** astonish**ment**

-NESS: "state or quality of being" light**ness,** full-**ness**

-OR: 1. "the person or thing performing the action expressed in the root verb" competit**or;** 2. "quality, state, or function of" demean**or**

-ORY: "serving for, used for, belonging to" dormi-t**ory,** audit**ory**

-TION: "suggests action" condemna**tion,** relax-a**tion,** reflec**tion**

As an exercise, can you delete when necessary and then add the appropriate suffix to make the root word into a noun?

1. real
2. thorough
3. free
4. detrimental
5. tremulous

ANSWERS: **1.** real**ism; 2.** thorough**ness; 3.** free**dom; 4.** detri**ment; 5.** tre**mor.**

Suffixes and Verbs

Let's review the definition of a **verb.** It is a member of a class of words that express existence, action, or occurrence. In *Handbook for Writers,* by Celia Millward (Holt, Rinehart & Winston, 1950), the author writes: "This definition [of a verb] by meaning is not always satisfactory, because other parts of speech, such as nouns, also express action or existence. But verbs can also be defined by their forms, that is, by characteristic endings, and by the function they serve in sentences."

Here, then, are verb suffixes you will see most often. There are not as many as there are with nouns and adjectives.

-ED: 1. "past tense" play**ed; 2.** "having, character-ized by" press**ed**

-ING: "the act or art of doing; a result" hunt**ing,** paint**ing**

-S: "third person singular, present tense" sing**s**

-ATE: "forming a verb from another part of speech" effectu**ate,** origin**ate**

-EN: 1. "made, or consisting of" short**en,** leav**en;** 2. "cause to become" hard**en,** rip**en**

-FY: "make or form into" dei**fy,** quali**fy.** (From

the Latin **facere,** "to make." We had this word in Chapter 5.)

-IZE: "make, cause to become, resemble" civil**ize,** item**ize**

Can you turn the following five words into verbs?

1. sad
2. wide
3. invalid
4. verbal
5. exemplary

ANSWERS: **1.** sadden; **2.** widen; **3.** invalidate; **4.** verbalize; **5.** exemplify.

Suffixes and Adjectives

The definition of an **adjective** is a word that modifies a noun or a pronoun by describing, qualifying, or limiting it. As with nouns and verbs, often adjectives can be recognized by their endings and the positions they take in sentences.

Let's review some of the most common endings:

-ABLE, -IBLE: "given to, tending to, fit to" change**able,** eat**able,** poss**ible**

-AL, -AR: "of or pertaining to" person**al,** regul**ar**

-ANT: "in the act, in the process of doing" exult**ant**

-ARY: 1. "connected with or pertaining to what is expressed in the root word" element**ary;** 2. "whatever a person is engaged in or working at" judici**ary,** milit**ary**

-ATE, -ITE: "possessing or characterized by" or**nate,** favor**ite**

-ED: "used to form the past tense" jump**ed**

-EN: "made of, resembling" wool**en**

-ENT: "having the quality of" pot**ent**

-ESCENT: "beginning to be, have, or do" efferves**cent,** convale**scent**

-FUL: "full of, characterized by" joy**ful,** care**ful**

-IC: 1. "of or pertaining to" volcan**ic;** 2. "resembling, characteristic of" angel**ic**

-ICAL: (similar to -IC) evangel**ical,** mus**ical,** com**ic** or com**ical**

-ID: "ending indicating an adjective" cand**id,** fer**vid**

-INE: "like; pertaining to" can**ine**

-ISH: "of a native group, like" Swed**ish,** clown**ish,** fool**ish**

-IVE: "having a tendency or predisposition to, or in the nature of" disrupt**ive,** mass**ive**

-LESS: "deprived of, without, beyond the range of" mother**less,** harm**less,** count**less**

-LY: "like, characteristic of" friend**ly,** eager**ly**

-OUS: "full of, having, characterized by" glori**ous,** enorm**ous**

-SOME: "characterized by, tending to be" hand**some,** mettle**some**

-Y: "being, possessing, resembling" rain**y,** ston**y**

Convert each of the following five nouns into adjectives:

1. necessity
2. beauty
3. hope
4. red
5. possibility

ANSWERS: **1.** necessary; **2.** beautiful; **3.** hopeful; **4.** reddish; **5.** possible.

Points to Remember

Become familiar with the prefixes and suffixes we have listed. Take a few at a time. For prefixes, turn to the section in the dictionary that lists words beginning with those you are trying to remember. This is a good way to imprint them in the memory patterns of your mind.

Word-Power Test

I Select the correct word from the ones below to fill the blanks in the given sentences:

fortuitous, commodious, demagogue, lethal, finesse, affluent, circumvent, depreciate, staccato.

1. Many . . . . . . people take their wealth for granted.
2. It took great . . . . . . to straighten out the nasty situation.
3. She met her husband in a . . . . . . way when a Ferris wheel broke down.
4. Her heels hammered on the floor, resembling a . . . . . . phrase in music intruding on the heavy silence.
5. The hotel room was more than . . . . . . ; it was palatial.
6. They cleverly figured out how to . . . . . . the traffic tie-up.
7. To . . . . . . a child's efforts may be to destroy enthusiasm.
8. Thoughtlessness and inattentiveness can be . . . . . . to a patient in an emergency situation.

ANSWERS: **1.** affluent; **2.** finesse; **3.** fortuitous; **4.** staccato; **5.** commodious; **6.** circumvent; **7.** depreciate; **8.** lethal.

II Choose the word or phrase closest to the power word.

1. antediluvian   appearing as if A: broken down. B: existing before mankind. C: existing before the Flood.
2. deduction   A: subtraction. B: something made smaller. C: weakening.
3. dissident   one who is A: in disagreement with others. B: dishonest. C: cleverly sarcastic.
4. indigent   A: fury. B: native. C: needy.
5. matriculate   A: to reach maturity. B: enroll. C: graduate.
6. pagan   A: joyful song. B: unbeliever. C: foreigner.
7. nihilism   A: negative doctrine. B: rule by a few. C: humility.
8. magnanimity   A: enormous size. B: optimism. C: nobility of spirit.
9. dissonance   A: harmony. B: discord. C: stubbornness.
10. credible   A: plausible. B: desirable. C: praiseworthy.
11. euthanasia   A: old age. B: unconsciousness. C: painless death.
12. eclipse   A: to cut out. B: outshine. C: fasten.

ANSWERS: **1.** C; **2.** A; **3.** A; **4.** C; **5.** B; **6.** B; **7.** A; **8.** C; **9.** B; **10.** A; **11.** C; **12.** B.

III Answer the following sentences yes or no.

1. A person moving from the tropics to Alaska would probably need time to *acclimate.* Yes or no
2. Customs agents usually ignore *contraband* articles if they are on a government list. Yes or no
3. An *antipathy* can easily develop toward someone who blows cigarette smoke in one's face. Yes or no
4. The President displayed his *malleable* nature when he insisted that his program be accepted. Yes or no
5. The *protagonist* in the play enjoyed his minor role as a crank. Yes or no

ANSWERS: **1.** yes; **2.** no; **3.** yes; **4.** no; **5.** no.

IV Match the words with their synonyms. There are more possible answers than there are power words.

1. debilitating	a. brought forth prematurely; failing
2. disconcert	b. quickness
3. adulation	c. weakening
4. paternalism	d. saying much in few words
5. sententious	e. cause to lose composure
6. abortive	f. charge with a crime
7. extenuate	g. make excuses for
8. deleterious	h. extravagant praise
9. indict	i. inadequate; disproportionate
10. incommensurate	j. control of a group as if by its father
	k. voluptuous
	l. causing moral or physical injury

ANSWERS: **1.** c; **2.** e; **3.** h; **4.** j; **5.** d; **6.** a; **7.** g; **8.** l; **9.** f; **10.** i.

These words can be too close for comfort, either in looks or meaning, to other words. Select the right meaning. Which answer is correct—A or B?

1. bathos   A: descent from something important to something trivial in expression; excessive sentimentality. B: finding fault and complaining.
2. lugubrious   A: insincere, especially in flattery. B: mournful, especially in a ludicrous way.
3. centrifugal   A: directed away from the center. B: directed toward the center.
4. centripetal   A: directed away from the center. B: directed toward the center.
5. epigram   A: brief statement of a practical nature. B: short, witty, or thought-provoking saying.
6. aphorism   A: brief statement of a truth or a principle. B: sexual stimulus.
7. epithet   A: word or phrase used to describe a person or a thing, usually disparaging. B: final statement in a book.
8. epitaph   A: disparaging personal remark. B: carved inscription on a tomb.
9. immanent   A: existing in something as a natural characteristic. B: about to happen.
10. opportune   A: timely. B: moneymaking.

ANSWERS: **1.** A; **2.** B; **3.** A; **4.** B; **5.** B; **6.** A; **7.** A; **8.** B; **9.** A; **10.** A.

Your Score

45–40 . . . . Word master
39–27 . . . . Very good
26–20 . . . . Fair

7

Are These Words Native or Imported?

A rhyme from the nineteenth-century schoolroom gives a brief history of the origins of English.

"The Romans in Britain first held sway;
  The Saxons after them led the way;
  And they tugged with the Danes, till an overthrow
  They both of them got from the Norman bow."

Power Words

alleviate	junta
altruism	largess
amenable	lucrative
amok	nabob
cabal	nadir
caprice	pariah
clique	pogrom
collusion	polyglot
compunction	potpourri
contrite	punctilious
cull	raison d'être
harangue	savoir faire
hauteur	seraph
incognito	vendetta
jeopardy	virtuoso

*Special Words Having to Do with Domestic
and Imported Words*

avant-garde	mesa
bizarre	peccadillo
chiaroscuro	pundit
coup d'état	seraglio
fresco	shibboleth
Hegira	taboo
juggernaut	tycoon
maladroit	

The Deep Roots of English

How often during the day do you *think about* the words you use when conversing with others? Probably not often. Even we, who are professionally concerned with language, take them too much for granted.

The English of the fourteenth, fifteenth, and six-teenth centuries felt the exuberance and power of the language. A sixteenth-century poet exulted:

"And who in time knows whither we may vent
  the treasure of our tongue . . . ?"

This treasure that we use daily and often unthinkingly only partially has roots in England. It is not a native tongue. Most of it has been imported from all over the world.

Let's travel back in time and see how this treasure developed.

England was a remote island. The Celts crossed the English Channel in three main waves—beginning around 500 B.C. and eventually being pushed to the north and settling in Scotland, Ireland, and the Isle of Man. Their language survives today in Irish, Scotch Gaelic, and Manx.

Later, another group of Celts arrived and were finally driven into the mountains of Wales by a people related to the Gauls—coming from somewhere around what are now modern France and Belgium. When Caesar landed in England, in 55 B.C., these fierce fighters were waiting for him on the beach.

Surprisingly, the Romans occupied the island for over four hundred years. Very few Celtic words remain in the English language. In his book *The Treasures of Our Tongue*, Lincoln Barnett mentions that most of the words surviving have to do with place-names. For example, the Thames river, or Aberdeen, the Trent river, Dover, Exeter, and the like.

The island was a favorite place for other countries to invade, and throughout the years, the Vikings, fierce Scandinavian sea rovers, terrorized and pillaged the coasts of England, eventually making permanent settlements. Their terse, no-nonsense type of words merged with local dialects.

By 850, the descendants of Germanic tribes who also invaded the island referred to themselves and their language as English. It is what we today call Old English. If we could "light-beam" ourselves back to that era, we wouldn't understand what the people were talking about. It would be a foreign language.

The island was invaded again, in 1066, by the

Normans. This was a group of people of Scandinavian heritage who had settled in Normandy, in France, during the tenth century. They tried to impose their French on the natives, but the local gentry resisted for two hundred years. By 1250, the invaders were using many of the English words, and "in the process in became transformed into a new language (now called 'Middle English,') which is the immediate parent of our own 'Modern English.'"

Old English is also known as Anglo-Saxon. The Saxons were part of a Germanic tribe who settled and dominated part of England. The word "Anglo-Saxon" remained in our language, loosely meaning someone of English descent today. Modern English has retained some of the simple, earthy elements of Old English.

The Roman Connection

Since those rugged years, the English vocabulary has grown explosively. Becuase it has blotted up so many words from the Romance languages—French, Italian, Spanish, and Portuguese (all deriving from Latin)—that "dead" language Latin lives on in about 60 percent of English.

Romance languages are not necessarily "romantic." Yet the phrase does give us the modern meaning of "romance." There's a history behind the word that Wilfred Funk tells in his entertaining book *Word Origins and Their Romantic Stories.*

"Romance goes back to Rome. When a young girl's eyes are starry with /romance/ she is in innocent debt to the ancient city of Rome, or *Roma*, as it was then called. Should we speak of the /Romance languages/, we are dealing with the speech of the French, the Italians, the Spaniards, and with such others as came originally from the vernacular ('everyday language') Latin, and that, therefore, came at the beginning from Rome itself.

"The word /romance/ is from the Old French term /Romans/, a derivation of /Romanus/, 'Roman.' One of the early meanings of /romance/ was a song or story in the popular tongues of the day. Since these tales were almost always narratives of derring-do ('daring to do'), and written in a language deriving from /Roma/, /romance/ came to mean a tale in verse about a hero, or, preferably, a hero and his lady, which is approximately what it is now in prose form."

Not only have we received words directly from Latin, but a number from Greek as well, many of which give names to scientific words.

A Motley Collection

Let's sample some of the words that other times and nations have given us.

Old English has left many fossils embedded in our daily speech. The following are but a few.

Our pronouns: I, me, mine, you, your, him, his, she, her, and the like.

Basic verbs: break, drink, eat, go, learn, play, ride.

Nouns: book, errand, fiend, gospel (from Old English *godspell*), love, strength, token.

Names relating to the body: blood, foot, mouth.

Food and drink: ale, beer, egg, honey.

Farming: acre, field, sheep, deer, dune.

French The English language has been said to be French badly pronounced. This hyperbole carries a measure of truth. The 1066 invasion caused French to become our language of government, law, and the military. Once English-speakers got the habit of borrowing, the process never stopped. Even today, the word *détente* confirms that we are still making withdrawals from the great riches of French.

On the other hand, there is give as well as take. The French have been borrowers of English. The French, always proud of their language, periodically campaign to keep out the decadent Anglicisms. But it doesn't work. Words like **hamburger, disc jockey, hit parade, zoning,** and the spate of space-age terms continually flow through the ramparts. There is what linguists call *franglais,* a mixture of French and English: **le weekend, le snacque barre,** and the like.

Here is a list of six useful words that have come from French. How many do you know? Choose the right answer—either A or B.

1. clairvoyance (klair VOY ans)   A: suggestibility. B: extraordinary insight.
2. mirage (mih RAHZH)   A: unexplained event. B: optical illusion.
3. menagerie (meh NAJ er ee)   A: collection of wild animals. B: an establishment.
4. facile (FAS'l)   A: effortless. B: flexible.
5. chalice (CHAL is)   A: Swiss-style house. B: goblet.
6. bastion (BASS chun)   A: dungeon. B: stronghold.

Answers: **1.** B; **2.** B; **3.** A; **4.** A; **5.** B; **6.** B.

Words from Spain and Latin America. There are many Spanish words in everyday English, and more are coming as our Hispanic population increases. We know such words as **poncho, siesta, mustang, pinto, mañana.** If you are uncertain of their meanings, you may want to look them up. It's even possible you may have driven cars named after two of them.

Here are some other well-known words:

- wrangler—a cowboy
- hacienda (ha see EN da)—ranch
- El Dorado (el doh RAH doh)—place of wealth and opportunity
- machismo (mah CHIZ moh)—exaggerated masculinity
- junta (HOON tah; JUN tah)—political clique
- peccadillo (pek uh DILL oh)—slight fault
- fiesta (fee ES tah)—festival

Italian. As the editors of *Success with Words* (Reader's Digest Association, Inc., 1983) state, "Italian creativity has been conspicuously strong in the arts, warfare, and cookery. The Renaissance, which originated in Italy in the 14th century, transformed painting, architecture, literature, and all the other arts."

We see this in words such as **fresco** and **pastel, arcade, balcony,** and **colonnade, sonnet,** and **scenario.**

Military contributions are **battalion, brigade, cavalry, infantry, colonel, sentinel,** and **cannon.** We also have words dealing with violence, as **bandit, brigand, duel,** and **vendetta.**

Of a more tasty nature, the Italians give us **pasta, broccoli,** and **salami,** among others.

Or what about the potpourri of words such as **caprice, caress, intrigue, incognito, zany, carnival, casino, regatta, parasol,** and even **jeans?**

Chinese and Japanese. Are these words from the "inscrutable" Orient puzzling? How many of them do you know? Answer *true* or *false* to the questions. The first four are Chinese. The second six, Japanese.

1. Mah-jongg is a game.		true	false
2. Gung ho is a rice dish.		true	false
3. To kowtow is to bow to someone.		true	false
4. Typhoon is a hurricane.		true	false

ANSWERS: **1.** true; **2.** false (extremely enthusiastic); **3.** true; **4.** true.

1. Tempura is a type of painting.		true	false
2. Zen is a meditative discipline.		true	false
3. Tycoon is a wealthy businessman.		true	false
4. Shogun is a type of firearm.		true	false
5. Satori is sudden enlightenment.		true	false
6. Tofu is a type of robe.		true	false

1. false (pieces of seafood and sliced vegetables deep-fried in batter); **2.** true; **3.** true; **4.** false (a strong leader; originally, one of the military rulers of Japan who conducted all state business on the emperor's behalf); **5.** true; **6.** false (custard-like bean curd).

German. Germans give us much of our scientific and technical vocabulary—words such as **diesel, ecology, enzyme, Fahrenheit.**

At the same time, they are heavy in the culinary arts, with such offerings as **cold duck, delicatessen, frankfurter, hamburger, noodle.**

They also provide us with **blitzkreig, flak, strafe.** Don't forget **glitch, kitsch,** and **spiel.**

We also are indebted to them for **dollar, kindergarten, leitmotif, realpolitik** (ray AHL po lih TEEK), **semester, snorkel, superman, swindle,** and **waltz.**

If you are uncertain of any of these words, check them out in your dictionary. For example, **realpolitik** is an important word these days, pertaining to international relationships between countries.

The Arab Countries. The Arabs have brought us more than oil. They've contributed words we speak or read frequently. Some of the following appear also in other chapters of this book.

If you were on a **safari** (hunting expedition) in Kenya, though you'd be wearing a simple **khaki** outfit, you'd probably be considered a **nabob** (rich person). You'd be delighted with the **azure** (sky-blue) sky of a perfect summer day. In town you would sit in an **alcove** (recess) in a small cafe sipping your **coffee,** while your friend poured his wine from a **carafe** (bottle). You would be reminiscing about the high **caliber** of service of the people who organized your trip. The drinking water might have a bit too much **alkali** in it, and some **ghouls** (evil spirits) might have bothered your dreams. But, all in all, it was a delightful experience that **kismet** (fate) provided for you.

India. It may surprise you to learn that **bungalow** and **dungaree** come from India. So do **pajamas, seersucker, thug, veranda,** and **dinghy.** There are other words, of course.

Yiddish. Yiddish is the High German language of the Jews of Eastern Europe; they carried their language with them as they migrated to different countries. Yiddish includes about 15 percent Hebrew words and a smattering of borrowings from other languages.

Here are a few Yiddish gifts to English:

Bagel, blintz (thin pancake filled with cream cheese, berries, etc.), **borsht** (beet soup), **chutzpah** (HOOTS pah) (shameless audacity), **kibitz** (give unwanted advice), **schlock** (shoddy product or performance), **shtick** (something contrived to make one's personality distinct or memorable, as an actor's characteristic mannerism or a comedian's routine).

Word Cognates

Ruth Freedman, a nurse in the leper colony of Molokai, in Hawaii, decided that **cognates** were an overlooked method of learning foreign words. **Cognates,** as you know, are words having a common origin. The word itself is from Latin *co-* (together) and *gnatus* (born). **Word cognates** often look alike. If you look back in this chapter at the words under French, Spanish, Italian, et cetera, you will see the similarity between the English and the foreign words.

For example, our well-known food coffee:

Italian	caffè
Dutch	koffie
German	Kaffee
French	café
Spanish	café

Some other words:

coordinate	German *koordiniert*
presentable	Italian *presentabile*
felicity	Spanish *felicidad*
discretion	French *discrétion*

In an inventive and fascinating way, Nurse Freedman has made up lists of thousands of **word cognates.** Such lists would help you to learn a foreign language more quickly.

Points to Remember

1. English is a composite made up of words borrowed from other languages.

2. English has an exciting history, which is embedded in its words, like past time in fossils.

3. By being aware of the heritage of English, you become more keenly aware of other languages.

4. Think of using **word cognates** to help you to learn a foreign language.

Power-Word Test

I   What words would you use to describe the following people? Pick the appropriate words from the list given below:

pariah, polyglot, nabob, tycoon, virtuoso, pundit.

1. The wealthy businessman demanded great deference, and he was powerful enough to get it.

2. The pianist's mastery of the finger technique demanded by the playful, light scherzo delighted the audience.

3. The young economist's expertise in his criticisms and predictions won him a wide audience.

4. The woman, unfortunately, could not perceive why people avoided her. No one told her she was inconsiderate, aggressive, and boring.

5. The fact that he was fluent in four languages definitely helped him get the position.

6. His magnificent home, extensive holdings, and prominent position as a community leader made him a fearsome opponent.

ANSWERS: **1.** tycoon; **2.** virtuoso; **3.** pundit; **4.** pariah; **5.** polyglot; **6.** nabob.

II   Pick the phrase or sentence from a, b, or c that matches the sentence closely.

1. The nurse tried to *alleviate* his fears by giving sensitive and cheerful answers.
   a. She tried to make the fears easier to bear.
   b. She tried to permanently remove the fears.
   c. She tried to explain.

2. He was very *contrite* when he broke his mother's best mirror while roughhousing with his friend.
   a. He was sassy.
   b. He was filled with remorse.
   c. He argued that he had not done it.

3. They suggested he might be in *collusion* when he watched the crime and did not report it.
   a. He might be terribly confused and upset.
   b. He might have imagined he saw the crime.
   c. He might be in secret cooperation.

4. Often, the king liked to go *incognito* among his subjects to find out their true feelings.
   a. He liked to observe from his carriage.
   b. He went in disguise.
   c. He walked around the marketplace.

5. The wealthy woman was known for her *largess.*
   a. She was known for being overweight.
   b. She was known because she served good food.
   c. She was known for her generosity.

6. Don't put yourself in *jeopardy* by arguing with those hoodlums.
   a. Don't start a fight.
   b. Don't expose yourself to ridicule.
   c. Don't expose yourself to danger.

7. The South American country suffered one *coup d'état* after another.
   a. They suffered an unexpected overthrow of the government.
   b. They suffered business failure because of international economic conditions.
   c. Their crops failed from drought or too much rain.

8. Those close to the famous often emphasize their *peccadillos* more than the qualities that make these people important.
   a. They emphasize the money they make.
   b. They talk about their parties.
   c. They talk about their trifling faults.

9. The *Hegira,* which now means any flight from danger, originated with:
   a. The flight of Mohammed from Mecca to Medina.
   b. The flight of the Jews out of Egypt.
   c. The flight of the Russians from Napoleon's invasion.

10. The beautiful enclosed garden architecturally resembled a *seraglio.*
    a. The vine motif on the structure was reminiscent of an Eastern temple.
    b. It resembled an Egyptian temple.
    c. It resembled the harem section of a sultan's palace.

ANSWERS: **1.** a; **2.** b; **3.** c; **4.** b; **5.** c; **6.** c; **7.** a; **8.** c; **9.** a; **10.** c.

III Match the power words with the appropriate meanings. There are more possible meanings than words.

1. altruism		**a.**	startlingly odd
2. amok		**b.**	high, broad plateau with steep slopes
3. caprice		**c.**	embedded in mud
4. cull		**d.**	to pick or sort out
5. harangue		**e.**	proud, arrogant manner or spirit
6. hauteur		**f.**	clumsy or blundering
7. nadir		**g.**	unselfish devotion to the welfare of others
8. pogrom		**h.**	a Spanish dance with shawls
9. bizarre		**i.**	possessed with a murderous frenzy
10. maladroit		**j.**	high-style design by Parisian couturier
11. mesa		**k.**	officially instigated massacre, especially against Jews
12. taboo		**l.**	an oration, especially a loud, vehement speech
		m.	whim; unreasonable impulse
		n.	the lowest possible point
		o.	religious or social prohibition against doing something because it is sacred or dangerous

ANSWERS: **1.** g; **2.** i; **3.** m; **4.** d; **5.** l; **6.** e; **7.** n; **8.** k; **9.** a; **10.** f; **11.** b; **12.** o.

IV Fill in the blanks in the paragraphs or sentences from the words below:

amenable, cabal, compunction, raison d'être, savoir faire, vendetta, shibboleth.

1. The zoning board was surprisingly . . . . . . and let them put in the wide driveway.
2. For many of the well-to-do in society, good table manners became a . . . . . . dividing people.
3. The student unfortunately seemed to have no . . . . . . about cheating.
4. Our ambassadors must have a high degree of . . . . . . to deal with unusual situations in foreign countries.
5. The family carried on a . . . . . . for many years against the neighbors who had inadvertently killed their daughter.
6. Skiing was his . . . . . . , and he was out on the slopes all day, every day throughout the winter.
7. The . . . . . . secretly plotted to take over a powerful cartel.

ANSWERS: **1.** amenable; **2.** shibboleth; **3.** compunction; **4.** savoir faire; **5.** vendetta; **6.** raison d'être; **7.** cabal.

V Pick the word or phrase closest in meaning to the power word.

1. clique   A: clannish group of people. B: decoy. C: gathering of powerful businessmen.
2. junta   A: legislative emergency session. B: irresistible force. C: political group taking over government.

3. lucrative   A: fortunate. B: profitable. C: lavish.

4. potpourri   A: peppery food. B: mixture. C: informal gathering.

5. punctilious   A: compulsively fussy. B: obsessively punctual. C: minutely particular about fine points.

6. seraph   A: shepherd. B: servant. C: angel.

7. avant garde   A: protective group. B: barrier. C: a vanguard.

8. chiaroscuro   A: treatment of light and shade. B: surgical reflected light. C: blocking light.

9. fresco   A: wall. B: painting on plaster. C: outside statuary.

10. juggernaut   A: irresistible force. B: battleship. C: solemn pronouncement.

ANSWERS: **1.** A; **2.** C; **3.** B; **4.** B; **5.** C; **6.** C; **7.** C; **8.** A; **9.** B; **10.** A.

Your Score

45–40 . . . . Word master
39–27 . . . . Very good
26–20 . . . . Fair

8

Words on the Move—The Changing World of Words

Power Words

addicted	feline
antic	felony
apathy	genre
aplomb	harbinger
assiduous	illusory
atypical	imbibe
bombast	laity
choleric	legend
critique	ossify
deprecate	personification
dudgeon	potential
effete	sanguinary
eleemosynary	sanguine
elusive	toxic
exorbitant	

Special Words Having to Do With How Words Are Born, Die, Lose Force, Ascend, Narrow, Widen or Are "Set in Concrete"

analogy	provincial
casuistry	quatrain
composite	signification
hyperbole	simile
metamorphosis	spurious
metaphor	syllogism
misconstrue	variant
paradox	

"In 1914, Monica Baldwin, the niece of the future British prime minister Stanley Baldwin, entered a convent and remained there in total seclusion for twenty-eight years. When she finally emerged, the map of Europe was scarcely recognizable; technology had dramatically altered everyday life; most of the customs she had been bred to as a young girl had changed greatly.

"But she was even more puzzled by what she heard. She found it difficult to communicate with other members of her speech community, for not only had words been added or lost in the vocabulary, but the usage of once-familiar words was often different. New idioms had become popular; when people said to her, 'It's your funeral,' or 'believe it or not,' she looked at them befuddled. Seemingly, Monica Baldwin had returned to her own speech community, but in reality it was a different one in time even though it remained the same geographically and in the ethnic composition of its membership." (Peter Farb, *Word Play,* Alfred A. Knopf, Inc., 1974)

Who's to Blame?

Probably, you have heard "guardians" of English complain that our language is becoming vitiated—that is, weakened, spoiled, made ineffective. They tell us that words no longer mean what they did. For them, commentators on TV and radio are constantly mispronouncing words; advertisements frequently are ungrammatical. In short, our language is "going to hell."

And who is responsible for this supposed state of affairs?

You are! You and I, and the other 350 million people for whom English is the native tongue. Another 300 million in other countries who use English as an additional language also influence change. We are somewhat like Humpty Dumpty in *Alice in Wonderland.* He said: "When *I* use a word, it means just what I choose it to mean—neither more nor less."

A word is merely a symbol. It only *represents* an idea or an object. For example, scientists make up words to describe a discovery. **Entropy** was coined by a German physicist who combined *en-(ergy)* and Greek *trope* (a turning toward). In a general sense, the word means a trend toward disorder in our universe, or such a trend in any "system." For physicists it is a measure of the degree to which the energy of a system is unavailable for work. Someone else might have put another name on **entropy.**

Also, as our society changes, so do the meanings

of some of our words. Yet the process is a subtle one, for each has an influence on the others.

As linguists, the authors of this book are not against the tide of change. Even if we were, it wouldn't make any difference. Language changes. We find ourselves a bit in the position of Margaret Fuller, an nineteenth-century editor and feminist leader. At one point she stated: "I accept the Universe!"

Responded Thomas Carlyle, the English historian: "By God, she'd better."

And, "by God," *we'd* better accept the fact that language does change, since change is inevitable.

The Weakening of Words

In addition to careless usage, words tend to lose their impact and force by overuse and hyperbole. We Americans usually shy away from **litotes** (LIT uh tees)—understatement. Advertisers, trying to shock an audience into an awareness of their product, turn to **hyperbole.** They go far beyond what is needed. Or when a word moves over to the colloquial side of the street, the essence of the meaning becomes diluted. The original, keen edge is dulled.

An ad for a new book writes about an **awesome** literary talent. A sportscaster describes how a quarterback threw an **awesome** pass. A restaurant has come up with an **awesome** *flambé.*

Awe, according to Webster's New World Dictionary, refers to a feeling of fearful or profound respect or wonder, inspired by the greatness, superiority, grandeur, etc., of a person or thing and suggests an immobilizing effect. To be **awesome** you have to have a mighty talent to be able to create that result. The word is used loosely today.

What about **great?** Most of the time we use it to mean enjoyable or satisfactory. The original force of the word described something or someone as much above average in size, amount, or intensity. A **great** person had remarkable abilities; a **great** event was important. Now it is used mostly in a sense of having had a "great" vacation, a "great" golf game, a "great" party, and the like.

Or **love!** Poor old **love.** Take a week sometime, and listen to the many and trivial ways **love** is used. And we're as guilty as anyone, employing it as a kind of spread to cover a multitude of nice, warm feelings.

Sometimes adjectives are used unnecessarily, as, for example, "a brilliant genius." Geniuses are supposed to be brilliant, so why the need for "brilliant"?

We came across a "penniless pauper." We thought paupers were very poor. David B. Guralnik, at Webster's New World Dictionary, suggests that such verbal constructions come about because "the speaker is trying to make sure he will not be misunderstood." Possibly this is so, because people today do not have as sure an understanding of a word's meaning. Such usage saps a word's impact.

Finally, colloquial English and slang nearly always debilitate the essential meanings of words.

A Quick Quiz

Which of the following fourteen words have changed their primary meanings over the years?

1. ally	**8.** bribe
2. accost	**9.** facetious
3. dexterous	**10.** filibuster
4. baffle	**11.** garnish
5. imp	**12.** economist
6. lewd	**13.** charm
7. exploit	**14.** humor

ANSWER: Every one!

1. ally: In its younger days, hundreds of years ago, it meant "a connection by marriage."

2. accost: Its basic meaning has been "to approach and speak to." During the last few years it is more often used in an aggressive and intrusive sense.

3. dexterous: At one time this meant simply "seated at the right hand." Today it means "skillful and clever."

4. baffle: An early meaning was "to subject someone to disgrace." Today its meaning is to confuse or perplex.

5. imp: Once, this meant "a boy." Today we think of an **imp** as "a small devil" or "a mischievous child."

6. lewd: A word that once meant a layman, or someone without schooling. Gradually it took on a sexual connotation.

7. exploit: From meaning "to make effective use of," most of the time today it is used to mean "to take full advantage of for one's own use at the expense of others."

8. bribe: A bribe meant originally "a piece of bread to a beggar."

9. facetious: From meaning "having a polished and agreeable manner," to today's meaning, "intending to be humorous." Most of the time now, the word describes "joking at an inappropriate time."

10. filibuster: In the sixteenth and seventeenth centuries, a **filibuster** was a buccaneer in the West Indies. A long cry from the **filibustering** in Congress. Are you sure you know what the word means as used in Congress?

11. garnish: Once, this word was a warning to people in debt. Today it means to "decorate food" and the like.

12. economist: In ancient Greece, an **economist** was a housekeeper.

13. charm: If a girl were called **charming** in fourteenth-century England, she was a prime candidate for the torture chamber. A **charm** meant an association with evil and magic powers.

14. Here's an interesting metamorphosis of a word's meaning. In Latin, **humor** meant fluid. The ancient philosophers believed that the body was made up of four **humors**, or fluids: blood, phlegm, yellow bile, and black bile. Your temperament depended on the mixture of the humors. You have heard of people being in a "black mood." To the ancients, this was the result of too much "black bile." Or if you had too much yellow bile (in Latin, bile is *chole*) you were short-tempered and cranky. In other words, you were **choleric.** When these **humors** were out of balance, you were apt to be eccentric (away from the center), and so **humor** took on the sense of "oddness." Ultimately, the word became associated with personalities **(humorists)** that could "provoke laughter at the oddities and the incongruities of life."

Some Words Increase Their Muscle

Change works both ways. Some words grow in impact.

In its early days, **captious** simply meant "clever." Today it pins down the personality of one who tries to find fault with, or argue about, even the pettiest details; as, a *captious* critic.

At one time, **Frankenstein** was only a character in an 1818 novel written by Mary Wollstonecraft Shelley. In it the imaginative doctor of that name created a living thing who inadvertently became a monster. Now it is synonymous with anything that becomes dangerous to its creator.

When we speak today of a **garbled** text, we mean that the text has been changed and perverted, usually with a bad intent. But in the old days, **garble** meant only to sort and to sift. Gradually it came to suggest this as being done in a dishonest way.

Words like **foul** and **filth** were used in earlier English much as **dirt** is today, without implying something "offensive to the senses" or "loathsome." And **loathe** itself was not much more emphatic than **dislike.** The adjective **loath,** as in "He was **loath** to go downtown," still means only "reluctant." **Disaster,** from Latin **dis** (against) and **astrum** (star), which at one time signified merely "an unlucky or unfortunate event," has since strengthened so that it acts as a close synonym to "calamity."

The Way Words Become Abstract

In their early development, most words are concrete. Each had one specific meaning. Through use and misuse, the meanings gradually spread out.

Take the word **gossip.** Writing in *The Wall Street Journal,* Steele Commager notes that **"Gossip** itself has a respectable enough ancestry. The original spelling was 'godsib,' 'sib' being a relative. A 'godsib' was a sponsor at a child's christening, a godparent. And when godsibs, or godparents, gathered for a baptism, the talk would not be particularly elevated. Instead, it would dwell on such things as Uncle Peter's illness, Cousin Mary's dreadful child or a neighbor's financial disarray—matters familial, or at least familiar—which is still the basic material for gossips today."

Trivial is another word that has escaped. The Romans had a sense that where their roads crossed would be the spot women would meet and chat, perhaps gossip a bit on the way back from market. The words for this in Latin are *tri-* (three) and *via* (road or way), which becomes our "trivial."

Try matching the word and its current meaning, on the left side of the column, with one of its earliest meanings, on the right side.

1. trophy (prize)	**a.** dice game
2. trump (winning bridge hand)	**b.** crime
3. forfeit (a penalty)	**c.** fundamental or primary
4. hazard (danger)	**d.** triumphal entrance
5. radical (extreme)	**e.** a monument

ANSWERS: **1.** e; **2.** d; **3.** b; **4.** a; **5.** c.

Words Become Concrete

Words, like money, tend to inflate. By now you are probably more than ever aware that over a period of time they become encrusted with various synonymous meanings. However, a few—a *very* few—go in the opposite direction. They stress one particular meaning and become more concrete, more definite.

In earlier English, a bow with which you shoot an arrow was referred to as **buxom,** something that is "pliable, easily bent." In current English, however, it has settled on a rather concrete description of a woman who is plump and healthy-looking, or one who is full-bosomed.

Did you know that, in the early part of the nineteenth century, **blizzard** had the meaning of "a blow, a loud noise or a blast" and sometimes meant a flash of lightning? The year 1888 had a cold winter, and when gale winds with snow "blasted" over the Northeast, burying a good part of it, the storm was called a **blizzard.** An official **blizzard** today must have winds of forty miles an hour, a temperature close to zero Fahrenheit, and an abundance of fine, swirling snow.

In olden times, if you thought a friend was acting foolish, you might have called him **dizzy.** More precisely today we characterize a man as **dizzy** if he suffers from vertigo or feels confused.

How Do Changes Affect You?

The authors are not concerned with the broad changes in language. Such changes occur more slowly than we think. For example, we can quite easily read and understand most writings of the sixteenth century.

We do become distressed, however, when words are carelessly misused. Through such misuse, people have misunderstandings—both in communicating and in thinking. Using the wrong word is like pushing the wrong button on a machine: you come up with an error.

Sloppy usage means sloppy thinking, and then clear understanding and thinking becomes an "endangered species." In our world of possible instant annihilation, we cannot afford to be careless in the things that count.

Another aspect we find worrisome is the falling off of the quality of vocabulary among people in general. Tests show that though individuals may know more technical words today, the general vocabulary is shrinking. The brain has become top-heavy with technical terms. What is being lost is the irreplaceable general vocabulary—the vocabulary of communication, the vocabulary of concepts, of abstractions, of time and relationships, of history

and literature, of the words that go creatively into constructive ideas, words that bring greater understanding and better relations between people.

The quality and range of our thinking is dependent on the quality and range of our vocabulary. And a vocabulary is like any other sensitive piece of equipment: it may be used destructively or constructively.

As the quality of our people's vocabulary diminishes, all of us will be affected in one way or another. The quality of our lives is, to a large measure, rooted in language.

By enriching your word power, you are giving yourself an important asset that will be useful in nearly every area of your life. As we mentioned in Chapter 1, an efficient way of improving your brainpower is through word power.

Points to Remember

1. The nature of language is to be in a state of flux.

2. What we try to do is to use and pronounce our words as accurately as possible.

3. A quality vocabulary helps to improve the "richness" of our lives.

Word-Power Test

I In the following paragraph, fill in the spaces with the correct words from the ones given below:

bombast, misconstrued, imbibing, syllogism, hyperbole, simile, analogy, casuistry, aplomb.

After previously **(1)** . . . . . . wine freely at dinner, the speaker at the forum on zoning used **(2)** . . . . . . to make his points. With great **(3)** . . . . . . he used a false **(4)** . . . . . . in comparing residential to business zoning as "the idle" compared to "the producers." The **(5)** . . . . . . angered most of the audience. It was worse than **(6)** . . . . . . ; it was an insult. Such thinking is comparable to saying, idle people live in houses, therefore, all people living in houses are idle. A **(7)** . . . . . . can sound plausible, but the meaning may be **(8)** . . . . Such **(9)** . . . . . . fooled no one.

ANSWERS: **1.** imbibing; **2.** casuistry; **3.** aplomb; **4.** analogy; **5.** simile; **6.** hyperbole, **7.** syllogism; **8.** misconstrued; **9.** bombast.

II Pair off the synonyms or antonyms in the following two lists:

1. assiduous	a. fruitful
2. choleric	b. genuine
3. toxic	c. excessive
4. exorbitant	d. possible
5. effete	e. bitter
6. atypical	f. angry
7. apathy	g. unusual
8. spurious	h. harmless
9. provincial	i. indifference
10. potential	j. lazy
	k. urbane
	l. out of orbit

ANSWERS: **1.** j (ant.); **2.** f (syn.); **3.** h (ant.); **4.** c (syn.); **5.** a (ant.); **6.** g (syn.); **7.** i (syn.); **8.** b (ant.); **9.** k (ant.), **10.** d (syn.).

III Be careful with the following words, as they are close in meaning, appearance, or sound. Fill the blank spaces with the appropriate words.

1. The ancient warrior was **(a)** . . . . about winning the battle and **(b)** . . . . in pursuit of his objective, as he was merciless.   sanguinary sanguine

2. The woman, not wishing to **(a)** . . . . the motives of the salesman, still felt compelled to question his judgment in selling a **(b)** . . . . car with bad tires to an inexperienced buyer, at top value.   deprecate   depreciated

3. The idea was **(a)** . . . . in terms of explaining it without graphics, and purely **(b)** . . . . in terms of utility.   elusive   illusive

ANSWERS: **1. (a)** sanguine, **(b)** sanguinary; **2. (a)** deprecate, **(b)** depreciated; **3. (a)** elusive, **(b)** illusive.

IV Pick the word or phrase that best describes the meaning of the target word in the sentence from one of the three selections below it.

1. The clown's entertaining *antics* amused children and adults.
   a. acrobatics
   b. pranks
   c. placards

2. To graduate, the English majors had to write a *critique* of a well-known novel.
   a. analytical review
   b. standard form
   c. paraphrase

3. The young celebrity left in high *dudgeon* when the press ignored her presence to concentrate on the humble older woman who devoted her life to saving lost children.
   a. with a flounce
   b. sullen displeasure
   c. disgrace

4. By selling the top-secret materials, the captain not only committed a *felony* but destroyed his self-esteem forever.
   a. especially foolish act
   b. regrettable decision
   c. one of the gravest of crimes

5. The painting by Chardin of kitchen implements is in the *genre* of the times.
   a. archive
   b. catalog
   c. style

6. The redbud trees were a colorful *harbinger* of the return of spring.
   a. indication
   b. hidden sign
   c. bright picture

7. The *laity* were divided on accepting the pretty young minister for the staff.
   a. ecclesiastical hierarchy
   b. people not members of clergy
   c. Women's Prayer Group

8. To some it seemed a *paradox* that the older she became the more beautiful she appeared to be.
   a. contradicts common belief but is true
   b. an impossibility
   c. a marvelous surprising occurrence

9. The *metaphor* that her lover became a god of light and beauty was not an exaggeration to the young woman.
   a. statement
   b. figure of speech saying one object is another
   c. figure of speech saying an object is "like" or "as" another

10. The woman's entire stance and walk appeared *feline*.
   a. feminine
   b. catlike
   c. sensitive

ANSWERS: **1.** b; **2.** a; **3.** b; **4.** c; **5.** c; **6.** a; **7.** b; **8.** a; **9.** b; **10.** b.

V Pick the word or phrase closest to the meaning of the power word.

1. ossify   A: to convert into bone. B: be idle. C: be conspicuous.

2. personification   A: endowment of the inani-

mate with human qualities. B: movement stressing individual rights. C: promotion.

3. legend   an unauthenticated story A: from the past. B: from the current news. C: given to the police.

4. eleemosynary   pertaining to A: a sad poem. B: praise of a person's life. C: charity.

5. composite   A: compound. B: solid. C: fake.

6. metamorphosis   A: hypnotic sleep. B: great distress. C: transformation.

7. quatrain   A: stanza of eight lines. B: stanza of four lines. C: poem of fourteen lines.

8. signification   A: hand-stamped decree. B: meaning. C: signed document.

9. variant   A: indefinite. B: opposite. C: differing.

10. addicted   A: upset or disturbed. B: habitually dependent. C: despairing.

ANSWERS: **1.** A; **2.** A; **3.** A; **4.** C; **5.** A; **6.** C; **7.** B; **8.** B; **9.** C; **10.** B.

Your Score

42–40 . . . . Word master
39–27 . . . . Very good
26–20 . . . . Fair

9

How Words Get to Be the Way They Are—Origins and Histories

"We know only that there must have been a time when there was no language, and then there was a time when there was a language, but we do not know how, when, where, or by whom language came into being." (Charlton Laird, *The Miracle of Language,* The World Publishing Company)

Power Words

accredit	lithe
arbitrary	lunar
blasphemy	minutiae
charlatan	monogamy
comprehensible	primal
correlate	prodigy
corroborate	prolific
exotic	protocol
gestate	quell
grit	secular
hybrid	sequester
inadvertent	sinuous
incorrigible	transcend
insensible	uxorious
irascible	vehement

Words That Are Special Because of Their Origins and History

augury	phlegmatic
crestfallen	plagiarism
egregious	precocious
enthrall	recalcitrant
impediment	sinister
jaded	stigma
jingoism	supercilious
ostracize	

We continue Charlton Laird's observation: "In short we know nothing about how language started, and we have not even the materials from which we might hope to find out. Logically, of course, there must have been a time when some primordial creature—let us call him Og—opened his carnivorous jaws and said, 'Bup,' or 'Ickey,' and his bored wife, or his Electra-complex-ridden daughter, or his worst enemy in the next cave, or somebody, under-

stood him, and language was born. Something of the sort there must have been. Theoretically and symbolically there had to be an Og."

We do know generally that what is known as the Proto-Indo-European language may have originated as a spoken language in an area close to the Black Sea in Europe or Asia. This location is surmised by certain words describing types of trees and animals. It is the grandfather of many languages: English, German, Dutch, Swedish, Norwegian, Icelandic, French, Italian, Spanish, Portuguese, Armenian, Romanian, Latin, Greek, and various Near Eastern ones such as Hindi and Persian. Indo-European roots spawned eighty or more major tongues.

To some extent, they are all related, and so when you are speaking English, in a sense you are dipping into a well-seasoned word-stew.

Match the word in the left column with the language it comes from.

1. euphoria		Russian
2. condominium		Greek
3. garage		Spanish
4. ombudsman		French
5. karate		Swedish
6. apartheid		Latin
7. pronto		Japanese
8. sputnik		Afrikaans

ANSWERS: **1.** Greek; **2.** Latin; **3.** French; **4.** Swedish; **5.** Japanese; **6.** Afrikaans; **7.** Spanish; **8.** Russian.

Words are not ready-made for our use. To the contrary, most of them are custom-made, arising out of a need to describe or explain something.

Before we get on with the power-word games, let's take a look at the way words are formed. To some degree, this is a digression. But on the other hand, the history of words is a fascinating one, and the more familiarity you have with your language, the easier it is to understand. In his book *Word Origins and Their Romantic Stories,* Wilfred Funk wrote at the end of his Preface: "In the end this book has one main intent. I can only wish that the reader might be encouraged to walk among words as I do, like Alice in Wonderland, amazed at the marvels they hold." The authors of this book have a similar hope, that *Word Power Made Simple* will ensnare your curiosity and delight in the enticing web of words.

New Words
These are formed in a variety of ways: by combining forms, from myths, from words shortened or clipped, from echoing sounds, by extending meanings.

Combining
We know that historically many words in the English language are the result of the process of blending. Because of that, it is a hospitable host, spreading its net wide to catch all kinds of verbal fish, opening its doors freely to admit foreigners: Chinese, Arabic, Hebrew, various African languages, Eskimo, almost whatever words are spoken.

Joseph Shipley, in *The Origins of English Words,* points out that in addition to words coming from foreign countries, they may also be invented or formed by combining already existing roots or words. In the seventeenth century, Jan Baptista van Helmont coined **gas** from Greek **chaos. Blurb,** the praising of something in an advertisement, especially the write-up on a book jacket, was invented by Gelett Burgess in this century. He said it sounded like a publisher. **Kodak** was the brainchild of inventor George Eastman. He felt *K* had a commanding sound. **Chortle,** thought up by Lewis Carroll of *Alice in Wonderland* fame, is a combination of chuckle and snort. **Scuba,** an acronym, is formed from *s*elf-*c*ontained *u*nderwater *b*reathing *a*pparatus.

The technical name for an invented word is **neologism** (nee OL uh jiz em). One of the most prolific of the word coiners (neologists) was William Shakespeare. Out of the 17,700 different words he employed, 1,700 appeared for the first time in his works. One of them, which he used with tongue in cheek, is **honorificabilitudinitatibus.** Since it is obsolete and rare, not many dictionaries list it. The meaning is simply the shorter word **honorableness** or honor.

"O, they have lived long on the alms-basket of words. I marvel thy master had not eaten thee for a word; for thou art not so long by the head as honorificabilitudinitatibus: thou art easier swallowed than a flap-dragon." *Love's Labour's Lost,* Act v, scene i.

"Words are weird," observes Dr. Shipley.

There are many examples of words combining: **sidewinder** missile, **high-rise** apartment buildings, **railroad, freethinker, greyhound, lifeboat,** and on and on.

Many of our scientific words are combined from Latin and Greek. **Geology,** from Greek *geo,* "earth," and *logy,* "the science of."

Classical Myths
Myths are a source of words. **Psychology** developed from the goddess Psyche. In Roman folklore she was a maiden who, after undergoing many hardships due to Venus' jealousy of her beauty, is reunited with Cupid and made immortal by Jupiter. Someone with a **mercurial** disposition is unpredictably changeable, moving quickly from one mood to another. The word comes from Mercury, the messenger of the gods.

Words Are Shortened and Clipped
The history of words is sometimes also the story of people. For example, in the seventh century there was a pious girl who eventually became the head of a nunnery. During her childhood she had loved exquisite necklaces. In her later life she died of a throat disease, and she blamed her sickness on her one worldly vanity. On October 17 her birthday was celebrated by a fair, and scarves called "St. Audrey's laces" were sold. The local people clipped "St. Audrey's laces" to **tawdry** laces. At first, **tawdry** laces were supposed to have been fine and lovely, but when they began to be made in quantity, the quality was lost. Eventually, **tawdry** came to mean showy and gaudy, without either taste or elegance.

Television is often clipped to **TV.** We say, "I'll **phone** you." We look for a **taxi,** rather than a taxicab.

Echoic Words
These are words that seem to represent certain sounds, such as **crack, buzz,** and the like. Referring to Joseph Shipley again, he observes that "peoples of different tongues, however, also hear differently; it is enlightening as well as amusing to note, say, Japanese or even French, Danish, German and English **echoic** words for the crowing of a cock, the growl of a dog, the purr of a cat. Imitation has played an incalculable part in word formation."

Words Extend Their Meanings
At one time, **parameter** was only used in a technical sense. Webster's Illustrated Contemporary Dic-

tionary defines the word as "a variable or constant whose values determine the form of an expression, function, etc. 2. A number expressing some aspect of the behavior of a physical system." Now, however, the word is used in an **extended** sense by the public to mean "a fixed limit or guideline."

For the word **man,** Webster's New World Dictionary lists twenty-one meanings. The women's liberation movement, however, quite rightly challenges some of them. The movement objects to the use of **man** to represent the whole human race, or a **man** in a backgammon game. This movement is causing a shift in certain meanings, as well as giving them additional ones.

Words can develop contradictory meanings. The earliest sense of **fast** is "firmly fixed in place." It has nothing to do with speed.

Linguists surmise that the current meaning of **swift** comes from the idea of keeping close to what is pursued.

What do you make of the two meanings of **cleave?** One is "to split," the other "to cling to." The answer is they come from slightly different Old English roots: *cleofan* and *cleofian.*

Can You Use Each of the Following Five Words in Five Different Ways?

1. through
2. throw
3. let
4. up
5. play

For answers, check your dictionary.

Brief Reminder

1. There is no *single* valid theory for the beginnings of language.

2. Generally, new words come into our language by adopting words from other languages, combining existing forms of words, inventing new words (neologisms), using words that seem to be echoes of something else, and extending the meanings of words.

Word-Power Test

I   The origins to the following words are either amusing or thought-provoking, which thus makes them easier to remember. Fill each blank with a word from the power words you think matches the comment on the origin.

1. The crest of a rooster who has lost a fight actually falls, as a person's feelings fall when he loses. They feel . . . .

2. A sheep might be termed foolish that stands out from the herd, especially if a wolf is near. People stand out when they make a glaring mistake or an . . . . error.

3. To be brought into slavery or bondage is the basic idea when an idea . . . . you so that you forget everything else.

4. The picture of a Roman with his feet shackled or entangled meant it was difficult for him to accomplish what he wanted. The Latin word . . . . and our words for whatever hinders are similar. They are . . . .

5. When a public person seemed dangerous or unwholesome, the ancient Athenians voted to banish him by writing on a tile called "ostrakon." Today we may . . . . a person socially for the same reason, but it is not a law.

6. Something that is cooked or ripened beforehand, or comes into flower early, may be used to describe a . . . . child, who is unusually forward and mature.

7. In Rome when you raised your eyelids (cilia) or eyebrows, you appeared to be the picture of haughtiness. Today we still feel the same way about the gesture and use it to describe those . . . . people who disdain others.

8. In Greece a brand made by a pointed instrument came, in seventeenth-century England, to be used as the word for the brand on criminals. Today . . . . means disgrace, but it used to be much more painful.

ANSWERS: **1.** crestfallen; **2.** egregious; **3.** enthralls; **4.** impediment; **5.** ostracize; **6.** precocious; **7.** supercilious; **8.** stigma.

II   Match the word with its synonym:

1. transcend	a. trivia
2. sequester	b. confirm
3. quell	c. sacrilege
4. protocol	d. inattentive
5. minutiae	e. go beyond, exceed
6. secular	f. a marvel
7. corroborate	g. coordinate
8. blasphemy	h. isolate
9. inadvertent	i. rules of diplomatic etiquette
10. correlate	j. first, original
	k. suppress
	l. worldly

ANSWERS: **1.** e; **2.** h; **3.** k; **4.** i; **5.** a; **6.** l; **7.** b; **8.** c; **9.** d; **10.** g.

III If you wanted to describe these friends, which of the power words might come to mind? Use the list immediately below to fill the blanks:

jaded, lithe, uxorious, arbitrary, phlegmatic, irascible, exotic.

1. A . . . . . . friend of yours spun around the parallel bars like an otter frolicking in bubbling water.
2. Another pal of yours has a . . . . . . view of life; he says he's seen it all and hasn't the energy or desire to move from his comfortable chair.
3. Your . . . . . . next-door neighbor can find no fault with his wife and regrets every minute they are separated.
4. Even when you fell off the edge of the crater into the volcano, this . . . . . . friend didn't flicker an eye. He merely asked if you might like some help to get out.
5. You are frequently upset by your . . . . . . friend's prejudiced and capricious approach to decisions.
6. Another friend is so . . . . . . you are very careful not to say anything that might anger him.
7. The . . . . . . looks and vivacity of my Spanish friend caused her to be a favorite of everyone.

ANSWERS: **1.** lithe; **2.** jaded; **3.** uxorious; **4.** phlegmatic; **5.** arbitrary; **6.** irascible; **7.** exotic.

IV Pick the word or phrase closest to the power word.

1. comprehensible A: adjustable. B: extensive. C: understandable.
2. hybrid A: anything of mixed origin. B: of ancient lineage. C: mixed.
3. lunar pertaining to A: the moon. B: the stars. C: comets.
4. monogamy state of being married A: early in life. B: late in life. C: to one person.
5. sinuous A: strong. B: winding. C: suspicious.
6. incorrigible A: from back to front. B: unbelievable. C: incapable of being corrected.
7. vehement arising from A: strong feeling. B: careful thought. C: bewilderment.
8. charlatan A: clown. B: pretender to knowledge. C: a leader who captures devotion.
9. prolific A: wordy. B: fruitful. C: spread out.
10. grit A: skill. B: spite. C: pluck.
11. insensible A: incapable of feeling. B: extremely unintelligent. C: harmless.
12. gestate A: to form in womb or mind. B: make motions with arms and hands. C: guess.

ANSWERS: **1.** C; **2.** A; **3.** A; **4.** C; **5.** B; **6.** C; **7.** A; **8.** B; **9.** B; **10.** C; **11.** A; **12.** A.

V From the origin and a synonym, fill the blank with one of the power words.

1. origin: Latin *plagium* (kidnapping); synonym: stealing. . . . . . .
2. origin: Latin *re* (back) and *calcitrare* (to kick); synonym: obstinate. . . . . . .
3. origin: *sinister* (to the left): synonym: evil. . . . . . .
4. Latin *augurium* (divination by interpretation of bird flights, etc.) Latin *auspex* (bird); synonym: prophesy. . . . . . .

ANSWERS: **1.** plagiarism; **2.** recalcitrant; **3.** sinister; **4.** augur.

Your Score
41–39 . . . . Word master
38–27 . . . . Very good
26–20 . . . . Fair

10

The Name of the Game Is Fame—
Names of Places, People, and Things

Do you want to have a place in history? You can, if you do something the public will associate with you, your name, or where you live. Then you may land in the dictionary! This chapter presents a variety of examples. Good luck!

Power Words

aegis	maudlin
ampere	mentor
bowdlerize	mercurial
chauvinist	mesmerize
chimerical	narcissistic
dunce	pander
galvanize	philippic
gasconade	Procrustean
harpy	protean
hermetic	quixotic
Janus-faced	saturnine
jeremiad	silhouette
Junoesque	Socratic
laconic	stentorian
masochist	sybarite

Special Words on People—How to Become Famous

bacchanalian	Platonic
Braille	Pyrrhic victory
epicure	sadistic
gargantuan	simony
iridescent	solecism
Machiavellian	stoic
malapropism	thespian
nemesis	

What's in a Name?

Plenty! All through history, a person's name has been a prized possession.

> "Who steals my purse steals trash; 'tis
>   something, nothing . . .
>   But he that filches from me my good name
>   Robs me of that which not enriches him
>   And makes me poor indeed."
>   SHAKESPEARE, *Othello* III, iii, 165

> "Their bodies are buried in peace, but their name
> lives for ever."
>
>   Ecclesiasticus 44:14

> "A good name is like a precious ointment; it filleth
> all around about and will not easily away."
>   FRANCIS BACON, *Of Marriage and Single Life*

In ancient days, the idea of God was so awesome, the Judaic people would not even mention His name, and instead used synonyms or circumlocutions. In some primitive tribes, you could never mention your mother-in-law's name; in others, the name of someone who had died.

Names were thought to possess magical powers. You controlled the destinies of whomever or whatever you named.

Except for the more primitive areas in the world, this is no longer true, of course. Yet, for each of us, there is something in our name that binds us close to it. Our name is a symbol of ourselves.

You telephone Helen Jackson, and a "light" and cheery voice answers. "Helen" is her **given** name. That is, at birth her parents **gave** her the name "Helen." Many names have a history to them, and it so happens that "Helen" means light, or torch. "Jackson" is the **surname,** from Latin *super-* (over, upon, above) and *name.* It is over and above your **given** name. Originally, "Jackson" meant son of John.

Historically, **surnames** often represented one's job or work. It's obvious where names such as Miller, Baker, Carpenter, Cook, Hunter, Fisher, and Taylor come from. What about people with the **surname** Fox or Bull? And we then have the famous or infamous John **Doe** which appears so often on documents used as examples. During World War II, wherever they were, soldiers, sailors, and marines scribbled on walls and the like, "Kilroy was here." **Kilroy** was the name of a mythical soldier, but it was amusing and comforting when you were in a risky situation to notice that the amazing **Kilroy** had been there before you.

There are books that go into the subject of names. If you are in the library sometime, it might be entertaining to learn more about yours.

In the left column is a list of **given names.** Can you match them up with their earlier meaning in the right column?

1. Barry	**a.** lovable
2. Richard	**b.** gift of God
3. Peter	**c.** spear
4. Nathaniel	**d.** strong king
5. Harold	**e.** good and kind
6. Agatha	**f.** rock
7. Elizabeth	**g.** chief of the army
8. Diana	**h.** consecrated to God
9. Judith	**i.** Roman goddess of the forests
10. Mabel	**j.** praised
11. John	**k.** God is good
12. Susan	**l.** lily

ANSWERS: Barry (spear), Richard (strong king), Peter (rock), Nathaniel (gift of God), Harold (chief of the army), Agatha (good and kind), Elizabeth (consecrated to God), Diana (goddess of the forests), Judith (praised), Mabel (lovable), John (God is good), Susan (lily).

Where Did These Well-Known Words Come From?

The actor Gary Cooper was known as a **laconic** man. He was swimming quite far out in the ocean one day with a companion.

"Great day for a swim, isn't it?" his friend commented.

"Yup," he answered.

"Hey, that shore looks a *long* way off, doesn't it?"

"Yup," he answered, suddenly beginning to swim toward it, leaving his companion behind.

Obviously, a **laconic** man or woman is a person of few words, often blunt and forceful. The **Laconians** were Greek and were known for their brief and pithy speech. The people of Athens and the Laconians, whose capital was Sparta, were usually hostile to one another. An Athenian said once, "If we come to your city, we will destroy it." The **Laconian** reply: "If!"

Most of us would like to have a **mentor**—a wise and trusted teacher, guide, and friend. When Odysseus, the hero of Homer's epic poem the *Odyssey,* left home to fight in the Trojan War, he asked his good friend **Mentor** to watch over his wife, Penelope; Telemachus, his son; and the household. However, suitors for Penelope, thinking Odysseus was dead, moved in, impoverishing the household with their eating and drinking. The goddess Athena, seeing what was going on, assumed the form of **Mentor** and whispered good advice to the son.

Newly arrived in France, an American commented to a cab driver in enthusiastic French his admiration for the new President. Startled, the driver slammed on the brakes and whipped his head around toward him. With a relieved sigh, he told the American the solecism he had committed. Apparently, the tourist had said something like, "I am nude!" A **solecism** is "a grammatical error or a violation of approved idiomatic usage." The word has links to **Soloi,** a province in southeastern Asia Minor. Because of the distance from Greece, gradually the inhabitants developed their own dialect and idioms. And so when Greek travelers visited **Soloi,** they were shocked at the way the language had been perverted, much in the same way that the English feel the Americans have mutilated their language.

Anyone who has been on a large body of water or near the seashore knows that the sea seems to be continually changing its appearance. *Proteus* was a god of the sea, and so we can understand that the ancients accepted that he, too, could assume any shape he chose. Today, **protean** means readily assuming different forms or aspects, or changeable; as, Mozart was a man of **protean** moods.

Each of the following words has sprung from the name or a characteristic of a person, animal, or place—real or imaginary. Can you match up the meanings of the left column with those of the right?

1. nepotism	**a.** an ideal place
2. amazon	**b.** to abduct
3. Pollyanna	**c.** long-distance race
4. draconian (dray KOH nee un)	**d.** cure-all
5. babel (BAY b'l)	**e.** trite
6. hackneyed	**f.** confusion of voices
7. utopia	**g.** harsh
8. panacea (pan uh SEE uh)	**h.** optimistic person
9. shanghai	**i.** tall, strong woman
10. marathon	**j.** nephew

ANSWERS: 1-j (favoritism shown to relatives in appointing them to jobs; in the early days, often the popes placed their nephews—Latin *nepotes*—in favorable positions within the church); 2-i (in Greek mythology the **Amazons** were a race of female warriors); 3-h (Pollyanna, named after a young, invincibly optimistic heroine of a novel); 4-g (after Draco, a strict Greek lawgiver in the seventh century B.C. who prescribed death for almost every offense); 5-f (from the city and tower of Babel in the Bible, Gen. 11:4–9); 6-e (named for workaday riding horses from Hackney, a London borough); 7-a (from Utopia, a fictional country in the book of that name by Sir Thomas More; Greek *ou,* "no," and *topos,* "place"); 8-d (Asklepios, the Greek god of medicine, named one of his daughters Panakeia "the all-healing"); 9-b (from the practice of procuring sailors for long voyages, perhaps originally to Shanghai, by kidnapping); 10-c (in 490 B.C., ten thousand Athenians defeated a hundred thousand Persians at the battle of Marathon; a Greek, running the first **marathon,** brought the news to the city of Athens, over twenty-six miles away.

After World War II, there was a briefly popular movement for "One World Government." The idea was that each of the nations of the world would give up its sovereignty and be under an elected government. One army, comprising members from all nations, would be used to keep the peace. The critics called this concept **chimerical** (kuh MER ih k'l, ky MER ih k'l). They meant it is not realizable or possible. The plan was impracticable, visionary, imaginary, and fanciful—and wouldn't work. The word is related to the Greek mythological fire-vomiting monster **chimera,** which had the body of a goat, the head of a lion, and the tail of a serpent. It was imaginary, a figment of the imagination. Legend has it that a hero by the name of Bellerophon slew this fearful concoction.

You are on a diet. While out for dinner, you are exposed to a **tantalizing** dessert. You push it away so that it is just beyond your reach. You can sympathize with the Phrygian king **Tantalus.** Because he revealed some secrets of Zeus, the chief god punished him. He was plunged up to his chin in water, and luscious fruits dangled from a tree over his head. But when he reached for the food, it withdrew, as did the water when he tried to drink. The dictionary definition of **tantalize** is to tease or torment by promising or showing something desirable and then denying access to it.

On TV news you may hear that **vandals** have ransacked a park. The word refers to **Vandals,** a Germanic tribe that in 455 sacked Rome. Actually, after defeating the Roman Army, they did not do much harm to the precious statues and art. However, the sense of destruction persisted unfairly, and

so today **vandalism** is willful destruction or defacement of public or private property.

For some undiscoverable reason, the English author Aldous Huxley had an aversion to the word **cynic.** He said that he always wanted to say "Bow-wow-wow" when he heard the word. Instinctively he was right: Antisthenes, a pupil of Socrates and a contemporary of Plato as well as a teacher of Diogenes, held that virtue is the only good and that self-control and independence form the essence of virtue. He and his followers were ostentatiously ascetic, scorning wealth and pleasure. Later followers, though, were thought of as ignorant, insolent, self-righteous people, offending the public. They were given the nickname *cynics* from the Greek *kynikos,* which meant "like a dog." The word is used today as a person who tends to question the virtues, values, and sincerity of others. As Wilfred Funk said, "So if we don't like the *cynics* of today, we can truly say they are surly and currish and have the way of a growling dog."

Points to Remember

By linking "name" words from where they come from—place, person, myth, or animal—you will more easily recall them. Word "stories" tend to stay in our memories.

Word-Power Test

I Pick the word or phrase that comes closest to describing the following situations.

1. The small company was protected from a lawsuit by its parent company. You could say it was under the . . . . . . of the parent company.

2. The piercing tornado siren electrified the community to seek protection. You could say it . . . . the community.

3. The dancer seemed to hypnotize the audience as she wove her steps into the music of Ravel's Bolero. The audience was . . . . . .

4. Scientists had a difficult time making the module impervious to gases and liquids. It was hard to make it . . . . . .

5. The tabloid catered to the readers' baser instincts with its sensationalism. Did the newspaper . . . . . . to the public?

6. The dictator ruthlessly forced his officials to conform, even to the point of death as a punishment. Was he . . . . . . in his demands?

7. The foolish man believed he could buy the forgiveness of God with gifts to the Christian evangelist. He could be accused of . . . . . .

8. The impassioned speech, filled with invective, made no friends for the senator, and turned many away. The . . . . . . was a mistake.

9. The young man's extravagant boasting made his friends feel he had a psychological problem. His . . . . . . worried his friends.

10. The candidate's well-disguised unscrupulous opportunism deceived the labor leaders. Could we say the candidate was . . . . ?

ANSWERS: **1.** aegis; **2.** galvanized; **3.** mesmerized; **4.** hermetic; **5.** pander; **6.** procrustean; **7.** simony; **8.** philippic; **9.** gasconade; **10.** Machiavellian.

II Match the words in column A with antonyms from column B.

A	B
1. gargantuan	a. quiet
2. bacchanalian	b. Spartan
3. stoic	c. comfort-loving
4. sadistic	d. tiny
5. sybarite	e. cheerful
6. mercurial	f. sensitive
7. saturnine	g. verbose
8. Janus-faced	h. temperate
9. stentorian	i. short-tempered
10. laconic	j. kind
	k. constant
	l. honest

ANSWERS: **1.** d; **2.** h; **3.** f; **4.** j; **5.** b; **6.** k; **7.** e; **8.** l; **9.** a; **10.** g.

III Fill in the correct word in the blanks given in the following sentences with a power word. Choices are given directly below.

jeremiad, Pyrrhic, Socratic, Platonic, iridescent, malapropism, nemesis, chimera.

1. It became evident that the young man's fanciful business schemes were a . . . . , doomed to failure.

2. We tried to comfort the prisoner, whose incredible . . . . . . was found to be true.

3. The general's . . . . . . victory won the battle, but the cost of it eventually bankrupted the country.

4. The nymph waltzed onto the ballet stage wearing an . . . . . . costume, which reflected the sunlight in a rainbow flash of colors.

5. The robber was flabbergasted when he found his . . . . , the wily detective, standing just inside a house he had entered.

6. He was desperately in love with her and wanted more than the . . . . . . love she offered.

7. The students preferred the . . . . . . method of teaching by pointed questioning that leads to thoughtful answers.

8. The television show counted, for many laughs, on . . . . , on the misuse of ordinary words, often those sounding alike such as the Pope's bicycle for the Pope's encyclical.

ANSWERS: **1.** chimera; **2.** jeremiad; **3.** Pyrrhic; **4.** iridescent; **5.** nemesis; **6.** Platonic; **7.** Socratic; **8.** malapropism.

IV Pick the words or phrases closest to the power words.

1. ampere   unit for measuring A: light. B: heat. C: electricity.

2. bowdlerize   A: to censor. B: riot. C: confiscate.

3. dunce   a person who is A: rebellious. B: ignorant. C: foolish.

4. harpy   person who A: is a plunderer. B: wears wild hairdos. C: is musical.

5. maudlin   A: affectionate. B: sentimental. C: eccentric.

6. silhouette   A: graph. B: cartoon. C: outline picture.

7. Braille   A: printer's plate. B: study in foreign languages. C: raised writing for the blind.

8. thespian   A: tramp. B: gypsy. C: actor.

9. solecism   A: plausible but fallacious argument. B: grammatical error. C: wise saying.

ANSWERS: **1.** C; **2.** A; **3.** B; **4.** A; **5.** B; **6.** C; **7.** C; **8.** C; **9.** B.

V Occasionally we meet persons who fit the words describing those in the following sentences. What words fit them? Match the words below to the persons.

mentor, Junoesque, masochist, chauvinist, narcissistic, protean, quixotic, epicure.

1. The senator was such a . . . . . . he felt no other country could ever equal his own.

2. The model spent hours primping and posing in front of mirrors. His . . . . . . ways were amusing.

3. To our amusement, the old actor became . . . . , assuming his past character roles in his daily life.

4. We all hope for a wise . . . . to advise and help us in our careers.

5. The large, stately woman seemed . . . . among the fluttery girls.

6. The . . . . . . tortured himself ogling cakes in a bakery window while on a diet.

7. The . . . . . . refused to eat at the pedestrian local cafeteria. He said he would rather starve.

8. His gentle . . . . nature led him to protect and encourage not only women and children, but men who were more able to defend him.

ANSWERS: **1.** chauvinist; **2.** narcissistic; **3.** protean; **4.** mentor; **5.** Junoesque; **6.** masochist; **7.** epicure; **8.** quixotic.

Your Score

45–40	Word master
39–27	Very good
26–20	Fair

Second Review Quiz

You are now two thirds of the way through *Word Power Made Simple*. This is a good time to review the words you have come across, many of which will be found in the following quiz. Why not list the ones you have trouble with and restudy them.

1. antediluvian   A: against all reason. B: broken down; decrepit. C: appearing as if existing before the Flood.

2. indict   A: to reprove. B: catalogue. C: accuse.

3. depreciate   A: minimize. B: lessen the value of. C: reject or disclaim.

4. commodious   A: well-supplied. B: cramped. C: spacious.

5. dissonance   A: stubbornness. B: discord. C: shyness.

6. aphorism   A: inoffensive expression. B: positive statement. C: maxim.

7. sententious   A: pleasing to the senses. B: ready to argue. C: pompous and moralizing.

8. acclimate   A: to adapt to new conditions. B: hail. C: reach a climax.

9. Hegira   A: custom. B: syrup. C: flight.

10. juggernaut   A: heavy pottery. B: battleship. C: overwhelmingly powerful object.

11. shibboleth   A: holiness. B: strength. C: a watchword.

12. coup d'état   A: secret meeting. B: sudden seizure of power. C: imprisonment.

13. fresco   A: painting. B: nudity. C: wall.

14. nadir   A: faint shadow. B: lowest point. C: zenith.

15. junta   A: emergency session. B: political excursion. C: political clique.

16. cabal   A: monopoly. B: secret intrigue. C: trivial objection.

17. provincial   A: temporary. B: unsophisticated. C: urban.

18. simile   figure of speech that A: spoofs something. B: discloses something. C: likens one object to another.

19. casuistry   A: offhand manner. B: dishonest reasoning. C: brilliance.

20. paradox   A: self-contradictory statement. B: geometric figure. C: conventional belief.

21. harbinger   A: forerunner. B: bird of prey. C: soothsayer.

22. sanguine   A: optimistic. B: listless. C: bloodshot.

23. effete   A: egotistic. B: abstract. C: exhausted or barren.

24. atypical   A: imitative. B: average. C: uncharacteristic.

25. jingoism   A: patriotism to the extreme. B: music term. C: emptiness.

26. egregious   A: varied. B: selfish. C: outstandingly bad.

27. stigma   A: summary. B: disgrace. C: obstruction.

28. sequester   A: to follow. B: search for. C: seclude.

29. charlatan   A: beggar. B: clown. C: pretender to knowledge.

30. gestate   A: to empty out. B: form in the mind. C: signal.

31. blasphemy   A: malicious charge. B: violent outburst. C: irreverence.

32. primal   A: primitive. B: wild. C: aggressive.

33. nemesis   A: accomplice. B: one who imitates. C: agent of one's downfall.

34. Pyrrhic   A: a victory gained by ruinous loss. B: an overwhelming victory. C: a quick victory.

35. solecism   A: plausible but fallacious argument. B: grammatical error. C: wise saying.

36. stoical   A: silent. B: imperturbable. C: strong.

37. chimera   A: a mirage in the desert. B: the distribution or the blending of lights. C: a foolish fancy.

38. narcissism   A: tendency to self-worship. B: ability to cook well. C: power of belief.

39. pander   A: to comfort. B: cater to others' weaknesses. C: implore.

40. Procrustean   A: pertaining to shellfish. B: care-free and jovial. C: forcing conformity.

ANSWERS: **1.** C; **2.** C; **3.** B; **4.** C; **5.** B; **6.** C; **7.** C; **8.** A; **9.** C; **10.** C; **11.** C; **12.** B; **13.** A; **14.** B; **15.** C; **16.** B; **17.** B; **18.** C; **19.** B; **20.** A; **21.** A; **22.** A; **23.** C; **24.** C; **25.** A; **26.** C; **27.** B; **28.** C; **29.** C; **30.** B; **31.** C; **32.** A; **33.** C; **34.** A; **35.** B; **36.** B; **37.** C; **38.** A; **39.** B; **40.** C.

Your Rating

40–35 . . . . Excellent
34–25 . . . . Good
24–18 . . . . Fair

11

In Our Own Words—Americana

"The language, like the country, has a certain breadth and magnificence. A Western man 'sleeps so sound, it would take an earthquake to wake him' . . . 'Stranger,' he says, 'in b'ar hunts I am numerous' . . . He tells of a person 'as cross as a b'ar with two cubs and a sore tail.' He 'laughs like a hyena over a dead scalawag.' He 'walks through a fence like a falling tree through a cobweb.' He 'goes the whole hog' . . . 'Bust me wide open,' he says, 'if I didn't bulge into the creek in the twinkling of a bedpost, I was so thunderin' savageous.' " (Thomas L. Nichols, *Forty Years of American Life*, 1864)

Power Words

ambidextrous	fetid
antipode	flagrant
bona fide	forbearance
calumny	humane
cavil	iconoclast
cohesive	idiosyncrasy
dilatory	ignominy
doctrinaire	impasse
ductile	importune
ecclesiastic	incarnate
elicit	incipient
emaciated	incredulous
emeritus	obtuse
fallacious	perfidious
fastidious	sanctimonious

Special Words: In Our Own Words (the Language of the United States)

affiliation	gerrymander
bluff	gubernatorial
blurb	junket
bogus	lame duck
caucus	maverick
demoralize	preempt
fedora	scrimshaw
genocide	

The Americanization of English

Is there a big difference between the ways English is spoken in England and in America? Until the twentieth century you could say, "Yes." Today, however, though there are differences, the gap is not wide and seems to be closing year by year. Most of it has to do with pronunciation, slang, and technical words.

But it's easy to see why there were much wider differences in the past. Until the twentieth century, the two nations were months apart by arduous travel across a vast sea. Exchange of information was extremely limited. Only the major events were ultimately known. As we've become aware from past chapters in this book, language is always on the move. It is not like a brick, lying where it is thrown. Language is more like a tree with expanding branches. In England and in the American colonies, language was being continually modified because of local influences. Consequently, the split between them widened.

Today, international television, periodicals, books, and the like create a kind of homogenization (an American word) and cross-fertilization in the English-speaking world.

It was not always so. From the earliest days, visitors to the American colonies from England complained of the corruption going on with their mother tongue. They returned to England dismayed.

For example, Francis Moore in 1736 described the town of Savannah. "It stands upon the flat of a hill. The bank of that river (which they in barbarous English call a *bluff*) is steep and about forty-five foot perpendicular." (Francis Moore, "A Voyage to Georgia," 1735). Observed H. L. Mencken in his superb book *The American Language,* Moore set the tone that English criticism has maintained ever since.

Whenever a people migrate, naturally their language goes along. The colonists brought with them the rich heritage of Elizabethan English—the language of Shakespeare, Marlowe, Ben Jonson, and the King James translation of the Bible (1611). It was a time of glorious experimentation with language.

Mencken suggests that though many of the humbler immigrants were probably unaware of Shakespeare, "it is nevertheless a fact that their way of using the language had something in it of his glorious freedom and spaciousness. If they had any written guide it was the King James Bible."

Furthermore, Americans seemed to have an intuitive sense of the symbolic meaning of a word. For example, at one time the English Church replaced the Anglo-Saxon word *sick* with *ill.* The Americans would have none of that. *Ill* might sound more elegant, but the colonists felt that *sick* had a down-to-earth quality that seemed real. As poet Walt Whitman was to say later, "I like limber, lasting, fierce words."

The pioneers moved westward. Many of them settled in the mountains in places such as Appalachia. Elizabethan words and phrases, as well as speech used in colonial times, can still be heard in these isolated pockets of lost time. "Isolated communities tend to remain relatively stable. They retain their customs, their occupations, their speech, all their cultural traditions, very much the way they were at the time when the members of the community" settled in the area. (George Philip Krapp, "Is American English Archaic?" *Southwest Review,* Summer 1927, p. 296)

A curious fact is that while certain words and phrases became established in America, the same words slipped out of favor in England. When English visitors scoffed at such words as **flapjack, molasses, beef, homespun, cross purposes, greenhorn, loophole, ragamuffin, trash,** and the like, they said such inventions were needless and polluting the language. They forgot that these were good old English words with a long and honorable history. For whatever reason, they'd temporarily fallen into disuse in England.

Too Much Babel

Though the British Isles occupy a relatively small land area, the inhabitants spoke a number of local dialects. As a matter of fact, very often one region could not understand another. You can see that, when they came together in the New World, sound and form were altered and something new created.

Except for the London dialect—the King's English!—there didn't seem to be a reasonable standard. The proliferation of dialects stimulated reformers, during the seventeenth and eighteenth centuries, to attempt to create a standard as to spelling, pronunciation, and meaning. The famous lexicographer Samuel Johnson actively supported this effort. He admitted, however, that "sounds are too volatile and subtle for legal restraints, and that to enchain syllables and to lash the winds are equally the undertakings of pride." Yet he lashed out at such words as **to wobble, to budge, to coax, touchy, stingy, swimmingly, chaperone.**

Another reason for the differences in language: the colonists lived in a new world—a world of strange animals, different plants, unusual weather conditions, seemingly endless forests, and rugged mountains—where they engaged in unfamiliar occupations. They needed a flexible language to describe these novel experiences. They had to invent Americanisms, for there were no words at hand for these unusual conditions. Describing the linguistic innovations of Shakespeare, George H. McKnight compared the playwright's effect to that of "the renewed metaphors to be heard in the speech of . . . the frontier, where free from the blighting influence of learning, forms of language are created afresh." (George H. McKnight, *Modern English in the Making,* Appleton, 1928)

Commenting on the creative and relaxed way the early Americans used language, Mencken observed that they showed an easy disregard for linguistic niceties. Following Shakespeare's inventiveness, they reduced verb phrases to simple verbs, turned verbs into nouns, nouns into verbs, and adjectives into either or both. They shortened words. For example, the English law phrase "to convey by deed" was reduced to "to deed."

Not all Americans agreed that native linguistic ingenuity should be admired. In 1781, John Witherspoon, president of the College of New Jersey (now Princeton University), wrote: "I have heard in this country, in the senate, at the bar, and from the pulpit, and see daily in dissertations from the press, errors in grammar, improprieties and vulgarisms which hardly any person of the same class in point of rank and literature would have fallen into in Great Britain." Others agreed with him. Upset by the novelties he encountered, the redoubtable American lexicographer said, ". . . it is quite impossible to stop the progress of language—it is like the course of the Mississippi, the motion of which, at times, is scarcely perceptible, yet even then it possesses a momentum quite irresistible. Words and expressions will be forced into use, in spite of all the exertions of all the writers in the world."

The scholar and diplomat Alexis de Tocqueville wrote in 1835, after visiting America, "The genius of a democratic people is not only shown by the great number of words they bring into use, but also by the nature of the ideas these new words represent."

How Many of the Following Fourteen Words and Phrases Are Americanisms?

geriatrics	square deal
wetbacks	emigrant
egghead	feisty
brainwash	horse sense
break even	smidgen
finesse	equal rights
on a shoestring	sidekick

ANSWER: all of them

Exuberance Is Busting Out All Over

The hurly-burly life on the frontier brewed a vigorous language that is wonderfully imaginative and often poetic. It vibrates with life. It shouts with vigor.

One of your friends might be a **blustiferous** (violent or blustery) sort of fellow. Another may be **cavorting** (prancing or leaping about happily) to the strings of a fiddle. As the men partake of their **creature comforts** (whiskey), the voices and music make up an unbelievable **conbobberation.** Some of the people are dressed in a **grandiferous** (grand, extremely well) style, because they've hit a gold mine, while others have been **hornswoggled** (cheated), and their attire shows it. Among the crowd are a number of **skirmudgeons** (rascals) and a **swonny** (worthless person, dope) or two.

Or what about the following wild torrent of verbiage?

"This is *me,* and no mistake! Billy Earthquake, Esq., commonly called Little Billy, all the way from the No'th Fork of Muddy Run! . . . Whoop! won't *nobody* come out and fight me? Come out some of you, and die decently, for I'm spoiling for a fight . . . I'm a poor man, it's a fact, and smell like a wet dog, but I can't be run over . . . Maybe you never heard of the time the horse kicked me, and put both his hips out of joint—if it ain't true, cut me up for catfish bait! W-h-o-o-p! I'm the very infant that refused its milk before its eyes were open, and called out for a bottle of old rye . . . Talk about grinning the bark off a tree—'taint nothin'; one squint of mine at a bull's heel would blister it. Oh, I'm one of your toughest sort—live forever, and then turn to a white-oak post. I'm the ginewine article, a real double-acting engine, and I can out-run, out-jump, out-swim, chaw more tobacco and spit less, and drink more whiskey and keep soberer

than any man in these localities." (Mamie Meridith, "Tall Talk in America Sixty Years Ago," *American Speech,* 1919)

To some readers this fusillade of words, this tall talk, as it was known, might appear grotesque and absurd. But it has a virgin exuberance and power. No wonder the pioneers swept through the West carrying everything before them. Their language had a primitive energy that reflected an indomitable optimism and infectious high spirits. They may not have had culture, but they accomplished herculean deeds.

In a quieter way, some of our colorful slang is a heritage from those days. May we never lose this quality.

You are English. Do you know the American equivalents for the following words?

1. biscuit	**8.** caravan
2. cornet	**9.** torch
3. sweets	**10.** silencer
4. nappy	**11.** windscreen
5. paraffin	**12.** dustman
6. lift	**13.** spanner
7. tap	**14.** tower block

1. cookie or cracker; **2.** ice-cream cone; **3.** candy; **4.** diaper; **5.** kerosene; **6.** elevator; **7.** faucet; **8.** trailer, mobile home; **9.** flashlight; **10.** muffler; **11.** windshield; **12.** garbage man; **13.** monkey wrench; **14.** high-rise building
(There are a few differences between our words)

The Native Injuns

The early settlers had various names for the truly indigenous Americans: **injun, engian, indjion, Indian.** And they not only appropriated their lands unfairly, but they also took over portions of their language. Not much of Indian language remains today. Most of the Indian words have to do with food or animals.

In the winter we go **tobogganing.** In the summer we can eat **succotash** (corn and lima beans) and **squash,** and **canoe** on lakes and rivers. Many people wear **moccasins,** and all of us try to avoid **skunks. Pecan** (puh KAHN or PEE kan) pies are universally popular even if people don't agree on the pronunciation. If you are from the Southwest, you will select the first. **Raccoons** may have an appealing face, but they can cause a mess in suburbia, as they rummage through trash cans.

Of course, many places have Indian names: **Okla-**

homa (red people), **Minnesota** (muddy water), **Shinnecock** Bay (after a New York tribe). And then there's **Yuma** (from a tribe of North American Indians living along the lower Colorado River), which recently was voted the worst place to live in the United States. The townspeople vigorously denied this. Having driven through there once and stopping for luncheon, we concur.

Would You Believe This Man?

"Next to the savage struggle for land and dollars, party politics was the chief concern of the people," wrote Mencken.

Hell-bent, first appearing in print in 1835, means "recklessly determined." During election time we sometimes hear the term: he was **hell-bent for election.** In *Word Mastery Made Simple,* the authors wrote that an Indian was the "first American **to stump.** Usually when an Indian chief had important news to relate, he stood on a tree stump in the main meeting place. Contemporary politicians rarely depend upon tree stumps, but **stumping** (and by extension, **grass-roots**) campaigns are integral to American politics."

Favorite son was originally a complimentary title given to George Washington, in the phrase "Columbia's favorite son." A **gag** in politics means a law or ruling designed to restrict or prevent discussion on a particular subject. In 1810, a newspaper writer said, "It is to be hoped that the majority in Congress will extend the **Gag Rule** to fiddles, and the whole tribe of musical instruments."

Who would have thought that **straight out** comes from a distant political past? Around 1840 the term referred to the Whig party (more or less a precursor of the Republican party). Said the Nashville *Whig* paper: "The Straight Outs are the representatives of a hardy race of honest log cabin pioneers, who, however ridiculed for their primitive manners, never fail to make their influence felt at the ballot box." Today, to come **straight out** is to be straightforward, direct. A second meaning is thoroughgoing.

New uses for old words came into play with such terms as **plank, pull, machine, primary, filibuster.** Did you know that **bulldozer** was not first a machine to push earth around, but instead was someone who intimidated others by violence or threats, pushing them around? The word was used frequently for political purposes.

If something is a lot of **bunk,** it's nonsense, not worth much. "Around the year 1820 a debate was in progress in the House of Representatives on the complicated question of the Missouri Compromise. In the middle of the discussion a member from *Buncombe* County, North Carolina, arose and started a long, dull, and completely irrelevant talk. Many members walked out . . . Finally the speaker apologized with the now famous statement: 'I'm talking for *Buncombe,'* which meant, of course, for his constituents in *Buncombe,* which was a county in his district . . . The phrase 'talking to (or for) *Bunkum'* was well known in 1828. We clipped the word to *bunk.'*" (Wilfred Funk, *Word Origins and Their Romantic Stories*, Harper & Row, 1950.)

And So What's New?

We're carrying on the tradition of dreaming up new words or creating new uses for old words. They are being invented daily. The lexicographer Barnhart has put out two dictionaries of "New English" since 1963, trying to keep up with the flood of neologisms.

Touching on only a few: **Unisex** and **the beautiful people** come from fashion. Business gives us **the bottom line** and **condominium.** From computers we get **floppy** and **hard disks, debug, word processor** . . . In sports, the **Nautilus,** the **long bomb,** to **hustle.** From TV we have **soaps** and **VCRs** (video cassette recorders).

Science inundates us with words.

Words are born. And words die. But many more arrive than pass away. Is our language becoming overpopulated?

Points to Remember

Relish the vigor in your American English. As you build your word power, use strong and vivid words. Your language will become more exciting and so will you.

Word-Power Test

I Fill the blanks that make sense in the following paragraph from the words below:

elicited, lame-duck, caucus, unbelievable, demoralizing, junket, gerrymander, perfidious, impasses, forbearance, obtuse, gubernatorial.

During a **(1)** . . . . to discuss the next **(2)** . . . . election, a congressman learned of a

(3) . . . . . . plan to (4) . . . . . . his district. He immediately canceled his planned (5) . . . . . . He called a meeting to discuss the (6) . . . . . . and (7) . . . . . . scheme. He (8) . . . . . . some interest and concern. However, during a (9) . . . . . . session there are many (10) . . . . . . because of conflicting interests, so he had to show great (11) . . . . . . with his colleagues, though they appeared completely (12) . . . . . . to him. And so it goes.

ANSWERS: **1.** caucus; **2.** gubernatorial; **3.** perfidious; **4.** gerrymander; **5.** junket; **6.** demoralizing; **7.** unbelievable; **8.** elicited; **9.** lame-duck; **10.** impasses; **11.** forbearance; **12.** obtuse.

II Pick the definition in column B for the correct power word.

	A		B
1.	antipode	**a.**	capable of being hammered thin, or easily led
2.	ambidextrous	**b.**	just beginning, or in the first stages
3.	fetid	**c.**	systematic extermination of a racial group
4.	ductile	**d.**	tardy or slow
5.	dilatory	**e.**	retired from active service but held in an honorary position
6.	bona fide	**f.**	an exact opposite
7.	incipient	**g.**	carried out in good faith, or authentic
8.	fastidious	**h.**	emitting an offensive odor
9.	emeritus	**i.**	able to use both hands equally well
10.	genocide	**j.**	hard to please or overly sensitive

ANSWERS: **1.** f; **2.** i; **3.** h; **4.** a; **5.** d; **6.** g; **7.** b; **8.** j; **9.** e; **10.** c.

III Do you find the use of the power words in the following sentences right or wrong?

1. A person who *cavils* at the smallest detail, in a meeting, taxes everyone else's patience. Right or wrong?

2. A faddish food diet could leave you looking so *emaciated* that instead of looking better you might look sick. Right or wrong?

3. It is a *flagrant* act of discourtesy to interrupt the President during a press conference. Right or wrong?

4. An *iconoclast* will have nothing to do with any type of organized religion. Right or wrong?

5. The young couturier conformed to all the traditional concepts, making an outstanding reputation as a *maverick*. Right or wrong?

6. The enormous and famous Hope diamond was definitely proved to be authentic. They can now officially call it *bogus*. Right or wrong?

7. He wrote a clever, ten-page *blurb* for the book jacket. Right or wrong?

8. The *fedora* is a new kind of frisbee. Right or wrong?

9. The *scrimshaw* pin was unusual as there was a small mermaid carved in the center of the whalebone. Right or wrong?

10. The group was extraordinarily cohesive; they could not be split up. Right or wrong?

ANSWERS: **1.** right; **2.** right; **3.** right; **4.** right; **5.** wrong; **6.** wrong; **7.** wrong; **8.** wrong; **9.** right; **10.** right.

IV Find the word or phrase closest to the meaning of the given power word.

1. calumny   A: slander. B: hardship. C: cleverness.
2. ignominy   A: stupidity. B: privation. C: dishonor.
3. doctrinaire   A: tolerant. B: philosophical. C: dictatorial.
4. fallacious   A: quarrelsome. B: deceptive. C: superficial.
5. preempt   A: to foreclose. B: to appropriate. C: to take legal possession.
6. ecclesiastic   a person who is A: unusual. B: a cleric. C: a prophet.
7. idiosyncrasy   A: foolish action. B: a quirk. C: a prophet.

ANSWERS: **1.** A; **2.** C; **3.** C; **4.** B; **5.** B; **6.** B; **7.** B.

V Have you ever misused these words? It's easy to do. Pick the right answer between the two close choices in feeling, meaning, look, or sound.

1. bluff   A: pretense. B: mistake.
2. affiliation   A: association. B: affection.
3. humane   A: forgivably weak. B: kind.

4. importune   A: persuade. B: beg.

5. incarnate   A: embodied. B: sinful.

6. sanctimonious   A: making a pretense of holiness. B: holy.

Your Score

45–40 . . . . Word master

39–27 . . . . Very good

26–20 . . . . Fair

ANSWERS: **1.** A; **2.** A; **3.** B; **4.** B; **5.** A; **6.** A.

12

Say What You Mean—Simplicity and Clarity

Have you ever listened to a speaker or read a passage in a book and thought suddenly, "I don't know what the guy is talking about"? Obviously, the purpose of speaking and writing is to explain clearly. Too often, the meaning gets lost in a shuffle of confusing or unnecessary words.

Power Words

amalgam	machination
brackish	morose
complacent	muse
derogatory	mystic
ebullient	officious
eclectic	periphery
eke	petulant
idyll	pillage
implication	proliferation
inexorable	quiescent
injunction	quizzical
inquisitive	repertoire
limbo	schism
limpid	stolid
lowering	unconscionable

Special Words: Say What You Mean So People Will Understand You (Simplicity and Clarity)

circumspect	incisive
concomitant	insouciance
conversant	malign
duplicity	neologism
enhance	obsequious
fulsome	peregrination
garrulous	plethora
histrionic	

This chapter is concerned with how to avoid short-circuiting your message. Three basic rules will help: **keep it simple, be clear, be specific.**

Simplicity

"Clutter is the disease of American writing. We are a society strangling in unnecessary words, circular constructions, pompous frills and meaningless jargon . . . The secret of good writing is to strip every sentence to its cleanest components. Every word that serves no function, every long word that could be a short word, every adverb which carries the same meaning that is already in the verb, every passive construction that leaves the reader unsure of who is doing what—these are the thousand and one adulterants that weaken the strength of a sentence. And they usually occur, ironically, in proportion to education and rank." (*On Writing Well,* by William Zinsser, Harper & Row, 1950.)

A saying in business is expressed by the acronym KISS—Keep It Simple, Stupid. Sound advice to anyone who writes, whether a letter or a novel. The best writing is hard, clean, and bare. The rule is *simplify, simplify.*

Avoid the Big Word Just to Impress

Someone once said to us, "It's an azygous fact that at the hebetic stage of youth the ability to learn a new language is attenuated." If we'd been on our toes and with a dictionary of impossible words handy, we might have replied, "Your sesquipedalianism has unfortunately deliquesced your erudition into obfuscation."

In other words, he said. "It's a unique fact that at puberty the ability to learn a new language is weakened." And my reply would have been, "Your use of long words has dissolved your knowledge into confusion."

As an aunt of ours would say, speakers of such sentences sound as if they have a hot potato in their mouths.

For example, there is nothing wrong with *some* of the words in the left column. On balance, however, you will make your message clearer by using the ones on the right.

assemblage	gathering
dissemination	distribution, spreading
periphrastic	wordy, verbose
luculent	clear, lucid
pusillanimous	cowardly
ambience	atmosphere
malignity	malice
objurgatory	reproachful
parabolical	like a parable
oppugnant	antagonistic
sesquestrate	confiscate

Most of the time, try to avoid the long word that is no better than the short one: (numerous) "many," (implement) "do," (increment) "increase," (remand) "send back," and on and on.

Today there are many good, descriptive, punchy words coming into our language: dropout, uptight, unisex, paraprofessional, machismo, to name a few. They are colorful and descriptive. Use them.

In a previous edition of this book, the previous authors suggested that, on occasion, "big" words and foreign ones do indeed have a point and place. One polysyllabic employer (the right word for the following amusing anecdote) had valid reasons for his choice of words in this letter of recommendation handed to an associate when she left his employ. He liked her and wished her well, hiding her true qualifications in words that sounded complimentary—regrettably, a less than honest approach. "She is good-tempered, cheerful, obliging, *immund, otiose,* respectful, and *incorrigible.* With neatness, carefulness, and economy she would be an excellent worker." (Definitions: *immund,* "unclean"; *otiose,* "useless"; *incorrigible,* "beyond correction."

1. Be direct. Avoid **euphemisms**—from Greek **eu-** (good) and **pheme** (voice). As you probably know, the word means a mild or roundabout expression substituted for one considered improper, too harsh, or too blunt. Though today people are much more frank than fifty years ago, we still come across euphemisms often. A street cleaner becomes a **sanitation engineer.** In clandestine operations to **neutralize** means to asassinate. **Men's room** and **ladies' room** rather than toilet. A janitor is now a **custodial engineer.** Instead of so-and-so dying, the person **passed away, departed, reached his or her end, went to a better world** (we hope!).

Because it is usually a false refinement, euphemism ought to be used sparingly and only in special situations.

2. Avoid being wordy. Here are four words dealing with **wordiness** as defined by Webster's New World Dictionary: **verbose** suggests a wordiness that results in obscurity, tediousness, bombast, etc., as a *verbose* acceptance speech; **prolix** implies such a tiresome elaboration of trivial details as to be boring or dull, as *prolix* lectures; **diffuse** suggests such verbosity and loose construction as to lose all force and sharpness, as a rambling, *diffuse* harangue; **redundant,** in this connection, implies the use of unnecessary or repetitious words or phrases, as a *redundant* literary style.

Prune all the "dead" words out of your sentences as you would the dead branches from a tree. Well-known, successful authors often rewrite their articles and books seven and eight times. They are ruthless pruners of their own work. Vigorous writing is concise. Try to reduce clauses to phrases and phrases to single words.

In their book *The Elements of Style,* William Strunk, Jr., and E. B. White tell us, "An expression that is especially debilitating is *the fact that.* It should be revised out of every sentence in which it occurs."

Recast the following sentences into one or more words, removing *the fact that.* FOR EXAMPLE: owing to the fact that   ANSWER: since, or because

1. in spite of the fact that
2. call your attention to the fact that
3. I was unaware of the fact that
4. the fact that he had not succeeded
5. the fact that I had arrived

ANSWERS: **1.** though, although; **2.** remind you, notify you; **3.** I was unaware that, did not know; **4.** his failure; **5.** my arrival.

Clarity

1. Think Clearly. Unfortunately, clear writing or speaking demands clear thinking. Not many of us polish our minds so that our thoughts are clearly reflected. Cloudy thinking produces murky writing. And thinking clearly is an act we must force ourselves to do. A statement may sound impressive, but does it have meaning?

Wilfred Funk was a fine and clever poet. As a joke, he once wrote a poem by simply stringing together magnificent-sounding words. Because the words were chosen at random, no meaning was to be found in the poem. He sent it along to a prestigous poetry magazine, which awarded him a prize. Many readers must have been puzzled. It sounded beautiful, but what exactly did it mean?

2. Say What You Mean. You must ask yourself constantly, "What am I really trying to say?" You may be surprised when you realize that you don't actually know. But when, after thinking and analyzing, you do find out, then you find that the act of writing or giving a speech comes more easily.

Since we write or speak to communicate our thoughts, our goal is to be clear. "Muddiness is not merely a disturber of prose, it is a destroyer of life, of hope: death on the highway caused by a badly worded road sign, heartbreak among lovers caused by a misplaced phrase in a well-intentioned letter, anguish of a traveler expecting to be met at a railroad station and not being met because of a slipshod telegram." (*The Elements of Style,* William Strunk, Jr., and E. B. White, Macmillan, 1962.)

The Japanese term *mokusatsu* is believed to have brought on the tragedy of Hiroshima and all that followed, because it was not accurately translated. It has two meanings: "to ignore" and "to refrain from comment." Apparently, the emperor and the cabinet were ready to surrender to the ultimatum of the Allies, but they wanted a little more time to talk over the terms. They prepared a press release announcing a policy of *mokusatsu,* with the "no comment" implication. Unfortunately the translators inferred the meaning "to ignore." And the fateful Bomb was dropped. The Japanese leaders should have sent a more clearly worded message.

Governments are notorious offenders of clarity in their statements. **Bureaucratese** is a verbal disease of most government officials. "Thus, when a government report states that 'the agency is **parameterizing viable** resource **utilization strategies** within the projected personnel **funding matrix,'** the adept comprehends that they're just figuring out what they can do this year with the staff and money they expect to get. Or, when 'Phase-two **feasibility studies** indicate that current programs have **impacted suboptimally** upon quality of housing stock in **catchment areas,'** the insider knows that the housing program has bombed, and badly." (*The Book of Jargon,* by Don Ethan Miller, Macmillan, 1981.)

What to do about such jargon? Sailors would say in *their* jargon: "Deep-six it." That is, throw it overboard. Get rid of it. Clear off the decks of your mind and try to rephrase your thought.

Another pothole of muddy writing is **tautology** (needless repetition).

Try to substitute one word for each of the following phrases.

1. small in size
2. skirt around
3. advance planning
4. any and all
5. at the present time
6. by means of
7. if and when
8. matinee performance
9. not to
10. strangled to death
11. true facts
12. for the simple reason that

ANSWERS: **1.** small; **2.** skirt; **3.** planning; **4.** either *any* or *all;* **5.** now; **6.** by; **7.** if; **8.** matinee (a matinee *is* an afternoon *performance*); **9.** not; **10.** strangled (death is what *strangled* implies); **11.** true (if they're *facts,* they *are* true); **12.** because (five words are reduced to one! and the thought is that if it's so *simple,* why didn't you think of it, you dope?)

Be Specific

Specific words help you to convey your meaning clearly and simply. Gustave Flaubert, a nineteenth-century French writer whose works are still read *(Madame Bovary),* stated, "Whatever be the thing one wishes to say, there is only one word to express it, only one verb to animate it, only one adjective to qualify it." Admittedly, this was an impossible ideal even for him. But we understand what he means. Choose with care the words that fit.

Avoid general words. Use definite, specific, concrete language.

Compare the following sentences. The second in each case is the more vivid and interesting.

1. In 1985 when Eric Knight traveled to Denver, when he arrived he realized he didn't have much money.

When Eric Knight arrived in Denver in 1985, he was so broke he couldn't even buy himself a meal.

2. John had been outside. Now he ran down to the kitchen and opened the door. He told me that somehow the field was on fire and that it would be a good idea for me to take a look at it.

John yanked open the kitchen door. "Dad!" he yelled. "The wind's making the field catch on fire. We need you. Hurry!"

3. A period of unfavorable weather set in.

It rained every day for a week.

Be specific. The finest writers you read—from the classics to modern works—deal in particulars and not the general. It is this that holds our attention.

Why do people use nouns and verbs of a vague or general meaning? Because they will not take the trouble to think of the exact expression required. They consequently favor nouns like **thing,** verbs like **do** and **fix.**

Here are some further examples of weak and strong writing:

WEAK: His book took up one topic and then another and then another.

STRONG: His book rambled from one topic to another.

WEAK: He took hold of the running man.

STRONG: He grabbed the running man.

WEAK: He walked along in an idle and sluggish manner.

STRONG: He dawdled.

WEAK: He spoke with his lips partly closed, so that his words came forth in a mutter.

STRONG: He mumbled.

WEAK: The troops displayed courage under the fall of exploding shells.

STRONG: The troops displayed courage under shellfire.

WEAK: The Lord is to me as one who guards, herds, leads, and drives sheep.

STRONG: The Lord is my shepherd.

Watch your idioms. "An idiom describes an expression that is not readily understandable from its literal meaning—for example, *put up with* in the sense of 'tolerate, endure.' 'Put up with' by itself doesn't really mean anything. An example of a foreign idiom that has found a permanent place in our language is *pièce de résistance,* whose literal meaning in French is 'resistance piece.' But what on earth is a resistance piece? Not even a Frenchman could tell you for sure . . . Here are a few examples of original American idioms that are probably understood by English speakers worldwide:

as all get-out   as mad as **all get-out**
  (greatly)
catch on   understand; become fashionable
run-in   hostile encounter."
(*Success with Words,* The Reader's Digest Association, Inc.)

Idioms, if they have not become trite from overuse, can add color and even precision to your language. Ones like "cut loose," "lock, stock and barrel," "saddle with," "simmer down," are useful and good verbal shortcuts. Your listener will catch on.

Certainly, we could never get along without that verbal factotum "OK."

"It's time for us to leave. We have another date," a husband said to his wife while at a party.

"I know, but it's kind of awkward to leave now."

"We'll make a clean **surgical cut.** We'll just say good-bye."

The wife understood from the idiom it was best not to make a lot of excuses.

Points to Remember

For clear writing:
1. Try to simplify.
2. Avoid the **big word** just to impress.
3. Be direct.
4. Avoid wordiness.
5. Think clearly.
6. Be specific.
7. Sometimes idioms can be helpful.

Word-Power Test

I Pick the word or phrase that best describes the meaning of the power word in the sentence from the three selections below it.

1. She became *circumspect* when her broker offered implausible reasons for switching her investment.
   a. confused
   b. cautious
   c. suspicious
2. After the rebellion, the pattern of *machinations* leading to it became evident.
   a. secret or hostile plans
   b. artillery deployment
   c. oversupply of war vehicles
3. The *garrulous* couple stayed too long at the party.
   a. slow-moving
   b. given to tedious talk
   c. irritated and critical
4. The young executive was annoyed by the *obsequious* salesman.
   a. fawning
   b. gloomy
   c. deceptive
5. With great *insouciance,* the tightrope walker waved at his girl during the most difficult maneuver of the act.
   a. fearlessness
   b. adroitness
   c. carefree unconcern
6. The programmer of the new software used some confusing *neologisms* that had no sound basis etymologically.

a. innovations
b. new words
c. transpositions

7. The speaker's *histrionics* caught the audience's rapt attention.
   a. historically sound presentation
   b. excessive or artificial display of emotion
   c. psychoneurotic condition
8. She was not *conversant* with the studies done on immigration.
   a. familiar with as a result of experience
   b. able to talk without confusion
   c. able to coordinate information

ANSWERS: **1.** b; **2.** a; **3.** b; **4.** a; **5.** c; **6.** b; **7.** b; **8.** a.

II Match the power word with its synonym in column B.

A	B
1. brackish	**a.** split, division
2. enamored	**b.** error
3. periphery	**c.** salty, undrinkable
4. pillage	**d.** bounds, confines
5. quiescent	**e.** in love, captivated
6. schism	**f.** inactive
7. unconscionable	**g.** unyielding
8. inexorable	**h.** unscrupulous
9. proliferation	**i.** plundering
10. muse	**j.** entertain
	k. ponder
	l. a multiplication, increase

ANSWERS: **1.** c; **2.** e; **3.** d; **4.** i; **5.** f; **6.** a; **7.** h; **8.** g; **9.** l; **10.** k.

III Put the power words listed below in the blanks that best suit the people in the sentences.

complacent, stolid, officious, morose, ebullient, petulant.

1. The . . . . . . customer fussed over the placement of each small curl, to the annoyance of almost everyone at the hairdresser's.
2. It's important not to seem . . . . . . when managing a group of workers.
3. . . . . , she threw her arms around him and jumped up and down with joy when he gave her the medal for winning the marathon.
4. He became extremely . . . . . . when he lost three hours work because of his technical error on the computer.

5. She complained she had wanted to marry a solid man but not a . . . . man whose apathy was totally boring.
6. After he was elected by such an overwhelming majority he unfortunately became . . . . resting on his laurels.

ANSWERS: **1.** petulant; **2.** officious; **3.** ebullient; **4.** morose; **5.** stolid; **6.** complacent.

IV Here are some more "mix-up" words. Look at them carefully to be sure *you* don't get mixed up. Pick the word or phrase that comes closest to the power word.

1. inquisitive   A: questioning; to satisfy curiosity. B: questioning, concerning a crime.
2. quizzical   A: testing, confronting. B: questioning; gently amused.
3. implication   A: a meaning hinted at. B: a conclusion by deduction.
4. lowering   A: overcast with clouds. B: sounding like cattle mooing.
5. duplicity   A: units of two. B: deception.
6. fulsome   especially concerning words A: sincere. B: cloying or excessive.
7. eke   A: to work at halfheartedly. B: to supplement with difficulty.
8. idyll   A: a literary piece about charming pastoral scenes. B: a worshiped person.
9. limbo   A: dangerous place. B: place of neglect.
10. limpid   A: relaxed. B: clear.
11. derogatory   A: belittling. B: reproving.
12. eclectic   A: selected from various sources. B: stunning effect.

ANSWERS: **1.** A; **2.** B; **3.** A; **4.** A; **5.** B; **6.** B; **7.** B; **8.** A; **9.** B; **10.** B; **11.** A; **12.** A.

V Fill the blanks in the following paragraphs with the appropriate words listed below:

plethora, mystic, injunction, repertoire, concomitantly, incisive, enhance, amalgam, maligned.

After the court issued an **(a)** . . . . . . forbidding further activity in the company plant until the monopoly accusation was settled, the officers decided to issue a booklet explaining the recent **(b)** . . . . . . of their new acquisitions that created a new and profitable entity.

The editors tried to make the **(c)** . . . . . . of information **(d)** . . . . . . and to **(e)** . . . . . . the presentation with spectacular photographs.

The company **(f)** . . . . issued a statement saying it had been **(g)** . . . . by a misinformed secret agent who had used a charlatan **(h)** . . . . . . for his facts. This fake holy man had many different schemes in his **(i)** . . . . . . of tricks that had made him rich.

ANSWERS: **a.** injunction; **b.** amalgam; **c.** plethora; **d.** incisive; **e.** enhance; **f.** concomitantly; **g.** maligned; **h.** mystic; **i.** repertoire.

Your Score

45–40	Word master
39–27	Very good
26–20	Fair

13

Style Is the Dress of Thought

"Reading makes a full person, discussion a ready one, and *writing* an exact one"—FRANCIS BACON. (Author's emphasis.)

Power Words

atheism	parasite
audacious	philistine
avaricious	precursor
avuncular	predilection
castigate	proclivity
clandestine	progeny
coalesce	raucous
doldrums	repine
ethics	restive
exiguous	risible
flotsam	salient
inherent	sardonic
jovial	supine
loggerheads	travesty
moot	truculent

Special Words: Style Is the Dress of Thought
(Avoiding the Cliché with Vivid Expression)

aesthetic	inchoate
comprehension	inept
conditioned	mnemonic
determinate	perfunctory
diction	piquant
didactic	poignantly
dissipate	recur
exigent	

Your challenge is to be able to write clearly and to be reasonably interesting.

Our challenge is to give you sensible guidelines, and to encourage you so you will enjoy writing.

We want you to take pleasure in the act of writing. There are certain principles that will make this easier. We will try to keep them to a minimum.

One of the authors of this book taught art in school. Rather than presenting a rigid way of painting a picture, she wanted the students to use their imaginations to paint naturally and not fill in lines, so to speak, that someone else had drawn.

This is the way we feel about your writing. We want you to write in a way that is natural for you. You will follow basic guidelines and use other writers as models. But you will be finding your own style.

Putting words on paper is a creative act, whether it's a letter, a business report, or a theme. Even though it may be somewhat difficult, you find that nothing is quite like pulling off a creative act. You experience a heady exhilaration. This is yours! This has come out of your brain and gut. The chances are no one will ever have put it in exactly the same way.

Tom Wolfe Makes It Seem Like Fun

Tom Wolfe is a writer who handles words and hyperbole like a juggler. His writing is funny, accurate, imaginative, and wildly energetic. Here is a section from *The Right Stuff,* a book telling about the first astronauts, humorously satirizing all the hoopla surrounding the early days of space flight. The scene is a gigantic barbecue welcoming the seven astronauts and their families. It takes place in a colossal auditorium, air-conditioned to a freezing temperature.

"The air was filled with the stench of burning cattle. They [the Texans] had set up about ten barbecue pits in there, and they were roasting thirty animals. Five thousand businessmen and politicians and their better halves, fresh from the 100-degree horrors of Downtown in July, couldn't wait to sink their faces in it. It was a Texas barbecue, Houston-style.

"First they took the seven brave lads and their wives and children up onto a stage that had been set up at one end of the arena, and there was a little welcoming ceremony in which they introduced them one by one, and a great many politicians and businessmen made speeches. All the while the great cow carcasses sizzled and popped and the smoke of the burning meat was wafted here and there in the chilly currents of the air conditioning. Only the extreme cold kept you from throwing up. The ganglia of the solar plexus were frozen. The wives tried to be polite, but it was a losing game. The children were squirming up on the stage and the wives were getting up and whispering to any locals they could get close to. The children were *in extremis.* They hadn't been near a bathroom for hours. The wives were frantically trying to find out where the johns were in this place . . ."

First Things First

One of the clearest and simplest books, and by far the best, relating to style in writing is Strunk and White's *The Elements of Style.* The book, a modern classic in its genre, is only seventy-one pages long and is in paperback. The publisher is The Macmillan Company. Buy your copy today!

In this chapter we can only touch on some of the ideas Strunk and White suggest.

We want to recommend another book. Good writing is based on at least a rudimentary knowledge of grammar: punctuation, sentence structure, and the like. A thorough, readable, and well-organized one is *Handbook for Writers,* by Celia Millward (Holt, Rinehart and Winston). It covers a multiplicity of topics and should be a part of your reference library.

Incidentally, writing is an act of discovery—of discovering what you have to say. One author put it this way. "How can I tell what I think until I see it in writing?" In other words, you don't have to have all your ideas completely formalized before you begin to write. A topic outline is handy—virtually a necessity. It's a scaffolding for your ideas. You know generally what you want to do, though at the beginning you may not be sure of how you are going to get there.

Use the active voice

The active voice is more direct and vigorous than the passive.

"I will always remember the first time I met Genghis Khan" is better than "The first time I met Genghis Khan will always be remembered by me."

"Around four in the morning, pain awakened me" is better than "Around four in the morning I was awakened by pain."

Recast the sentence, putting it into a different order—rephrasing it, in other words. We know, of course, that "was," "are," and "is" end up being among the most useful verbs, and you and I will use them often. In fact it *is* impossible not to use them. But practice avoiding them. It makes for livelier, more interesting writing.

Most of the time, a shorter sentence is stronger than a longer one.

Not always. But most of the time.

Your First Sentence

The first sentence in a paragraph gives the initial clue to the idea you will be considering. It may also be a transition sentence, leading from a past thought to a new one.

Be Positive

Too often, we throw in qualifiers. Strunk and White state we should "avoid tame, colorless, hesitating, noncommittal language.

"We think that perhaps the government may possibly be wrong in supporting the insurgents" is not a strong statement. If we have doubts about the role of the government, the sentence can be rephrased as "We believe the government may be wrong in supporting the insurgents."

The authors of *The Elements of Style* also observe that *not* is an unsatisfactory word. "Consciously or unconsciously, the reader is dissatisfied with being told only what is *not;* he wishes to be told what *is*. Hence, as a rule, it is better to express even a negative in a postive form."

Try to recast each of the following phrases into a more positive word:

1. not usually
2. not rational
3. not having any importance
4. did not pay any attention to
5. did not have much confidence in.

ANSWERS: **1.** infrequently; **2.** irrational; **3.** insignificant; **4.** ignored; **5.** distrusted.

Be Specific

We urged you, in Chapter 12, to be specific. Another way of stating this principle is, Be concrete.

If you are writing a business letter, be direct. Pare down your unnecessary words. Avoid to the point of death such foolish, air-filled phrases as "yours of this instant."

If you are writing a letter to a friend about a happening in your life, or working on a theme or paper, be concrete in fixing pertinent details in the reader's mind by creating word pictures.

For example, Annie Dillard, in *Pilgrim at Tinker's Creek,* writes about seeing:

"It was sunny one evening last summer at Tinker's Creek; the sun was low in the sky, upstream. I was sitting on the sycamore log bridge with the sunset at my back, watching the shiners the size of minnows who were feeding over the muddy sand in skittery schools. Again and again, one fish, then another, turned for a split second across the current and flash! the sun shot out from its silver side."

You are with the author, seeing what she sees.

Loose Sentences Are a Menace

Loose sentences muddy up clear writing and thinking. They are so often linked together clumsily using *and, who, but, which, that, when, where.*

"The Pegasus Art Gallery held an exhibit for Jane Yates, *who* has been painting watercolors for years and *who* has developed an expertise for this medium, *which* also lends itself to flowers and other colorful subjects. But on the other hand she also likes sketching *where* she is known for her scenes of houses and gardens, and at the same time she enjoys doing interiors, *which* has earned her equal praise" et cetera et cetera, as the king said in *The King and I.* How easy it is to write poorly! The words just flow along one after the other.

Let Your Fancy Take Off

Reader's Digest has a feature called "Toward More Picturesque Speech." In it are phrases that catch a moment or an incident in a picture of words. As an exercise, try to put the following incidents or situations into your own words. Then see how someone else has phrased it in *Reader's Digest.* This is not to say that one or the other is better. Each has its own merits. Use as few words as possible.

1. What does a fire escape look like to you?
2. You are in a plane over a city. Describe in ten words or less what the streets look like.
3. You are on a city street, looking up at the many tall skyscrapers. What are they like?
4. You are watching clouds touching high mountains. Describe them.
5. A mountain lion is running down the side of a hill. What does it remind you of?
6. You see tumbleweeds along a barbed-wire fence. Do they create an image?
7. You spy some turtles inching their way along the edge of a desert. What are they like?

ILLUSTRATIONS: **1.** Fire escapes slashing down sides of buildings like wrought-iron lightning (James Carroll); **2.** A spider's web of streets (Bill Granger); **3.** The upward flight of skyscrapers (Bonnie May Malody); **4.** Clouds lassoing the peaks of the mountains (Bonnie May Malody); **5.** A mountain lion flowing like smoke down the hillside (Jim Berry); **6.** Tumbleweeds clutching at a barbed-wire fence (Ruth E. May); **7.** Turtles tanking over the desert floor (Flo Waga)

Grammar May Not Be Glamour. But It Is Necessary.

As we mentioned a few paragraphs earlier, a basic understanding of grammar is important. Here are a few highlights gleaned from Webster's Illustrated Contemporary Dictionary, Doubleday & Company, Inc.

Agreement of Subject and Verb. It may seem needless to say that a singular subject takes a singular verb, while a plural subject takes a plural verb; however, when phrases or other elements come between the subject and the verb, the agreement may not be clear.

The small table around which the children played **was** in the hall.

The small tables owned by the church **were** in the hall.

The onlookers, as well as the policeman, **were** aghast at the sight.

The following words are generally considered singular and take singular verbs: *each, either, neither, none, one, someone, anyone, everybody, nobody, somebody, much, anybody, everyone.*

None of us **is** perfect.

Everybody thinks **he** or **she** has a sense of humor.

When you are referring to two or more persons who are of different sexes, or to a group of people of mixed gender, the pronouns **they, them,** and **their** are often used to refer to **anyone, each, everybody,** to avoid the awkward **he or she, him or her, his or her.** Although widely accepted, it is incorrect.

Often it is best to give the sentence a plural subject:

All weavers should choose their looms carefully
    is better than
Each weaver should choose his or her loom carefully

Collective Nouns. A collective noun, such as **class, company, club, crew, jury, committee,** takes a singular verb when the whole is considered as a unit, and a plural verb when members of the whole are being considered separately.

The jury **has** deliberated for six hours.

The crew **were** near exhaustion after their many hours of exposure.

Some collective nouns, as **police** and **cattle,** are used only in the plural sense; others, as **mankind** and **wildlife,** are generally used in the singular sense.

The cattle **were** almost destroyed by the severe storm.

The New England wildlife **has** been protected.

Agreement of Pronoun with Its Antecedent

An **antecedent** is the word or words to which a pronoun refers. In the sentence below, **John** is the antecedent of **he.**

John thinks he is the reincarnation of Elvis Presley.

If the antecedent is singular, the pronoun is singular. If the antecedent is plural, the pronoun is plural.

The girl did **her** best in the contest.

The girls did **their** best in the contest.

Spelling

When in doubt as to the correct spelling of a word, consult the dictionary.

Keep a list of your spelling errors and study them.

Learn the most commonly misspelled words.

Learn to spell by syllables, carefully pronouncing each syllable. Faulty spelling is often due to faulty pronunciation.

Euphony

Euphony means "pleasing sound." It comes from the Greek words **eu-** (well) and **phone** (sound).

Do you have words that are favorites of yours because of the way they sound? Wilfred Funk did. A poet and lexicographer, he made up a list of what he considered the ten most beautiful words in the English language. His list created interest around the world. Make up your list, and then check with what he considered the most **euphonious.** You will find it interesting to compare.

Wilfred Funk's list: chimes, dawn, golden, hush, lullaby, luminous, melody, mist, murmuring, tranquil.

What are the ten worst-sounding English words for you? Check it against the list arrived at by the National Association of Teachers.

The NAT list: cacophony, crunch, flatulent, gripe, jazz, phlegmatic, plump, plutocrat, sap, treachery.

Needless to say, all such lists are highly subjective. The writer Dorothy Parker liked **cellar door.** The Dutch writer and artist Hendrik Willem van Loon opted for **cuspidor.** One's choice depends to a large extent on private and sometimes erratic association.

Finally the Poor Old Cliché

"Pity the poor, unloved cliché. Dictionary definitions are contemptuous:

'A trite phrase or expression . . . a hackneyed

theme or situation' (Webster's New Collegiate Dictionary)

"Experts in usage are dismissive. The lexicographer Eric Partridge described his Dictionary of Clichés as being 'full of things better left unsaid . . . phrases so hackneyed as to be knock-kneed and spavined.'

"Some writers have argued that one hallmark of the genuine cliché is that it was once a fresh and imaginative coinage—so fresh and imaginative, in fact, that it was repeated until it finally became tiresome." (*Success with Words,* The Reader's Digest Association, Inc.)

Eric Partridge could find enough clichés to form a dictionary. Unfortunately, with limited space, we can only give a few examples here. You are already familiar with clichés. They surround us like "wolves in sheep's clothing": **"like a bolt from the blue, strictly speaking, bleary-eyed, hook, line, and sinker, the impression of, abject apology, between the devil and the deep blue sea, as cool as a cucumber, fate worse than death, keep a stiff upper lip, I've got news for you, lay one's cards on the table, skeleton in the closet, thanks for nothing, vicious circle, weaker sex, a little knowledge is a dangerous thing."**

Epilogue (A Short Concluding Section)

"Writing is, for most, laborious and slow. The mind travels faster than the pen; consequently, writing becomes a question of learning to make occasional wing shots, bringing down the bird of thought as it flashes by. A writer is a gunner, sometimes waiting in his blind for something to come in, sometimes roaming the countryside hoping to scare something up. Like other gunners, he must cultivate patience; he may have to work many covers to bring down one partridge." (Strunk and White, *The Elements of Style*).

Points to Remember

1. Enjoy the act of writing.
2. Be specific.
3. Watch for loose sentences.
4. "See" with your fancy.
5. Get hold of the elements of grammar.
6. Shut the door on clichés.

Word-Power Test

I What power word best describes the following remarks? Pick the word from the list below:

truculent, jovial, perfunctory, didactic, poignantly, sardonic, audacious, avuncular

1. "Well now, as you are my only nephew, I will give you a treat and take you to the Men's Night Out Club," he said in a kindly . . . . . . way.
2. "Notice the prehensile tail of the monkey. It has many uses. Wouldn't it be marvelous if we had one?" The professor laughed in a . . . . . . way.
3. "No one can help those miserable bag ladies, especially such an inept young woman as you." The . . . . . . remark just spurred the heroine on.
4. "File your cards here," the clerk said in a . . . . voice, without looking up.
5. The young convert tried to "reform" his grandmother with many biblical quotations. She smiled gently at his . . . . . . remarks, holding her well-used Bible in her lap.
6. "We'll never find my little dog," the small child cried . . . . . .
7. Astounding her parents, the . . . . . . young woman talked her way past guards and a battery of secretaries and spent a few charmed moments with the Pope.
8. "I'll get you," the savage criminal spat out in a . . . . . . way, frightening his accuser but not delaying justice.

ANSWERS: **1.** avuncular; **2.** jovial; **3.** sardonic; **4.** perfunctory; **5.** didactic; **6.** poignantly; **7.** audacious; **8.** truculent.

II Pick the word or phrase closest to the power word.

1. atheism   the belief A: there is no god. B: the truth cannot be known. C: there are many gods.
2. clandestine   A: hostile. B. intimate. C: secret.
3. ethics   A: standards of behavior. B: race or tribe. C: proverb.
4. flotsam   A: worthless objects. B: valuables. C: a small fleet.
5. philistine   A: boor. B: materialist. C: selfish miser.
6. progeny   A: ancestors. B: offspring. C: a genius.
7. dissipate   A: dilute. B: scatter. C: sample.
8. avaricious   A: greedy. B: vehement. C: hungry.
9. piquant   a taste that is A: mild. B: agreeably tart. C: sour.
10. salient   A: sharp. B: aggressive. C: prominent.
11. risible   A: light in weight. B: odd. C: amusing.

12. determinate   A: specific. B: thoughtful. C: puzzling.

ANSWERS: **1.** A; **2.** C; **3.** A; **4.** A; **5.** B; **6.** B; **7.** B; **8.** A; **9.** B; **10.** C; **11.** C; **12.** A.

III Fill in the blanks in the following paragraphs from the appropriate power words listed below:

conditioned, inchoate, castigated, restive, raucous, parasites, aesthetics, mnemonics, diction, comprehension, inept.

A few of the pupils noticed the mild professor became increasingly **(a)** . . . . . . as their responses to his questions grew **(b)** . . . . . . But he totally startled them when he suddenly jumped up, shaking his fist, and wildly **(c)** . . . . . . them.

He called them **(d)** . . . . . . willing to live off others, not trying to study hard in order to support themselves. He shouted that they were **(e)** . . . . . . by a deteriorating society. They had no **(f)** . . . . . . of the **(g)** . . . . . . found in the arts and never even used simple **(h)** . . . . . . to help them retain their lessons. Far beyond merely correcting their **(i)** . . . . . . , he was not surprised to find they had become **(j)** . . . . . . and even **(k)** . . . . . .

The strange incident had an effect. No one ever forgot it, and a few even tried to improve themselves.

ANSWERS: **a.** restive; **b.** raucous; **c.** castigated; **d.** parasites; **e.** conditioned; **f.** comprehension; **g.** aesthetics; **h.** mnemonics; **i.** diction; **j.** inchoate; **k.** inept.

IV Decide whether these sentences are true or false.

1. *Doldrums,* meaning those parts of the ocean near the equator where calms or fitful winds prevail, seems to have a logical tie with the metaphoric use "in the doldrums," meaning depressed or bored. True or false?
2. If you are at *loggerheads* with your friends, it means you are in sympathy with them. True or false?
3. It has definitely been proved that "life on other planets" is not a *moot* question any longer. True or false?
4. When minute particles on a slide *coalesce,* it means they grow or come together. True or false?
5. If you were subjected to a *travesty* of justice, it is probable you would consider legal action. True or false?

ANSWERS: **1.** true; **2.** false; **3.** false; **4.** true; **5.** true.

V The following words are interesting from a variety of aspects. Think about them and try to fill the blanks with the correct power words from the ones listed below.

repine, exiguous, supine, exigent, inherent, recur, proclivity, precursor, predilection

1. Would you be discontented and . . . . if you were forced to be . . . . . . in bed for two weeks?

2. If you were living on . . . . . . means, would it be . . . . . . to find a way to make money?

3. The letters were a . . . . to the blackmail, and if he did not stop it now it would . . . .

4. When thwarted, his strong . . . . for peace and quiet triggered his . . . . . . to a quick temper. Whether . . . . . . or not, it was no longer debatable.

ANSWERS: **1.** repine, supine; **2.** exiguous, exigent; **3.** precursor, recur; **4.** predilection, proclivity, inherent.

Your Score

40–35	Word master
34–25	Very good
24–18	Fair

14

Are You Sure You Can Express What You Feel?— Denotation and Connotation

A few years ago we experimented in schools with a reading program. Teachers told us that youngsters who were more difficult, who tended to "explode" more often, were those whose vocabularies were limited. They didn't have adequate words to express their frustrations and anger—to themselves as well as to others. Consequently, they expressed themselves physically.

Power Words

abjure	hiatus
apocryphal	hypothetical
apposite	illicit
artifact	imprimatur
conclave	insidious
connive	intransigent
corporeal	intrepid
coup	laudable
desultory	materialism
execrable	portentous
fallow	preposterous
farcical	proselyte
foray	punctilious
gamut	sporadic
gratuitous	sullen

Special Words: Can You Express What You Feel?

amorphous	patent
caustic	preclude
equivocal	proponent
feasible	referent
imperturbable	rhetoric
irony	subjective
metonymy	synecdoche
onomatopoeia	

If you think about it, even when you have an adequate vocabulary, communicating with words can be frustrating. Essential and elementary though it may be, having someone else understand what we're thinking is only partially satisfying. Even at this moment of writing, we're not conveying to you *exactly* what we have in mind. We have a stew of words inside our brains, and though we dish out what we think will be the right mix, some of the flavor is lost in the transfer. Besides, we have different taste buds.

The problem is that words are only symbols. That is, they are something that represents something else, and that is why some of the flavor is lost. They are *not* the thing itself. They only stand for it. The word green is a symbol for the actual color. When we mention that a character in a story wore a green dress, your perception of the color green and ours may vary. Who knows? One of us may be color-blind.

Extend this problem to abstract notions such as love, democracy, patriotism, freedom. No wonder the human race trembles on the edge of an abyss. The more fully we understand the meaning of everyday words as well as the more complex ones, the keener sense we will have of each word's use. We can evaluate it better when we see or hear it.

United, Words Fall; Divided, They Stand

This is a lighthearted way of stating a truth about words. Fortunately with many words, we can divide the sense of their meaning into two areas, though these are not rigid compartments. There is an overlapping.

The two areas are **denotation** and **connotation.**

According to the dictionary, **denotation** is the actual, explicit meaning. **Explicit** is a no-nonsense word that means plainly stated, clearly expressed, having no disguised meaning. Lexicographers (dictionary makers) like to put a word into a particular meaning-slot that fixes its definition as permanently as possible. A certain word has a specific meaning and that's where it stays. **Denotation** comes from Latin *de-* (down) and *notare* (to mark).

But **connotation** stretches a word. It is the emotional content or significance of a word *in addition* to its explicit meaning. Many of the important words influencing our lives are "escape artists." They refuse to keep their meanings in the explicit, predetermined slots. They become colored by our personal emotions and associations. The word **connotation** is from the Latin prefix *com-* (together), which you came across in Chapter 6, and *notare.*

For example, atheists can accept the explicit definition, the **denotative** explanation, of prayer as "a solemn request or thanksgiving to God." Nonetheless, they believe it is a useless exercise, for to them God is nonexistent. Persons who are religious, however, also accept the literal definition, but to them prayer has a much richer **connotation.** It becomes a way of understanding God, a way of their reflecting to others the love that God has for the world. Their own lives and perspectives are altered. They learn about forgiveness and of finding a relative peace in a chaotic world. Their ideas and emotions are added to *prayer*'s basic definition.

The way an entire society approaches a word colors its meaning. Loyal Russian citizens insist they live in a democracy. Americans in the United States *know* they live in one. Who is right? What exactly is a Communist, a democracy, a faith? In a room with ten people, you are apt to get ten somewhat different definitions.

We are awash with words—newspapers, periodicals, paperbacks, TV, radio. We are inundated with people trying to persuade us with their words: go on this vacation, believe this is better, buy that. All use biased, or "loaded," words. Relying on **connotation,** the words are designed to appeal to our emotions, rather than to our intelligence. Try to see them for what they are.

The authors of *Word Mastery Made Simple* reported on an English word game. It is based on the varying **connotations** of synonymous words. It joins "I" to a word of a favorable **connotation,** "you" to a less favorable one, and "he" to a derogatory one.

> I am **resolute.**
> You are somewhat **stubborn.**
> He is **pigheaded.**
>
> I am pleasingly **plump.**
> You are **overweight.**
> He is **fat.**
>
> I am **slender.**
> You are **skinny.**
> She is a **bag of skin and bones.**

Try these comparisons. This could be a good party game. On the other hand, the participants might take it personally and the party could become sticky.

Use your thesaurus if your mind blanks out. You can come up with answers equally as good as the ones we suggest.

1. I am conservative.
   You are . . . .
   He is . . . .
2. I am liberal.
   You are . . . .
   She is . . . .
3. I am thrifty.
   You are . . . .
   She is . . . .
4. I am generous.
   You are . . . .
   He is . . . .
5. I am candid.
   You are . . . .
   He is . . . .
6. I am diplomatic.
   You are . . . .
   He is . . . .
7. I am petite.
   You are . . . .
   She is . . . .
8. I am content.
   You are . . . .
   He is . . . .
9. I am masterful.
   You are . . . .
   He is . . . .
10. I am persistent.
   You are . . . .
   She is . . . .

ANSWERS: **1.** You are not keeping up with the times. He is a narrow-minded reactionary. **2.** You are leftist. She is a wild-eyed radical. **3.** You are being too economical. She is stingy (miserly, niggardly, penurious, tight). **4.** You are being too open-handed. He is extravagant (spendthrift, prodigal). **5.** You are blunt. He is boorish (insulting, tactless, impolite). **6.** You are a wishy-washy Charlie Brown. He is insincere and deceitful. **7.** You are undersized. She is puny (pint-sized). **8.** You are self-satisfied. He is smug. **9.** You are a bit too overbearing. He is arrogant (overbearing). **10.** You are stubborn. She is pigheaded (bullheaded, dogmatic).

Points to Remember

1. Words are symbols.
2. Denotation is an explicit meaning.
3. Connotation offers an emotional content.
4. To some degree, your national language conditions your understanding of words.

Word-Power Test

I Pick the sentence a, b, or c that comes closest to describing the following situations.

1. General Gómez made an announcement that an Army *coup* took place at 5 o'clock this morning and the President resigned.
   a. At last the Army and General Gómez had their revenge.
   b. The Army had taken sudden and successful action to obtain power.
   c. General Gómez instituted needed reform measures.

2. Shirley explained that there was a *hiatus* of two years before she returned to graduate school.
   a. For whatever reason, Shirley's education was interrupted for two years.
   b. Shirley explained she'd been sick for two years.
   c. She said that she'd passed the two-year period in seclusion and inactivity.
3. His *amorphous* speech left his audience dissatisfied.
   a. The speech was without definite form or shape.
   b. His speech touched on sensitive subjects.
   c. His speech, given in a disinterested and low-key mood, dissatisfied people.
4. The Roman Catholic Church refused to put their *imprimatur* on the amoral novel.
   a. They would not give it publicity.
   b. They refused to give a permission, or sanction, to publish the book.
   c. The Pope would not write an introduction.
5. The choice of which museum pictures are most appealing is usually a *subjective* one.
   a. The choice has to do with going along with the crowd.
   b. It has to do with a consensus.
   c. The choice is involved with highly personal feelings and opinions.
6. The *farcical* attempt to impersonate the President of the United States ended when a child pulled off the man's wig.
   a. The attempt was a ridiculous failure.
   b. The attempt was extremely humorous.
   c. The attempt was a crime regarded by law as serious.
7. "Her philosophy," wrote a book reviewer about author Ayn Rand, "encourages materialism."
   a. The critic believed she had an undue regard for material and worldly values, rather than spiritual ones.
   b. The critic believed that Ayn Rand encouraged her followers to be free-thinking in regard to moral values.
   c. He felt that Ayn Rand encouraged her followers to make careful plans.

ANSWERS: **1.** b; **2** a; **3.** a; **4** b; **5.** c; **6.** a; **7.** a.

II Fill in the blank, in each sentence below, with an *antonym* of the word in capital letters.

1. Contradicting her position after ABJURING agreements last year concerning the arms race, Russia stated recently she would consider . . . . them.
2. Ten years ago the fields were FALLOW. Now they are . . . .
3. The storm rose, waves slammed over the boat, water leaked into the hold, while the IMPERTURBABLE skipper read a detective novel. A normal reaction would be . . . .
4. Our decision to vacation in Yuma city this year PRECLUDES our going to Death Valley . . . . . .
5. He was an avid PROPONENT of women's rights. On the other hand, she was a (an) . . . .
6. His SPORADIC cussing in public mortified his wife. "Look at it this way," he said. "Be glad I'm not the kind of guy that does it . . . ."

ANSWERS: **1.** upholding, uphold, maintain; **2.** productive, fertile, fruitful; **3.** excitable, frantic, panicky, upset; **4.** permits, allows, facilitates, effect; **5.** opponent, critic, adversary; **6.** frequently, regularly, continually.

III Pick the description a, b, or c that describes the power word in capital letters.

1. They enjoyed the DESULTORY talk of old friends, interrupted by periods of silence and lapses.
   a. Their discussions were slow and deliberate.
   b. They were clumsy in their renewal of friendship.
   c. The conversations were going erratically from one thing to another.
2. The group tried to assess the INSIDIOUS plans.
   a. The plans were immediately seen as dangerous and compromising.
   b. The plans were in bad taste and the group was embarrassed.
   c. Attracting little attention, the treacherous, crafty plans were more dangerous than seemed apparent.
3. The SULLEN young man obviously resented the questions.
   a. The young man was slow and sluggish.
   b. He was ill-humored and morose.
   c. He was extremely stubborn and uncooperative.
4. The senator's CAUSTIC remark caught everyone by surprise.
   a. The senator's remark was coldly cruel. It was unfeeling.
   b. The woman legislator's comment was an angry one.

c. Her remark was biting and sarcastic.

5. The movie was the story of an INTREPID man who decided to study wolves by living as they did.
   a. The man was foolhardy, careless, and unaware of danger.
   b. He was unshaken in the presence of danger.
   c. He was a man with a deep curiosity and a scientific approach to life.

6. My brother-in-law can be one of the most INTRANSIGENT men I've ever known.
   a. In fact he often refuses to agree or compromise.
   b. He can be utterly helpless and irrational.
   c. At times he relies on theory when he'd be better off using actual experience.

7. "The man you will work for," she told me, "is PUNCTILIOUS; so be careful."
   a. She warned me he was compulsively fussy.
   b. My new boss would be meticulous about observing fine points, rules, and conventions.
   c. She was letting me know he was a person guided mostly by his conscience.

ANSWERS: **1.** c; **2.** c; **3.** b; **4.** c; **5.** b; **6.** a; **7.** b.

IV From the dictionary definition, pick the word that suits it from the Power Words list in this chapter.

1. Of doubtful authenticity.
2. The use of words to signify the opposite of what they usually express; a condition of affairs or events exactly the reverse of what was expected or hoped for.
3. A figure of speech in which a part stands for a whole or a whole for a part, as "roof" for a house or "mink" for mink fur.
4. The entire range of anything.
5. Full of warnings of ill; ominous.
6. Appropriate; pertinent.

ANSWERS: **1.** apocryphal; **2.** irony; **3.** synecdoche; **4.** gamut; **5.** portentous; **6.** apposite.

V Answer *yes* or *no* to each of the following questions:

1. Is an *artifact* a piece of handiwork? Yes or no?
2. *Equivocal* means "the same as." Yes or no?
3. A *referent* is something referred to. Yes or no?
4. *Rhetoric* carries the sense of "I don't give a damn." Yes or no?
5. *Conclave* is a secret council or meeting. Yes or no?
6. If you make a *hypothetical* statement, you are making a definite assumption about a thing. Yes or no?
7. *Metonymy* is a figure of speech in which a word closely connected to another word is used in place of that other word. Example: "crown" for king. Yes or no?

ANSWERS: **1.** yes; **2.** no; **3.** yes; **4.** no; **5.** yes; **6.** no; **7.** yes.

VII Pick the word or phrase that is closest to the power word.

1. corporeal   pertaining to A: being stout. B: having a material existence. C: related to a military grade.
2. foray   A: raid. B: country picnic. C: a signal that everything is A-OK.
3. laudable   A: foolishly gushing. B: praiseworthy. C: benevolent.
4. preposterous   A: absurd. B: annoying. C: greedy.
5. proselyte   to try to A: develop. B: escape. C: convert.
6. gratuitous   A: Spanish phrase for thanks. B: willing. C: given freely.
7. feasible   A: possible. B: desirable. C: useful.
8. patent   A: evident. B: suitable. C: hidden.
9. connive   A: conspire. B: incite. C: plan.
10. illicit   A: unlawful. B: secret. C: broad-minded.
11. onomatopoeia   A: words imitating sounds. B: silly, sentimental poetry. C: one-upmanship.

ANSWERS: **1.** B; **2.** A; **3.** B; **4.** A; **5.** C; **6.** C; **7.** A; **8.** A; **9.** A; **10.** A; **11.** A.

Your Score
44–40 . . . .   Word master
39–27 . . . .   Very good
26–20 . . . .   Fair

15

Confusibles and Other Things to Trip You

Caution! You will have to *pare* away the meanings from the *pairs* of homonyms in this chapter. Some of the words may tie you in a *knot* but we hope *not* all of them. If you get *one* correct you've *won* half the battle. And as you *ring* up your score we hope you will not want to *wring* our necks.

Power Words

adjudicate	effrontery
aggrandize	elliptical
anachronism	enervate
benison	epoch
cache	erratic
chicanery	ethnic
complement	factious
compliment	flaccid
contravention	flagging
counterpoint	kinetic
demise	lambent
disburse	pathos
dormant	

Special Words

colloquy	inculpate
discreet	ingenious
discrete	ingenuous
emollient	obloquy
emolument	precipitate
empirical	precipitous
hypercritical	turbid
hypocritical	turgid
imperial	venal
inculcate	venial

" 'Let thy words be few,' counsels the unknown author of the Book of Ecclesiastes. Sound advice, too. In everyday life, however, it is an injunction not so easy to obey. Words are not *few*. We are obliged to use words plentifully, even prolifically, if we are to communicate. So, round the clock, we speak words, hear words, read words, think words, and dream words. And it is hardly surprising, therefore, that, when communicating, we get our wires crossed occasionally. We say one word when we mean another, half-comprehend or misunderstand words, and encounter unfamiliar and 'hard' words daily." (Adrian Room, The Penguin Dictionary of Confusibles, Penguin Books)

Furthermore, certain words are more easily confused than others. One word sounds like another and suggests a different image—**guerrilla** and **gorilla.** Are you sure you know the difference between **flaunt** and **flout?**

You have met some of the culprits in earlier chapters. The list we present you with is not complete, of course. It couldn't possibly be. Adrian Room has already made up an excellent one from which we have just quoted, and says another is in the works. But this chapter is a good start, for the words you will find here are ones frequently misused or confused.

A suggestion for you: When you come across such words, add them to your list of **confusibles.** You will find you will be creating your own book.

Some of the following words are based on *Word Mastery Made Simple.*

Confusibles

ability, capacity

Though the meanings of these two words overlap when used with human characteristics, they suggest differences. **Ability** is the more general word. It is the quality that makes an action possible. A person of **ability** has the natural aptitude *and* the skill of experience for a practical achievement. **Capacity** is more the potential power to do something. It implies a natural aptitude, rather than acquired skill.

She had the **capacity** for playing championship tennis, while he had a rare **ability** to teach it.

accept, except

Though frequently confused, these words are nearly antonyms. **Accept** means "to take what is offered." **Except** (as a verb) means "to exclude."

He was willing to **accept** any invitations, but most people **excepted** him from their parties.

abjure, adjure

Only one small letter separates the enormous difference between these two words.

Whereas **abjure** means "to renounce or give up rights, allegiance, and the like," **adjure** is "to command or urge solemnly; earnestly entreat."

When the young king **abjured** his throne to enter a monastery, his advisers **adjured** him to change his mind.

adverse, averse

Adverse means "unfavorable, bringing misfortune or harm." **Averse** means "unwilling; disliking."

The **adverse** criticism the play received made him **averse** to seeing it.

affect, effect

As a verb, **affect** means "to act upon; influence." **Effect** means "to produce; accomplish."

Wild living will **affect** his health. But a change to a sensible, well-balanced life will **effect** his cure.

As a noun, **affect** has psychological overtones connoting "feeling, desire, emotion." **Effect** denotes "results; consequence."

The **effect** of an **affect** is to influence behavior or consciousness.

allude, refer

Allude means "to touch on indirectly; hint at." **Refer** means "to mention directly."

Though she **referred** to no novelist, everyone felt sure she was **alluding** to the controversial James Michener.

amount, number

Amount applies to mass or bulk, **number** to separate units.

They had a large **number** of children and a small **amount** of money.

apposite, opposite

Apposite means "appropriate or suitable for a purpose or occasion; to the point." **Opposite**, of course, means "contrasting in position or belief."

Though her political beliefs were **opposite** to his, he admitted that her observations were often **apposite.**

appraise, apprise

Appraise is "to estimate, evaluate, determine the worth or merit of," while **apprise** means "to inform; give notice to; tell."

When the accused was **apprised** of his rights by the police, he tried to **appraise** exactly what this meant to him at the moment.

apt, likely, liable

Apt means: (1) "suitable; appropriate," as an **apt** explanation; (2) "tending or inclined to," as He is **apt** to forget; (3) "quick at learning," as The Japanese are **apt** students.

Likely and **liable** are synonymous.

Likely suggests: (1) "probability or an eventuality," as He's **likely** to win; (2) "likely to do or suffer something," as If he slips, he's **likely** to fall into the water.

Liable implies (1) "exposure or susceptibility to something undesirable," as The boat is not steady, and it is **liable** to be blown over by the wind; (2) "responsible for damages," as He is **liable** for all their debts.

He is not an **apt** writer, and it is **likely** that Mrs. Sharp will hold him **liable** for his insulting letter.

He is not an **apt** mountain climber, and he is **likely** (or he is **liable**) to fall off the cliff.

beside, besides

Beside means "at the side of"; **besides** means "additionally."

No one sat **beside** me; as a matter of fact, no one **besides** me sat, since I had the only chair.

between, among

Between is used when speaking of two things or persons, **among** when speaking of more than two.

What I have to say is just **between** you and me, but I believe there is an extraterrestrial creature **among** us.

However, we can use *between* when more than two things are mentioned if the items are related. According to Bergen Evans in A Dictionary of Contemporary American Usage: "we say 'the difference between the three men' when we are thinking of each man compared with each of the others separately and individually. But we would say 'the three men quarreled among themselves' because we are thinking of them as a group of three, and not as a series of pairs"—that is, not as separate entities.

case, instance

Case is a general word, meaning a fact or occurrence or situation typical of a class.

His insensitive remark demonstrates a **case** of supercilious academic elitism—knowing what is best for all of us.

Instance is a concrete factual **case** that explains a general idea or illustrates the truth of something.

George Washington's refusal to be vindictive to those who were critical of him is an **instance** of his remarkable ability to put the welfare of his country before his personal feelings.

climatic, climactic

Just the one letter *c* separates the completely different meanings of these two words. **Climatic** means "pertaining to or depending on weather" (**climate**). **Climactic** means "pertaining to or forming the highest point" (**climax**).

The **climactic** event of the journey occurred among the geographic and **climatic** wonders of the Yangtze River.

complacent, complaisant, compliant

We've all known **complacent** people, who are "self-satisfied and pleased with themselves." They delight in their special advantages.

And sometimes we've been blessed with **complaisant** companions, who are willing to do what pleases us, often by their kindness, friendliness, or courtesy.

On the other hand, those who are **compliant** usually have a weak character, yielding meekly to the demands of others: his timidity made him **compliant** to his boss's unfair treatment.

contemptible, contemptuous

Contemptible means "deserving scorn or disdain." On the other hand, someone behaving **contemptuously** shows **contempt** or scorn for someone or something else.

In spite of his **contemptuous** attitude toward the holy rabbi, his own moral position is **contemptible**.

continual, continuous

Continual implies a regular but interrupted succession, **continuous** a constant and uninterrupted succession.

Both the **continual** rains and the **continuous** roar of the cataract depressed the honeymooners.

council, counsel

A **council** is "an assembly met for consultation or summoned to give advice." **Counsel** is "advice or deliberation."

The dictator dismissed the **council** when their actions displeased him.

credible, creditable, credulous

Credible means "believable, plausible, or trustworthy." Its essence is believability. **Creditable** means "deserving credit, worthy," while **credulous** describes "a condition of being gullible or too ready to believe."

When the eighty-year-old runner told his friends he ran the twenty-six-mile marathon in two hours, his **credulous** listeners thought it was a **creditable** performance, though we know it was not a **credible** story.

deprecate (DEP rih kate), depreciate (dih PREE she ate)

When we **deprecate** offensive graffiti on walls, we "firmly disapprove of it."

Depreciate is to "lessen the price or value of a thing or person." The moment you step into the new car you just bought, you **depreciate** its value by almost 20 percent. The word also carries the meaning of "belittle," as They **depreciated** his efforts to balance the budget.

disburse, disperse

Disburse is "to pay out," and **disperse** is "to scatter; break up; move in different directions."

The spy **disbursed** money to agitators to create a riot so the crowd would **disperse.**

disinterested, uninterested

Disinterested suggests being "impartial; not taking sides." **Uninterested** means "without interest or curiosity."

A good judge is always **disinterested** but never **uninterested** in the case before him.

elicit, illicit

To **elicit** information or a response is to draw it out. **Illicit** means "unlawful."

The attorney was able to **elicit** details of the **illicit** business.

emigrant, immigrant

An **emigrant** leaves one country to enter another. An **immigrant** enters one country from another.

Every **immigrant** must first have been an **emigrant.** The English **emigrants** left London at the same time the Irish **immigrants** arrived in New York.

eminent, imminent

When you are **eminent,** you are "famous and distinguished." You can also be "conspicuous and outstanding." If something is **imminent,** it is "likely to occur at any moment; impending."

Churchill, the **eminent** statesman, warned President Roosevelt of **imminent** problems if the Yalta treaty was signed.

farther, further

Strictly speaking, **farther** is used in reference to measuring physical distance, and **further** suggests a degree or quantity in a figurative or metaphorical sense.

How much **farther** do I have to run each day to **further** my endurance?

fewer, less

Fewer applies to number—to things that are counted. **Less** applies to quantity—to things that are measured.

The **fewer** one's possessions, Thoreau claimed, the **less** one's anxiety.

flaunt, flout

Two words that cause much confusion. **Flaunt** means "to show off in an ostentatious way," while **flout** means "to treat with scorn, disdain, or contempt."

An airline advertised: "When you've got it, **flaunt** it."

She **flouted** the order to wear shoes in the store, and walked in barefoot.

former, latter

Former applies to the first of two things mentioned, **latter** to the second.

She pointed to the seagull sitting on the post, and the **former** was almost the whitewashed color of the **latter.**

fortuitous, fortunate

Fortuitous means "accidental," and **fortunate,** "lucky."

Not all **fortuitous** events are **fortunate.**

healthy, healthful

In discriminating usage, **healthy** means "having health, strong, vigorous"; **healthful** suggests "promoting health."

A **healthful** diet will help one remain **healthy.**

illusion, delusion

William and Mary Morris, in Harper Dictionary of Contemporary Usage, suggest that the way to remember the difference between these two words "is to associate each with another word which begins with the same letter." **Delusion** is a form of deceit, even though it be self-deceit. **Illusion** is imaginary, in that it is "unreal, or nonexistent."

incredible, incredulous (in KREJ you lus)

Incredible means "not believable"; while **incredulous** means "unbelieving; not showing belief."

The children recounted an **incredible** tale about killing a talking snake. Their parents listened, then smiled **incredulously.**

individual, party

An **individual** is "a simple, separate entity; one person." A party is "a group met for some purpose."

The **individual,** though he may at times be a member of a political **party,** must never submerge his identity as an individual.

However, in a legal sense, **party** may refer to "a person involved in a transaction."

If the **party** to the deed signs the affidavit, he will be released from further responsibility.

imply, infer

Two confusibles that tend to make people stumble: **Imply** means "to suggest or hint"; and **infer,** "to conclude, or reach an opinion from facts or reasoning."

The chairman of the board **implied** the company would be sold. The employees, however, **inferred** from his remarks that their jobs were safe.

ingenious (in JEEN yus), ingenuous (in JEN you us)

While **ingenious** means "clever, inventive, resourceful," **ingenuous** means "unsophisticated, artless, open, frank."

He developed an **ingenious** invention to break the enemy code.

The embezzler didn't have the heart to disillusion such an **ingenuous** and obviously loving young woman.

insidious, invidious

Insidious carries the meaning of "treacherous; having a gradual and cumulative effect; subtle." **Invidious** is "repugnant; injurious; creating ill will or envy."

By **insidious** comments, the evil character Iago, in Shakespeare's play *Othello,* created the **invidious** atmosphere that led Othello to murder his own wife.

last, latest

Last refers to the final item in a series, **latest** to "the most recent."

Their **latest** horse ran **last.**

learn, teach

Learn means "to gain knowledge, or acquire skills." **Teach** is "to impart knowledge, or show how."

He **learned** how to juggle so that he might **teach** the art to his students.

leave, let

Leave is "to go away from or depart," and **let,** "to allow or permit."

Let me untie the lines from the dock, and then we'll **leave.**

lie, lay

Lie, an intransitive verb, means "to be in a resting or reclining position." (An *intransitive* verb is one that does not take a direct object.) **Lay** is a transitive verb, meaning "to put or place."

Lie down quickly. This morning I **lay** right here. I have just **lain** down.

Lay the books down here. Last evening you **laid** them on my bed. And now you have **laid** them there again.

laudable, laudatory

Laudable means "worthy of praise"; **laudatory,** "giving praise."

The reviewer is uniformly **laudatory,** even when the work is not at all **laudable.**

legendary, mythical

Though both are fictitious, there is a difference between them. According to Webster's New World Dictionary, if something is **legendary,** it may have a historical basis, but through popular tradition it has undergone great elaboration and exaggeration. On the other hand, **mythical** applies to the highly imaginary explanation of natural and historical phenomena by a people and therefore connotes that what it qualifies is a product of the imagination.

Over time, the exploits of baseball coach Casey Stengel have become **legendary.** Sportswriters of the twenty-first century will perhaps regard him as a **mythical** god of early baseball.

majority, plurality

Majority denotes "more than half," while **plurality** refers to "the number by which the winner's votes exceed those of the runner-up."

A total of one thousand ballots were cast for the three candidates. Abe received one hundred votes, Bill three hundred, and Charlie six hundred. Charlie, therefore, garnered the **majority** of the votes. His **plurality** was three hundred votes.

monetary, monitory

Monetary means "financial; relating to a country's finances; having to do with money." **Monitory** indicates "a warning; an admonishing."

Instead of good news, the Secretary of State wrote a **monitory** report on the dangerous **monetary** situation of the nation.

obtuse, abstruse

Obtuse means "dull; not sensitive or observant; slow-witted." **Abstruse** means "hard to understand; profound."

Teachers are frustrated when they try to teach **abstruse** subjects to **obtuse** students. We know a man who confused the words, who in public bragged about one of his associates, saying that Edward was very **obtuse.**

parameter (puh RAM uh tur), **perimeter**

Basically, **parameter** is "a measurable factor which helps with other such factors to define a system." Temperature, wind, and moisture are **parameters** which help to forecast weather.

In a more general sense, the word means "a guideline or criterion." The President discussed his foreign-policy **parameters.**

Perimeter is "the outer edge or boundary, or the length of a boundary." A hedge was planted along the **perimeter** of the garden.

persons, people

Persons refers to particular human beings. **People** refers to human beings collectively, especially when they form a characteristic group.

The **people** of the United States have always believed that no **persons** ought to be convicted of any crime without trial by jury.

presentiment (pri ZEN tih ment), **presentment**

And again, just one letter differentiates these two words. **Presentiment** indicates "a premonition; a foreboding." **Presentment** is "presentation; the act of presenting a formal statement of a legal matter in a court."

The lawyer had a gloomy **presentiment** that the judge would not consider the **presentment** in a favorable light.

presumptive, presumptuous (pri ZUMP chew us)
  Presumptive means "based on probability or an assumption; supposed; providing grounds for reasonable opinion or belief." But **presumptuous** has to do with being "arrogant; unduly confident; overbearing; domineering."

  The bachelor's **presumptuous** male chauvinism alienated women even though they had **presumptive** evidence that he would become a wealthy man.

principal, principle
  Principal means "chief; first in rank or importance." But **principle** suggests "a general truth or rule on which other truths, or conduct or action, are based."

  The **principal** points of the speech related to the **principles** of democracy.

sarcasm, irony
  Sarcasm is "a cutting or unpleasant remark that mocks or makes fun of something or someone." **Irony,** however, denotes "a form of expression in which the intended meaning is the opposite of the literal meaning."

  The editor's **irony** was clearly apparent. "You're too good for us," he told the impoverished novelist. The writer replied with cheerful **sarcasm:** "Anybody would be."

Points to Remember

  1. Quite a few words, "confusibles," appear or sound alike, and we are apt to use one for the other if we are not alert to the differences between them.

  2. When in doubt, look them up in your dictionary, adding them to this list. Eventually you will have your own book. The definitions and illustrations will contrast them, helping you to de-confuse.

Word-Power Test

I In the following sentences there are many malapropisms, but some words are used correctly. Answer wrong or right.

  1. The *ethnic* committee was set up to determine college rules pertaining to morality. Right or wrong?
  2. The heat of the tropics *enervated* him. Right or wrong?
  3. The *contravention* with the Congress pleased the President. He was sure he could get the bill passed. Right or wrong?

  4. The young man dressed in a knight's suit of armor might seem an *anachronism* except that he was riding a motorcycle and had a guitar on his back. Right or wrong?
  5. The *flagging* winners were so peppy and filled with energy they waved at everyone. Right or wrong?
  6. They were worried about the *erratic* secretary, as their material had to be so precise. Right or wrong?
  7. Bach was the dazzling master of *counterpoint,* the art of adding a melody that is related to but independent of the main theme. Right or wrong?
  8. The *pathos* of the politician's ridiculous speech made us laugh. Right or wrong?
  9. The epic about the *epoch* of the industrial revolution sold very well even though it was pretentious. Right or wrong?
  10. *Kinetic* energy can also apply to the writing down of words you try to remember. This very act seems to help your memory. Right or wrong?

ANSWERS: **1.** wrong; **2.** right; **3.** wrong; **4.** right; **5.** wrong; **6.** right; **7.** right; **8.** wrong; **9.** right; **10.** right.

II Pick the word or phrase you think is closest to the power word given.

  1. flaccid   A: flabby. B: calm. C: jolly.
  2. disburse   A: broadcast. B: waste. C: pay out.
  3. dormant   A: relaxed. B: inactive. C: hidden.
  4. chicanery   A: vulgar jokes. B: deception. C: amusing prank.
  5. adjudicate   A: to establish boundaries. B: determine judicially. C: accuse.
  6. cache   A: trick. B: ready money. C: hiding place.
  7. aggrandize   to A: assemble. B: steal. C: increase.
  8. effrontery   A: meaningless activity. B: shameless insolence. C: virtuosity.
  9. factious   relating to A: a contentious group. B: burning. C: a well-informed group.
  10. lambent   A: spontaneous. B: curving. C: flickering.
  11. elliptical   speaking or writing that is A: flowery. B: clear. C: abbreviated and obscure.
  12. benison   A: flesh of wild animals. B: a blessing. C: charity.

ANSWERS: **1.** A; **2.** C; **3.** B; **4.** B; **5.** B; **6.** C; **7.** C; **8.** B; **9.** A; **10.** C; **11.** C; **12.** B.

III The following words are easily mixed up. Sometimes the whole meaning is altered by changing one letter. Put the correct words in the blanks from the list of power words given below:

colloquy, emolument, turgid, precipitating, inculpate, venial, imperial, precipitous, hypocritical, discreet, empirical, discrete, inculcate, venal, emollient, turbid, compliments, ingenuous, complementing, hypercritical, ingenious, obloquy.

1. There was an . . . . command that all scientists must avoid basing their conclusions on theory; they must now base their conclusions on . . . . methods.
2. The couple clung on the ledge of a . . . . , rocky incline, not daring to move for fear of . . . . an avalanche.
3. The . . . . ambassador made sure there was a . . . . program for each nationality attending the opening ceremony of the embassy.
4. Unfortunately, the pupil's whole behavior seemed to . . . . him in the crime, though they had tried to . . . . a strong sense of right and wrong.
5. A person may be excused for some . . . . faults but . . . . weakness is inexcusable.
6. The trip to Hawaii was an . . . . for the hard-working executive. It was, also, to serve as an . . . . to soothe his frayed nerves.
7. He received many . . . . on the manner in which he worked out the . . . . material they had for the presentation, giving it a satisfying unity.
8. The . . . . young girl had an . . . . plan to solve the basic problems causing the enormous national debt.
9. The . . . . water from the flood poured over the farmland . . . . with debris from the banks.
10. The . . . . used during the . . . . on civil rights was disrupting and totally nonproductive.
11. The . . . . producer fussed over the smallest detail, but at least he was not . . . . ; he was straightforward with the actors.

ANSWERS: **1.** imperial, empirical; **2.** precipitous, precipitating; **3.** discreet, discrete; **4.** inculpate, inculcate; **5.** venial, venal; **6.** emolument, emollient; **7.** compliments, complementing; **8.** ingenuous, ingenious; **9.** turgid, turbid; **10.** obloquy, colloquy; **11.** hypercritical, hypocritical.

Your Score

44–40	Word master
39–27	Very good
26–20	Fair

Final Review Quiz

Congratulations! Here is the last review test. An advertisement says: "You've come a long way, baby." And you have. You've worked with over six hundred power words. The articles in each chapter exposed you to an abundance of useful information.

We hope you have enjoyed this verbal journey and that you are encouraged to continue to explore the "wonderful world of words."

Pick the correct definitions:

1. discreet A: apparently true. B: careful to keep confidences. C: having a practical approach.
2. empirical A: based on experience. B: proud and disdainful. C: relying on theory.
3. complement A: that which makes a thing complete. B: flattering comment or praise. C: strong force.
4. kinetic A: produced by movement. B: disruptive. C: occurring at regular intervals.
5. discrete A: being very cautious. B: individually distinct. C: showing good sense.
6. emollient A: any liquid. B: a soothing external application. C: complete self-satisfaction.
7. ethnic of or relating to A: principles. B: discrimination. C: nationality.
8. factious A: caustic. B: creating dissension. C: manufactured.
9. desultory A: unsystematic. B: thoughtless. C: slanderous.
10. punctilious A: minutely particular about fine points and forms. B: compulsively fussy. C: obsessively punctual.
11. onomatopoeia A: imitative words. B: flowery writing. C: beautiful sounds.
12. amorphous A: affectionate. B: formless. C: sleepy.
13. portentous A: ominous. B: solemn. C: crucial.
14. hiatus A: high point. B: an interruption. C: a retreat.
15. gratuitous A: thankless. B: willing. C: given freely.

16. apposite   A: appropriate or fitting. B: highly unpleasant. C: on a higher level.

17. castigate   A: criticize severely. B: mock or scorn. C: cross-examine peremptorily.

18. exiguous   A: precise. B: nearby. C: scanty.

19. coalesce   A: become thicker. B: move back and forth. C: fuse or blend.

20. inherent   A: restrained. B: possessive. C: naturally characteristic.

21. proclivity   A: aversion. B: skill. C: tendency.

22. sardonic   A: gloomy. B: scornful. C: sullen.

23. truculent   A: perversely reluctant. B: groveling. C: defiant and aggressive.

24. exigent   A: exciting. B: urgent. C: hateful.

25. limbo   A: state of neglect. B: firmament. C: jargon.

26. periphery   A: straight line. B: diameter. C: outer bounds.

27. histrionic   A: hypersensitive. B: overly dramatic. C: overactive.

28. insouciance   A: impertinence. B: unconcern. C: humor.

29. fulsome   A: offensively cloying. B: having a bad odor. C: buxom.

30. concomitant   A: something coming too late. B: something that accompanies or attends. C: friendly.

31. garrulous   A: noisy. B: quarrelsome. C: talkative.

32. peregrinations   A: mathematical calculations. B: uncertainties. C: wanderings.

33. doctrinaire   A: philosophical. B: tolerant. C: dictatorial.

34. affiliate   A: to effect. B: attract. C: join.

35. incarnate   A: vulgar. B: personified. C: inflammatory.

36. incipient   A: beginning. B: unnoticed. C: exhausted.

37. flagrant   A: careless. B: openly scandalous. C: spiteful.

38. ignominy   A: stupidity. B: disgrace. C: selfishness.

39. obtuse   A: sharp. B: stubborn. C: dull.

40. lame duck   A: politician serving out a last term. B: someone with a grievance. C: unhappy or unfortunate person.

Answers: **1.** B; **2.** A; **3.** A; **4.** A; **5.** B; **6.** B; **7.** C; **8.** B; **9.** A; **10.** A; **11.** A; **12.** B; **13.** A; **14.** B; **15.** C; **16.** A; **17.** A; **18.** C; **19.** C; **20.** C; **21.** C; **22.** B; **23.** C; **24.** B; **25.** A; **26.** C; **27.** B; **28.** B; **29.** A; **30.** B; **31.** C; **32.** C; **33.** C; **34.** C; **35.** B; **36.** A; **37.** B; **38.** B; **39.** C; **40.** A.

Your Rating

40–35 . . . .   Excellent
34–25 . . . .   Good
24–18 . . . .   Fair

Dictionary of Power Words

These entries are from The Doubleday Dictionary. Throughout this book, the authors have indicated pronunciation by phonetically spelling out each word and putting the emphasized syllable in capitals. Many dictionaries use a different system, which we have reproduced below. To avoid confusion, please note that sometimes a word will appear in the text in one form—verb, adjective, noun—and appear in the dictionary in another. Finally, since this is only a partial list, occasionally you will find a cross-reference to a word we have not reproduced here. This list is not a substitute for your own dictionary. NOTE: The *italic* number at the end of each work entry refers to the chapter in which you will find it.

Pronunciation Key

The primary stress mark (′) is placed after the syllable bearing the heavier stress or accent; the secondary stress mark (′) follows a syllable having a somewhat lighter stress, as in **com·men·da·tion** (kom′ən·dā′shən).

a	add, map
ā	ace, rate
â(r)	care, air
ä	palm, father
b	bat, rub
ch	check, catch
d	dog, rod
e	end, pet
ē	even, tree
f	fit, half
g	go, log
h*	hope, hate
i	it, give
ī	ice, write
j	joy, ledge
k	cool; take
l	look, rule
m	move, seem
n	nice, tin
ng	ring, song
o	odd, hot
ō	open, so
ô	order, jaw
oi	oil, boy
ou	pout, now
o͝o	took, full
o͞o	pool, food
p	pit, stop
r	run, poor
s	see, pass
sh	sure, rush
t	talk, sit
th	thin, both
t̲h	this, bathe
u	up, done
û(r)	burn, term
yo͞o	fuse, few
v	vain, eve
w	win, away
y*	yet, yearn
z	zest, muse
zh	vision, pleasure
ə	the schwa, an unstressed vowel representing the sound of

    a in *above*   *o* in *melon*
    e in *sicken* *u* in *focus*
    i in *clarity*

*Superscript *h*, as in *white* (ʰwīt) or *whale* (ʰwāl), and *y*, as in *due* (dʸo͞o) or *Tuesday* (tʸo͞oz′dā) represent sounds that commonly occur in certain regions but are commonly omitted in others.

FOREIGN SOUNDS

à	as in French *ami, patte.* This is a vowel midway in quality between (a) and (ä).
œ	as in French *peu,* German *schön.* Round the lips for (ō) and pronounce (ā).
ü	as in French *vue,* German *grün.* Round the lips for (o͞o) and pronounce (ē).
kh	as in German *ach,* Scottish *loch.* Pronounce a strongly aspirated (h) with the tongue in position for (k) as in *cool* or *keep.*
ṅ	This symbol indicates that the preceding vowel is nasal. The nasal vowels in French are œṅ *(brun),* aṅ *(main),* äṅ *(chambre),* ôṅ *(dont).*
'	This symbol indicates that a preceding (l) or

(r) is voiceless, as in French *débâcle* (dā·bä′kl')
or *fiacre* (fyȧ′kr'), or that a preceding (y) is
pronounced consonantly in a separate syllable
followed by a slight schwa sound, as in French
fille (fē′y').

a·bet (ə·bet′) *v.t.* **a·bet·ted, a·bet·ting** To encourage and support, esp. to support wrongdoing. [<OF *abeter* incite, arouse] **—a·bet′ment, a·bet′tal, a·bet′ter, a·bet′tor** *n.* 2

ab·hor (ab·hôr′) *v.t.* **ab·horred, ab·hor·ring** To regard with repugnance, horror, or disgust. [<L *ab-* from + *horrere* shrink] **—ab·hor′rer** *n.* **—Syn.** loathe, detest, despise, abominate. 4

ab·ject (ab′jekt, ab·jekt′) *adj.* **1** Of the lowest kind or degree; wretched. **2** Servile; cringing. [<L *ab-* away + *jacere* throw] **—ab·jec′tive** *adj.* **ab′ject·ly** *adv.* **—ab′ject·ness, ab·jec′tion** *n.* 4

ab·jure (ab·jŏŏr′) *v.t.* **ab·jured, ab·jur·ing** **1** To renounce under oath; forswear. **2** To retract or recant, as an opinion. [<L *abjurare* deny on oath] **—ab·jur·a·to·ry** (ab·jŏŏr′ə·tôr′ē, -tō′rē) *adj.* **—ab′ju·ra′tion, ab·jur′er** *n.* 14

ab·o·rig·i·ne (ab′ə·rij′ə·nē) *n.* **1** One of the original native inhabitants of a country. **2** *pl.* Flora and fauna indigenous to a geographical area. [<L *ab origine* from the beginning] 1

a·bor·tive (ə·bôr′tiv) *adj.* **1** Brought forth or born prematurely. **2** Imperfectly developed. **3** Coming to naught; failing, as an effort. **4** Causing abortion. **—a·bor′tive·ly** *adv.* **—a·bor′tive·ness** *n.* 6

ab·ro·gate (ab′rə·gāt) *v.i.* **·gat·ed, ·gat·ing** To annul by authority, as a law. [<L *ab-* away + *rogare* ask, propose] **—ab·ro·ga·ble** (ab′rə·gə·bəl), **ab′ro·ga′tive** *adj.* **ab′ro·ga′tion, ab′ro·ga′tor** *n.* **—Syn.** abolish, repeal, cancel, nullify. 5

ab·scond (ab·skond′) *v.i.* To depart suddenly and secretly, esp. to hide oneself. [<L *ab-* away + *condere* store] **—ab·scond′er** *n.* 1

ac·cred·it (ə·kred′it) *v.t.* **1** To furnish or send with credentials, as an ambassador. **2** To certify as fulfilling requirements. **3** To give credit for. **4** To attribute to. **5** To accept as true; believe. **6** To confer acceptance or favor on. [<F *à* to + *crédit* credit] 9

ac·cre·tion (ə·krē′shən) *n.* **1** Growth or increase in size, as by external additions. **2** The result of such growth or increase; also, that which is added to effect such a result. **3** An accumulation, as of soil on a seashore. [<L *accrescere* to grow to] **—ac·cre′tive** *adj.* 5

ac·cli·mate (ak′lə·māt, ə·klī′mit) *v.t.* & *v.i.* **·mat·ed, ·mat·ing** To adapt or become adapted to a different climate, environment, or situation. [<F *à* to + *climat* climate] **—ac·cli·ma·ta·ble** (ə·klī′mə·tə·bəl) *adj.* **—ac·cli·ma·tion** (ak′li·mā′shən), **ac·cli·ma·ta·tion** (ə·klī′mə·tā′shən) *n.* 6

ac·ri·mo·ni·ous (ak′rə·mō′nē·əs) *adj.* Bitterly sarcastic; caustic; sharp. **—ac′ri·mo′ni·ous·ly** *adv.* **—ac′ri·mo′ni·ous·ness** *n.* 1

a·cu·men (ə·kyōō′mən, ak′yōō·mən) *n.* Quickness of insight or discernment; keenness of intellect. [<L, sharpness (of the mind) <*acuere* sharpen] **—Syn.** acuteness, cleverness, keenness, insight. 3

ad·a·mant (ad′ə·mant, -mənt) *n.* In legends, a very hard but imaginary mineral. **—adj.** **1** Very hard. **2** Immovable and unyielding, as in purpose. [<Gk *adamas* the hardest metal (hence, unyielding)] **—ad·a·man·tine** (ad′ə·man′tin, -tēn, -tīn) *adj.* 3

ad·dict (ə·dikt′) *v.t.* **1** To give or devote (oneself) persistently or habitually: usu. used in the passive voice with *to*: He is *addicted* to drugs. **2** To cause to pursue or practice continuously: with *to*: This task *addicted* him to obscure research. **—n.** (ad′ikt) One who is addicted to some habit, esp. to the use of narcotic drugs. [<L *addicere* assign, devote to] **—ad·dict′ed·ness** *n.* 8

ad·ju·di·cate (ə·jōō′də·kāt) *v.* **·cat·ed, ·cat·ing** *v.t.* **1** To determine judicially, as a case; adjudge. **—v.i.** **2** To act as a judge. [<L *adjudicare*. See ADJUDGE.] **—ad·ju′di·ca′tion, ad·ju′di·ca′tor** *n.* 15

ad·u·late (aj′ə·lāt) *v.t.* **·lat·ed, ·lat·ing** To flatter or praise extravagantly. [<L *adulari* to fawn] **—ad′u·la′tion, ad′u·la·tor** *n.* **—ad·u·la·to·ry** (aj′ə·lə·tôr′ē, -tō′rē) *adj.* 6

ae·gis (ē′jis) *Gk. Myth.* The shield of Zeus, used also by Athena. **—n.** **1** Any protection. **2** Patronage; sponsorship. 10

aes·thet·ic (es·thet′ik) *adj.* **1** Of aesthetics. **2** Of, pertaining to, or appreciating beauty and art. **3** Having or characterized by fine taste. [<Gk. *aisthētikos* of sense perception] Also **aes·thet′i·cal.** **—aes·thet′i·cal·ly** *adv.* 13

af·fa·ble (af′ə·bəl) *adj.* Easy and courteous in manner; friendly; approachable. [<L *affabilis*, lit., able to be spoken to] **—af′fa·bil′i·ty, af′fa·ble·ness** *n.* **—af′fa·bly** *adv.* **—Syn.** amicable, cordial, genial, sociable, kind. 4

af·fil·i·ate (ə·fil′ē·āt) *v.* **·at·ed, ·at·ing** *v.t.* **1** To associate or unite, as a member or branch: with *to* or *with*. **2** To join or associate (oneself): with *with*. **3** To determine the origins of. **—v.i.** **4** To associate or ally oneself: with *with*. **—n.** (ə·fil′ē·it) An affiliated person or thing. [<L *affiliare* adopt] **—af·fil′i·a′tion** *n.* 11

af·flu·ent (af′lōō·ənt, ə·flōō′-) *adj.* **1** Abounding; abundant. **2** Wealthy; opulent. **—n.** A stream that flows into another. [<L *ad-* to + *fluere* flow] **—af′flu·ent·ly** *adv.* 6

ag·gran·dize (ə·gran′dīz, ag′rən·dīz) *v.t.* **·dized, ·diz·ing** **1** To make great or greater; exalt. **2** To make appear greater. [<L *ad-* to + *grandire* make great or large] **—ag·gran′dize·ment, ag·gran′diz·er** *n.* 15

al·lege (ə·lej′) *v.t.* **al·leged, al·leg·ing** **1** To assert to be true without proving; affirm. **2** To plead as an excuse, in support of or in opposition to a claim or accusation. [?<L *allegare* to send on a mission, dispatch] **—al·lege′a·ble** *adj.* **—al·leg′er** *n.* 1

al·le·vi·ate (ə·lē′vē·āt) *v.t.* **·at·ed, ·at·ing** To make lighter or easier to bear; relieve. [<L *alleviare* <*ad-* to + *levis* light] **—al·le′vi·a′tion, al·le′vi·a′tor** *n.* **—al·le·vi·a·tive** (ə·lē′vē·ā′tiv, ə·lē′vē·ə·tiv) *adj.* **—Syn.** allay, assuage, lessen, mitigate. 7

al·lude (ə·lōōd′) *v.i.* **al·lud·ed, al·lud·ing** To make indirect or casual reference: with *to*. [<L *alludere* play with, joke] **—Syn.** hint, imply, insinuate, intimate, suggest. 2

al·tru·ism (al′trōō·iz′əm) *n.* Unselfish devotion to the welfare of others. [<L *alter* other] **—al′tru·ist** *n.* **—al′tru·is′tic** *adj.* **—al′tru·is′ti·cal·ly** *adv.* 7

a·mal·gam (ə·mal′gəm) *n.* **1** An alloy of mercury with another metal. **2** Any mixture or combination. [<Med.L *amalgama*] 12

am·bi·dex·trous (am′bə·dek′strəs) *adj.* **1** Able to use both hands equally well. **2** Very dexterous or skillful. **3** Dissembling; double-dealing. —**am′bi·dex′trous·ly** *adv.* —**am′bi·dex′trous·ness** *n.* *11*

am·big·u·ous (am·big′yōō·əs) *adj.* **1** Capable of being understood in more senses than one. **2** Doubtful or uncertain. [<L *ambigere* wander about] —**am·big′u·ous·ly** *adv.* —**am·big′u·ous·ness** *n.* *2*

a·mel·io·rate (ə·mēl′yə·rāt) *v.t. & v.i.* **·rat·ed, ·rat·ing** To make or become better; improve. [<L *ad-* to + *miliorare* to better] —**a·mel′io·rant** (-rənt), **a·mel′io·ra′tion** *n.* —**a·mel·io·ra·tive** (ə·mēl′yə·rā′tiv, -rə·tiv) *adj.* *4*

a·me·na·ble (ə·mē′nə·bəl, ə·men′ə-) *adj.* **1** Agreeable; tractable. **2** Accountable or responsible, as to authority. **3** Capable of being tested by rule or law. [<L *ad-* to + *minare* drive (with threats)] —**a·me′na·bil′i·ty, a·me′na·ble·ness** *n.* —**a·me′na·bly** *adv.* *7*

a·mok (ə·muk′) *adj.* Possessed with murderous frenzy. —*adv.* In a violent or frenzied manner. —**run** (or **go**) **amok 1** To run around attacking everybody one meets. **2** To exceed all bounds of restraint; go wild. Also **a·mock′.** [<Malay *amoq* engaging furiously in battle] *7*

a·mor·phous (ə·môr′fəs) *adj.* **1** Without definite form or shape; structureless. **2** Without definite characteristics or organization; anomalous. **3** Lacking definite crystalline structure. [<Gk. *a-* without + *morphē* form] —**a·mor′phism, a·mor′phous·ness** *n.* —**a·mor′phous·ly** *adv.* *14*

am·pere (am′pir, am·pir′) *n.* A unit of electric current, defined as the steady current that produces a force of 2×10^{-7} newtons per meter of length when flowing through parallel wires of negligible cross section and infinite length one meter apart in free space. [<A. M. *Ampère*, 1775–1836, French physicist] *10*

a·nach·ro·nism (ə·nak′rə·niz′əm) *n.* **1** The representation of something existing or occurring out of its proper time. **2** Anything placed out of its proper time. [<Gk. *anachronizein* refer to a wrong time] —**a·nach′ro·nis′tic, a·nach′ro·nis′ti·cal, a·nach′ro·nous** *adj.* *15*

a·nal·o·gy (ə·nal′ə·jē) *n. pl.* **·gies 1** A similarity or resemblance between things not otherwise identical. **2** *Biol.* A similarity in function but not in origin or structure. **3** *Logic* The assumption that things similar in some respects are probably similar in others. *8*

a·nath·e·ma (ə·nath′ə·mə) *n. pl.* **·mas** or **·ma·ta** (-mə·tə) **1** A formal ecclesiastical ban or curse, excommunicating a person or damning something, as a book or heresy. **2** A person or thing so banned or cursed. **3** Any curse or imprecation. **4** A person or thing greatly disliked or detested. [<Gk. *anathema* an offering] *5*

an·te·di·lu·vi·an (an′ti·di·lōō′vē·ən) *adj.* **1** Of the times, events, etc., before the Flood. **2** Antiquated; primitive. —*n.* Someone or something antediluvian. [<ANTE- + L *diluvium* deluge] *6*

an·thol·o·gy (an·thol′ə·jē) *n. pl.* **·gies** A collection of selected poems, stories, etc. [<Gk. *anthologia* a garland, collection of poems] —**an·tho·log·i·cal** (an′thə·loj′i·kəl) *adj.* *2*

an·thro·po·mor·phism (an′thrə·pō·môr′fiz·əm) *n.* The ascription of human attributes, feelings, motives, or characteristics to nonhuman objects, beings, or phenomena. —**an′thro·po·mor′phic** *adj.* —**an′thro·po·mor′phi·cal·ly** *adv.* —**an′thro·po·mor′phist** *n.* *5*

an·tic (an′tik) *n.* A ludicrous or clownish action; a prank; caper. —*adj.* Odd; ludicrous; incongruous. —*v.i.* **an·ticked, an·tick·ing** To perform antics. [<Ital. *antico* old, grotesque] *8*

an·tip·a·thy (an·tip′ə·thē) *n. pl.* **·thies 1** A feeling of aversion or dislike. **2** The cause of such feeling. [<Gk. *anti-* against + *pathein* feel, suffer] —**Syn.** repugnance, abhorrence, antagonism, hostility. *6*

an·ti·pode (an′ti·pōd) *n.* An exact opposite. *11*

an·tith·e·sis (an·tith′ə·sis) *n. pl.* **·ses** (-sēz) **1** The balancing of contrasted words, ideas, etc., against each other. **2** The direct contrary or opposite. [<Gk. *antitithenai* oppose] —**an·ti·thet·i·cal** (an′tə·thet′i·kəl), **an′ti·thet′ic** *adj.* —**an′ti·thet′i·cal·ly** *adv.* *2*

ap·a·thy (ap′ə·thē) *n.* **1** Lack of emotion, motivation, etc. **2** Lack of concern; indifference. [<Gk. *a-* without + *pathos* feeling] *8*

aph·o·rism (af′ə·riz′əm) *n.* A brief, pithy statement of a truth or principle; maxim. [<Gk. *aphorismos* definition] —**aph·o·rist** (af′ə·rist) *n.* —**aph′o·ris′tic** or **·ti·cal** *adj.* —**aph′o·ris′ti·cal·ly** *adv.* *6*

a·plomb (ə·plom′, ə·plum′) *n.* Assurance; self-confidence. [F, perpendicularity, assurance] —**Syn.** poise, self-assurance, self-possession, equanimity. *8*

a·poc·ry·phal (ə·pok′rə·fəl) *adj.* Of doubtful authenticity. —**a·poc′ry·phal·ly** *adv.* *14*

ap·po·site (ap′ə·zit) *adj.* Appropriate; pertinent. [<L *apponere* put near to] —**ap′po·site·ly** *adv.* —**ap′po·site·ness** *n.* *14*

ap·pre·hend (ap′ri·hend′) *v.t.* **1** To seize; arrest. **2** To grasp mentally; understand. **3** To expect with fear or anxiety. [<L *ad-* to + *prehendere* seize] —**ap′pre·hend′er** *n.* *1*

ar·bi·trar·y (är′bə·trer′ē) *adj.* **1** Based on mere opinion or prejudice; capricious. **2** Absolute; despotic. [<L *arbiter.* See ARBITER.] —**ar′bi·trar′i·ly** *adv.* —**ar′bi·trar′i·ness** *n.* *9*

ar·cha·ic (är·kā′ik) *adj.* **1** Belonging to a former period; ancient or antiquated. **2** Characterizing a verbal form or phrase no longer in current use except for special purposes, as poetry, the law, and church ritual. Also **ar·cha′i·cal.** [<Gk. *archaios* ancient] *2*

ar·ti·fact (är′tə·fakt) *n.* Anything made by human work or art. Also **ar′te·fact.** [<L *ars* art, skill + *factus,* p.p. of *facere* make] *14*

as·sid·u·ous (ə·sij′ōō·əs) *adj.* Carefully attentive and diligent. [<L *assidere* sit by] —**as·sid′u·ous·ly** *adv.* **as·sid′u·ous·ness** *n.* *8*

as·suage (ə·swāj′) *v.* **as·suaged, as·suag·ing** *v.t.* **1** To lessen or reduce the intensity of. **2** To reduce to a quiet or peaceful state. **3** To end by satisfying. [<L *ad-* to + *suavis* sweet] —**as·suage′ment** *n.* —**Syn. 1** ease, alloy, mitigate. **2** calm, pacify, mollify. **3** appease, slake, quench. *2*

as·tute (ə·st′ōōt′) *adj.* Having or showing keen intelligence or shrewdness: an *astute* businessman. [<L *astus* cunning] —**as·tute′ly** *adv.* —**as·tute′ness** *n.* —**Syn.** acute, sagacious, cunning, crafty. *2*

a·the·ism (ā′thē·iz′əm) *n.* The belief that there is no God. [<Gk. *a-* without + *theos* god] —**a′the·ist** *n.* —**a′the·is′tic** or **·ti·cal** *adj.* —**a′the·is′ti·cal·ly** *adv.* *13*

a·typ·i·cal (ā·tip′i·kəl) *adj.* Not typical. Also **a·typ′ic.** —**a·typ′i·cal·ly** *adv.* *8*

au·da·cious (ô·dā′shəs) *adj.* **1** Fearless; bold. **2** Defiant of convention, decorum, etc.; brazen; insolent [<L *audax* bold] —**au·da'cious·ly** *adv.* —**au·da'cious·ness** *n.*   *13*

au·gu·ry (ô'gʸə·rē) *n. pl.* **·ries 1** The art or practice of divination. **2** A portent or omen.   *9*

aus·pi·cious (ôs·pish'əs) *adj.* **1** Favoring or conducive to future success. **2** Attended by good fortune or indications of good fortune. —**aus·pi'cious·ly** *adv.* —**aus·pi'cious·ness** *n.* —**Syn.** propitious, favorable, hopeful, promising. **2** successful, prosperous, fortunate, lucky.   *4*

au·ton·o·mous (ô·ton'ə·məs) *adj.* **1** Functioning or existing independently. **2** Of or having self-government, as a state, group, etc. [<Gk. *autos* self + *nomos* law, rule] —**au·ton'o·mous·ly** *adv.*   *5*

a·vant-garde (ə·vänt'gärd', *Fr.* ȧ·väṅ·gȧrd') *n.* A group, as of artists or writers, who support or use the most advanced or unconventional ideas, techniques, etc.; vanguard. —*adj.* Of this group or their ideas, techniques, etc. [<F, lit., advance guard] —**a·vant-gard'ism** *n.* —**a·vant-gard'ist** *adj., n.*   *7*

av·a·rice (av'ə·ris) *n.* Passion for riches; covetousness; greed. [<L< *avarus* greedy] —**av·a·ri·cious** (av'ə·rish'əs) *adj.* —**av'a·ri'cious·ly** *adv.* —**av'a·ri'cious·ness** *n.*   *13*

a·vun·cu·lar (ə·vung'kyə·lər) *adj.* Of or pertaining to an uncle. [<L *avunculus* maternal uncle]   *13*

ba·nal (bā'nəl, bə·nal', ban'əl) *adj.* Trite; commonplace. [<OF, ordinary, common] —**ba·nal·i·ty** (bə·nal'ə·tē) *n.* —**ba'nal·ly** *adv.* —**Syn.** hackneyed, stale, boring, dull.   *3*

ba·roque (bə·rōk') *adj.* **1** Of, like, or characteristic of a style of art, architecture, and music that flourished in 16th- and 17th-century Europe, characterized by elaboration and profuse ornamentation. **2** Excessively elaborate and decorative. **3** Irregularly shaped: said of pearls. —*n.* **1** The baroque style. **2** An object, composition, or design in this style. [<Ital. *barroco*]   *2*

ba·thos (bā'thos) *n.* **1** A descent from the lofty to the trite in discourse. **2** Insincere pathos; sentimentality. [<Gk. *bathys* deep] —**ba·thet·ic** (bə·thet'ik) *adj.*   *6*

be·guile (bi·gīl') *v.t.* **be·guiled, be·guil·ing 1** To deceive; mislead by guile. **2** To cheat; defraud: with *of* or *out of.* **3** To while away pleasantly, as time. **4** To charm; divert. —**be·guile'ment, be·guil'er** *n.* —**be·guil'ing·ly** *adv.*   *4*

ben·i·son (ben'ə·zən, -sən) *n.* A benediction; blessing. [<LL *benedictio* benediction]   *15*

bi·o·de·grad·a·ble (bī'ō·di·grā'də·bəl) *adj.* Capable of being broken down by natural processes, such as bacterial action, etc. [< BIO- + DEGRADABLE]   *1*

bi·zarre (bi·zär') *adj.* Startlingly odd. [F] —**bi·zarre'ly** *adv.* —**bi·zarre'ness** *n.* —**Syn.** outré, outlandish, fantastic, grotesque, freakish.   *7*

blas·phe·my (blas'fə·mē) *n. pl.* **·mies 1** Words or action showing impious irreverence toward God or sacred things. **2** Any irreverent act or utterance. —**blas'phe·mous** *adj.* —**blas'phe·mous·ly** *adv.*   *9*

bla·tant (blā'tənt) *adj.* **1** Offensively loud or clamorous. **2** Obtrusively obvious; glaring: a *blatant* lie. [?<L *blatire* babble] —**bla'tan·cy** *n.* —**bla'tant·ly** *adv.*   *3*

blurb (blûrb) *n.* A brief, commendatory statement, as on a book jacket, that serves as publicity for a book, author, etc. [Coined by Gelett Burgess, 1866–1951, U.S. humorist]   *11*

bo·gus (bō'gəs) *adj.* Counterfeit; spurious; fake. [?]   *11*

bom·bast (bom'bast) *n.* Pompous, high-flown language.

[<OF *bombace* cotton padding] —**bom·bas'tic, bom·bas'ti·cal** *adj.* —**bom·bas'ti·cal·ly** *adv.* —**Syn.** grandiloquence, prolixity, verbosity, wordiness.   *8*

bo·na fide (bō'nə·fīd', -fī'dē) **1** Acting or carried out in good faith. **2** Authentic; real. [<L, in good faith]   *11*

boor (boor) *n.* A rude, coarse, or unpleasant person. [<Du. *boer* farmer, rustic] —**boor'ish** *adj.* —**boor'ish·ly** *adv.* —**boor'ish·ness** *n.*   *1*

bowd·ler·ize (boud'lər·īz) *v.t.* **·ized, ·iz·ing** To expurgate or edit prudishly. [<Thomas *Bowdler,* 1754–1825, Brit. editor of a "family" edition of Shakespeare] —**bowd'ler·ism, bowd'ler·i·za'tion** *n.*   *10*

brack·ish (brak'ish) *adj.* **1** Somewhat saline; briny. **2** Unpleasant to taste. [<Du. *brak* salty] —**brack'ish·ness** *n.*   *12*

Braille (brāl) *n.* **1** A system of printing or writing for the blind in which the characters consist of raised dots to be read by feeling with the fingers. **2** The characters themselves. Also **braille.** [<Louis *Braille,* 1809–52, French educator, who invented it]   *10*

buoy·ant (boi'ənt, boō'yənt) *adj.* **1** Having buoyancy. **2** Vivacious; cheerful; hopeful. [Prob. <Sp. *boyar* float] —**buoy'ant·ly** *adv.*   *1*

ca·bal (kə·bal') *n.* **1** A number of persons secretly united, as in a plot or conspiracy. **2** Intrigue; conspiracy. —*v.i.* **ca·balled, ca·bal·ling** To form a cabal; plot. [<Med. L *cabbala* cabala]   *7*

cache (kash) *v.t.* **cached, cach·ing** To store or hide in a secret place. —*n.* **1** A place for hiding or storing provisions. **2** Supplies stored or hidden in such a place. [<F *cacher* hide]   *15*

ca·jole (kə·jōl') *v.t. & v.i.* **·joled, ·jol·ing** To persuade or coax with flattery; wheedle. [<F *cajoler*] —**ca·jole'ment, ca·jol'er, ca·jol'er·y** *n.* —**ca·jol'ing·ly** *adv.*   *3*

can·dor (kan'dər) *n.* **1** Openness; frankness. **2** Freedom from prejudice; impartiality; fairness. *Brit. sp.* **can'dour.** [<L, sincerity, purity, whiteness]   *4*

ca·price (kə·prēs') *n.* **1** A sudden, unreasonable impulse or change of mind; a whim. **2** A tendency to such acts or impulses. **3** *Music* CAPRICCIO. [<Ital. *capriccio*]   *7*

cap·tious (kap'shəs) *adj.* **1** Apt to find fault. **2** Intended to confuse or trip up: *captious* questions. [<L *captiosus* fallacious] —**cap'tious·ly** *adj.* —**cap'tious·ness** *n.* —**Syn.** critical, carping, caviling.   *3*

cas·ti·gate (kas'tə·gāt) *v.t.* **·gat·ed, ·gat·ing** To punish or scold severely; chastise. [<L *castigare* chasten] —**cas'ti·ga'tion, cas'ti·ga'tor** *n.* —**cas·ti·ga·to·ry** (kas'ti·gə·tôr'ē, -tō'rē) *adj.*   *13*

cas·u·ist·ry (kazh'ōō·is·trē) *n. pl.* **·ries 1** The resolving of questions of right and wrong according to standard ethical principles. **2** Overly refined or false reasoning, esp. about matters of conscience.   *8*

cau·cus (kô'kəs) *n.* A meeting of members of a political party to select candidates or plan a campaign. —*v.i.* **cau·cused** or **·cussed, ·cus·ing** or **·cus·sing** To meet in or hold a caucus. [<Algon.]   *11*

caus·tic (kôs'tik) *adj.* **1** Capable of corroding or eating away tissue. **2** Stinging; biting; sarcastic. —*n.* A caustic substance. [<Gk. *kausos* burning < *kaiein* to burn] —**caus'ti·cal·ly** *adv.* —**caus·tic'i·ty** (-tis'ə·tē) *n.*   *14*

cav·il (kav'əl) *v.i.* **cav·iled** or **·illed, cav·il·ing** or **·il·ling**

To pick flaws or raise trivial objections; quibble: with *at* or *about*. —*n.* A trivial objection. [<L *cavilla* a jeering, a scoffing] —**cav′il·er, cav′il·ler** *n.* 11

cel·i·bate (sel′ə·bit, -bāt) *adj.* Unmarried or sexually abstinent, esp. by vow. —*n.* One who practices celibacy. 4

cen·trif·u·gal (sen·trif′yə·gəl, -ə·gəl) *adj.* 1 Directed or tending away from a center; radiating. 2 Employing centrifugal force: a *centrifugal* pump. [<L *centrum* center + *fugere* flee] —**cen·trif′u·gal·ly** *adv.* 6

cen·trip·e·tal (sen·trip′ə·təl) *adj.* 1 Directed, tending, or drawing toward a center. 2 Employing centripetal force: a *centripetal* pump. [<L *centrum* center + *petere* seek] 6

char·la·tan (shär′lə·tən) *n.* A person who claims to possess a knowledge or skill he does not have; a fake; quack. —**char′la·tan·ry, char′la·tan·ism** *n.* [<Ital. *ciarlatano* babbler] 9

char·y (châr′ē) *adj.* **char·i·er, char·i·est** 1 Cautious; wary. 2 Slow to give; sparing. [<OE *cearig* sorrowful, sad] 4

chau·vin·ist (shō′vən·ist) *n.* One who believes excessively and often belligerently in the superiority of his own country, race, sex, etc.: a male *chauvinist*. [<Nicolas *Chauvin*, an overzealous supporter of Napoleon Bonaparte] —**chau′vin·ism** *n.* —**chau′vin·is′tic** *adj.* —**chau′vin·is′ti·cal·ly** *adv.* 10

chi·a·ro·scu·ro (kē·är′ə·skyoōr′ō) *n. pl.* **·ros** 1 The distribution and treatment of light and shade in a picture. 2 A technique of painting or drawing using only light and shade to achieve its effects. 3 A painting or drawing using this technique. Also **chi·a·ro·o·scu·ro** (kē·är′ə·ō·skyoōr′ō). [Ital. < *chiaro* clear + *oscuro* dim, obscure] 7

chi·can·er·y (shi·kā′nər·ē) *n. pl.* **·er·ies** 1 The use of tricky or deceptive talk or action. 2 An instance of this. [<F *chicaner* to quibble] 15

chide (chīd) *v.t. & v.i.* **chid·ed** or **chid** (chid), **chid·ed** or **chid·den** (chid′n), **chid·ing** To scold or reprove. [<OE *cidan*] —**chid′er** *n.* —**chid′ing·ly** *adv.* 4

chi·mer·i·cal (kə·mer′i·kəl, kī-) *adj.* 1 Not realizable or possible; impractical; visionary. 2 Imaginary; fanciful. Also **chi·mer′ic.** —**chi·mer′i·cal·ly** *adv.* 10

chol·er·ic (kol′ər·ik, kə·ler′ik) *adj.* Easily aroused to anger; bad-tempered. —**Syn.** irascible, irritable, cranky. 8

cir·cum·spect (sûr′kəm·spekt) *adj.* Attentive to all possibilities; cautious. [<L *circum-* around + *specere* look] —**cir′cum·spec′tion, cir′cum·spect′ness** *n.* —**cir′cum·spec′tive** *adj.* —**cir′cum·spect′ly** *adv.* —**Syn.** prudent, wary, watchful, heedful. 12

cir·cum·vent (sûr′kəm·vent′) *v.t.* 1 To avoid by or as by going around; bypass. 2 To get the better of by strategy or craft; outwit. [<L *circum-* around + *venire* come] —**cir′·cum·vent′er, cir′cum·vent′or, cir′cum·ven′tion** *n.* —**cir′cum·ven′tive** *adj.* 6

clan·des·tine (klan·des′tin) *adj.* Kept secret; surreptitious. [<L *clandestinus* < *clam* in secret] —**clan·des′tine·ly** *adv.* —**clan·des′tine·ness** *n.* 13

clique (klēk, klik) *n.* An exclusive or clannish group of people; coterie. —*v.i.* **cliqued, cli·quing** To unite in a clique; act clannishly. [<F *cliquer* click, clap] 7

co·a·lesce (kō′ə·les′) *v.i.* **·lesced, ·lesc·ing** To grow or come together into one; fuse; blend. [<L *coalescere* unite] —**co′a·les′cence** *n.* —**co′a·les′cent** *adj.* 13

co·her·ent (kō·hir′ənt) *adj.* 1 Cleaving or sticking together.

2 Logical, intelligible, or articulate, as in thought, speech, etc. 3 *Physics* Exhibiting coherence. —**co·her′ent·ly** *adv.* 2

co·he·sive (kō·hē′siv) *adj.* Having or causing cohesion. —**co·he′sive·ly** *adv.* —**co·he′sive·ness** *n.* 11

col·lo·qui·al (kə·lō′kwē·əl) *adj.* 1 Characteristic of or suitable to the informal language of ordinary conversation or writing. 2 Of or pertaining to conversation; conversational. —**col·lo′qui·al·ly** *adv.* —**col·lo′qui·al·ness** *n.* 2

col·lo·quy (kol′ə·kwē) *n. pl.* **·quies** A more or less formal conversation or conference. [<L *colloquium* conversation] —**col′lo·quist** *n.* 15

col·lu·sion (kə·lōō′zhən) *n.* Secret cooperation in fraud or in illegal activities. [<L *colludere* to collude] —**col·lu′sive** *adj.* —**col·lu′sive·ly** *adv.* —**col·lu′sive·ness** *n.* 7

com·mo·di·ous (kə·mō′dē·əs) *adj.* Spacious; roomy. [<L *commodus* convenient] —**com·mo′di·ous·ly** *adv.* —**com·mo′di·ous·ness** *n.* 6

com·pen·di·um (kəm·pen′dē·əm) *n. pl.* **·di·ums** or **·di·a** (-dē·ə) A brief, comprehensive summary; abridgment. [<L *com-* together + *pendere* weigh] 2

com·pla·cent (kəm·plā′sənt) *adj.* Feeling or showing complacency, esp. smugly self-satisfied. [<L *com-* thoroughly + *placere* to please] —**com·pla′cent·ly** *adv.* 12

com·ple·ment (kom′plə·mənt) *n.* 1 That which fills up, completes, or makes perfect. 2 The number needed to fill or make complete. 3 Either of two parts that together form a whole; a counterpart. 4 Full number: the vessel has her *complement* of men. 5 *Geom.* The amount by which an angle or arc falls short of 90 degrees. 6 *Gram.* A word or phrase used after a verb to complete the meaning of the predicate, as *happy* in *She is happy.* —*v.t.* To supply a lack in; make complete; supplement. [<L *complere* complete] —**com·ple·men·tal** (kom′plə·men′təl) *adj.* See SUPPLEMENT. 15

com·pli·ment (kom′plə·mənt) *n.* 1 An expression of admiration, praise, congratulation, etc. 2 *pl.* A formal greeting or remembrance. —*v.t.* (kom′plə·ment) 1 To pay a compliment to. 2 To show regard for, as by a gift or other favor. [<Sp. *cumplimiento*, lit., completion of courtesy <L *complementum* completion] 15

com·pos·ite (kəm·poz′it) *adj.* 1 Made up of separate parts or elements. 2 *Bot.* Belonging to a large family of plants, as the aster, sunflower, etc., having massed heads of modified florets that resemble single flowers. —*n.* That which is composed of parts; a compound. [<L *compositus*, pp. of *componere* to put together] —**com·pos′ite·ly** *adv.* 8

com·pre·hen·si·ble (kom′pri·hen′sə·bəl) *adj.* That can be comprehended; understandable. —**com′pre·hen′si·bil′i·ty, com′pre·hen′si·ble·ness** *n.* —**com′pre·hen′si·bly** *adv.* 9

com·pre·hen·sion (kom′pri·hen′shən) *n.* 1 The act of comprehending or understanding. 2 The ability to do this. 3 The knowledge so gained. 4 The state or quality of being comprehensive. 13

com·punc·tion (kəm·pungk′shən) *n.* 1 Self-reproach for wrong-doing; guilt. 2 A feeling of slight regret. [<L *com-* greatly + *pungere* to prick, sting] —**com·punc′tious** *adj.* 7

con·cise (kən·sīs′) *adj.* Expressing much in brief form; compact. [<L *concisus*, pp. of *concidere* to cut thoroughly] —**con·cise′ly** *adv.* —**con·cise′ness** *n.* —**Syn.** brief, terse, pithy, short, compact. 3

con·clave (kon′klāv, kong′-) *n.* **1** A secret council or meeting. **2 a** The apartments in the Vatican in which the college of cardinals meets to choose a pope. **b** The meeting itself. [<L, a place which can be locked up] *14*

con·com·i·tant (kon·kom′ə·tənt, kən-) *adj.* Existing or occurring together; attendant. —*n.* An attendant circumstance. [<L *com-* with + *comitari* accompany] —**con·com′i·tance, con·com′i·tan·cy** *n.* —**con·com′i·tant·ly** *adv.* *12*

con·di·tion (kən·dish′ən) *n.* **1** The state or mode in which a person or thing exists. **2** State of health. **3** A sound state of health or fitness. **4** *Informal* An ailment. **5** A modifying circumstance. **6** An event, circumstance, or fact necessary to the occurrence, completion, or fulfillment of something else: *Luck is often a* condition *of success.* **7** *Usu. pl.* Any circumstances that affect a person or activity: *good working* conditions. **8** Rank or social position. —**on condition that** Provided that; if. —*v.t.* **1** To place a stipulation upon; prescribe. **2** To be the prerequisite to. **3** To specify as a requirement. **4** To render fit. **5** *Psychol.* To train to a behavior pattern or conditioned response. **6** To accustom (a person or animal) to something. —*v.i.* **7** To stipulate. [<L *com-* together + *dicere* say] —**con·di′tion·er** *n.* *13*

con·du·cive (kən·d⁽ʸ⁾ōō′siv) *adj.* Contributing; helping: with *to.* —**con·du′cive·ly** *adv.* —**con·du′cive·ness** *n.* *4*

con·gru·ent (kong′grōō·ənt) *adj.* **1** Having mutual agreement or conformity. **2** *Geom.* Describing two geometric figures that are identical part for part. [<L *congruere* agree] —**con′gru·ent·ly** *adv.* *5*

con·nive (kə·nīv′) *v.i.* **·nived, ·niv·ing** **1** To encourage or assent to a wrong by silence or feigned ignorance: with *at.* **2** To be in collusion: with *with.* [<L *conivere* shut the eyes] —**con·niv′er** *n.* *14*

con·sen·sus (kən·sen′səs) *n.* A collective opinion; general agreement. [<L *com-* together + *sentire* feel, think] *4*

con·tig·u·ous (kən·tig′yōō·əs) *adj.* **1** Touching or joining at the edge or boundary. **2** Adjacent; close. [<L *contingere* to contact] —**con·tig′u·ous·ly** *adv.* —**con·tig′u·ous·ness** *n.* *5*

con·tra·band (kon′trə·band) *adj.* Forbidden or excluded, as by law or treaty. —*n.* **1** Illegal or forbidden trade. **2** Contraband goods. **3** CONTRABAND OF WAR. [<LL *contra* against + *bannum* law, proclamation] —**con′tra·band′ist** *n.* *6*

con·tra·vene (kon′trə·vēn′) *v.t.* **·vened, ·ven·ing** **1** To act against or infringe upon, as a law. **2** To argue or disagree with. [<L *contra-* against + *venire* come] —**con′tra·ven′er, con·tra·ven·tion** (kon′trə·ven′shən) *n.* —**Syn.** **1** disregard, violate, disobey, defy. **2** dispute, contradict, contest, refute. *15*

con·trite (kən·trīt′, kon′trīt) *adj.* **1** Remorseful or guilty because of one's sins or shortcomings. **2** Proceeding from or showing remorse or guilt. [<L *contritus* bruised, pp. of *conterere* to rub together] —**con·trite′ly** *adv.* —**con·trite′ness, con·tri′tion** (-trish′ən) *n.* *7*

con·ver·sant (kon′vər·sənt, kən·vûr′sənt) *adj.* Familiar, as a result of study, experience, etc.: with *with* [<L *conversari.* See CONVERSE¹] —**con′ver·sant·ly** *adv.* *12*

con·vert (kən·vûrt′) *v.t.* **1** To change into another state, form, or substance; transform. **2** To apply or adapt to a new or different purpose or use. **3** To change from one belief, doctrine, creed, opinion, or course of action to another. **4** To exchange for an equivalent value, as goods for money. **5** To exchange for value of another form, as preferred for common stock. **6** *Law* To assume possession of illegally. —*v.i.* **7** To become changed in character. **8** In football, to score the extra point after touchdown, as by kicking a field goal. —*n.* (kon′vûrt) A person who had been converted, as from one opinion, creed, etc., to another. [<L *convertere* to turn around] *5*

cor·po·re·al (kor·pôr′e·əl, -pō′rē·əl) *adj.* **1** Of or of the nature of the body. **2** Having physical or material existence. [<L *corpus* body] —**cor·po·re·al·i·ty** (kôr·pôr′ē·al′ə·tē, -pō′rē-), **cor·po′re·al·ness** *n.* —**cor·po′re·al·ly** *adv.* *14*

cor·re·late (kôr′ə·lāt, kor′-) *v.* **·lat·ed, ·lat·ing** *v.t.* **1** To place or put in reciprocal relation. —*v.i.* **2** To be mutually or reciprocally related. —*adj.* Having mutual or reciprocal relations. —*n.* CORRELATIVE (def. 1). [<COM- + RELATE] *9*

cor·rob·o·rate (kə·rob′ə·rāt) *v.t.* **·rat·ed, ·rat·ing** To confirm or support (evidence, a statement, etc.) [<L *com-* together + *robur* strength] —**cor·rob′o·ra′tor, cor·rob′o·ra′tion** *n.* —**cor·rob·o·ra·tive** (kə·rob′ə·rā·tiv, -rob′ər·ə·tiv), **cor·rob·o·ra·to·ry** (kə·rob′ər·ə·tôr′ē, -tō′rē) *adj.* —**cor·rob′o·ra′tive·ly** *adv.* *9*

coun·ter·point (koun′tər·point′) *n.* **1** The art of adding to a melody a part or parts related to but independent of it, according to fixed rules. **2** The part or parts so arranged. [<Med. L *(cantus) contrapunctus* (a melody) with contrasting notes] *15*

coup (kōō) *n. pl.* **coups** (kōōz, *Fr.* kōō) **1** A sudden and successful action; a masterstroke. **2** A coup d'état. [<L *colaphus* a blow with the fist] *14*

coup d'é·tat (kōō′ dā·tä′) A forceful, unexpected political move, esp. a sudden overthrow of government and seizure of power. [F, lit., stroke of state] *7*

cred·i·ble (kred′ə·bəl) *adj.* Capable of being believed; reliable. [<L *credibilis* < *credere* believe] —**cred′i·ble·ness** *n.* —**cred′i·bly** *adv.* *9*

crest·fall·en (krest′fô′lən) *adj.* **1** Dejected; depressed. **2** Having the crest lowered. *9*

cri·tique (kri·tēk′) *n.* **1** A critical review. **2** The art of criticism. *8*

cull (kul) *v.t.* **culled, cull·ing** **1** To pick or sort out; collect. **2** To select and gather. —*n.* Something picked or sorted out and rejected. [<L *colligere* collect] —**cull′er** *n.* *7*

cur·so·ry (kûr′sər·ē) *adj.* Rapid and superficial; hasty, with no attention to detail. [<L *cursor* a runner < *currere* run] —**cur′so·ri·ly** *adv.* —**cur′so·ri·ness** *n.* *2*

cur·tail (kər·tāl′) *v.t.* To cut off or cut short; abbreviate; lessen; reduce. [<obs. *curtal* short; infl. in form by TAIL] —**cur·tail′er, cur·tail′ment** *n.* *1*

de·ba·cle (dā·bä′kəl, -bak′əl, di-) *n.* **1** A sudden and disastrous overthrow or collapse; ruin. **2** The breaking up of ice in a river, etc. **3** A violent flood. [<F *débâcler* unbar, set free] *1*

de·bil·i·tate (di·bil′ə·tāt) *v.t.* **·tat·ed, ·tat·ing** To make feeble; weaken. [<L *debilis* weak] —**de·bil′i·ta′tion** *n.* —**de·bil′i·ta′tive** *adj.* *6*

de·duc·tion (di·duk′shən) *n.* **1** The act of deducting or the sum or amount deducted. **2** Reasoning from stated premises to the formally valid conclusion; reasoning from the general to the particular. **3** An inference; conclusion. —**de·duc′tive** *adj.* —**de·duc′tive·ly** *adv.* *6*

de·fin·i·tive (di·fin′ə·tiv) *adj.* **1** Decisive and final; conclusive. **2** Most nearly accurate, complete, etc.: a *definitive* study. **3** Sharply defining or limiting; explicit. **—de·fin′i·tive·ly** *adv.* **—de·fin′i·tive·ness** *n.* *2*

deft (deft) *adj.* Skillful; adroit; dexterous. [<OE *gedæfte* meek, gentle] **—deft′ly** *adv.* **—deft′ness** *n.* *1*

del·e·te·ri·ous (del′ə·tir′ē·əs) *adj.* Causing moral or physical injury. [<Gk. *dēlētērios* harmful] **—del′e·te′ri·ous·ly** *adv.* **—del′e·te′ri·ous·ness** *n.* *6*

de·lin·e·ate (di·lin′ē·āt) *v.t.* **·at·ed, ·at·ing** **1** To draw in outline; trace out. **2** To portray pictorially. **3** To describe verbally. [<L *de-* completely + *linea* a line] **—de·lin′e·a′tion, de·lin′e·a′tor** *n.* **—de·lin′e·a′tive** *adj.* *3*

dem·a·gogue (dem′ə·gôg, -gog) *n.* One who attempts to gain power by arousing the prejudices and passions of the people. Also **dem′a·gog.** [<Gk. *dēmos* people + *agein* lead] **—dem′a·gog′ic** (-goj′ik) or **·i·cal** *adj.* **—dem′a·gog′i·cal·ly** *adv.* **—dem′a·gog′ism** (-gog′iz·əm) or **dem′a·gogu′ism, dem′a·gogu′er·y** (-gog′ər·ē), **dem·a·go·gy** (dem′ə·gō′jē, -gôg′ē, -gog′ē) *n.* *1*

de·mise (di·mīz′) *n.* **1** Death. **2** *Law* A transfer or conveyance of rights or estate. **—v. ·mised, ·mis·ing,** *v.t.* **1** To bestow (sovereign power) by death or abdication. **2** *Law* To lease (an estate) for life or for a term of years. **—v.i.** **3** To pass by will or inheritance. [<OF *demettre* send away] **—de·mis′a·ble** *adj.* *15*

de·mor·al·ize (di·môr′əl·īz, -mor′-, dē′-) *v.t.* **·ized, ·iz·ing** **1** To undermine the morale of. **2** To throw into disorder. **—de·mor′al·i·za′tion, de·mor′al·iz′er** *n.* *11*

den·i·zen (den′ə·zən) *n.* **1** A resident; inhabitant. **2** A person who frequents a place. **3** A person, animal, or thing at home in a region, although not a native. **—v.t.** *Brit.* NATURALIZE. [<AF *deinz* inside] **—den′i·zen·a′tion** *n.* *2*

dep·re·cate (dep′rə·kāt) *v.t.* **·cat·ed, ·cat·ing** **1** To express disapproval of or regret for. **2** To belittle; depreciate. [<L *de-* away + *precari* pray] **—dep′re·ca′ting·ly** *adv.* **—dep′re·ca′tion, dep′re·ca′tor** *n.* • The use of *deprecate* as a synonym for *depreciate* is regarded as incorrect by many, but it is increasingly common: While not wishing to *deprecate* their motives, he did question their judgment. *8*

de·pre·ci·ate (di·prē′shē·āt) *v.* **·at·ed, ·at·ing** *v.t.* **1** To lessen the worth of; lower the price or rate of. **2** To disparage; belittle. **—v.i.** **3** To become less in value, etc. [<L *de-* down + *pretium* price] **—de·pre′ci·a′tor** *n.* **—de·pre′ci·a·to′ry** *adj.* • See DEPRECATE. *6*

de·rog·a·to·ry (di·rog′ə·tôr′ē, -tō′rē) *adj.* Harmful to the reputation or esteem of a person or thing; disparaging. **—de·rog′a·to′ri·ly** *adv.* *12*

des·e·crate (des′ə·krāt) *v.t.* **·crat·ed, ·crat·ing** To divert from a sacred to a common use; profane. [<DE- + L *sacrare* make holy] **—des′e·crat′er** or **des′e·cra′tor, des′e·cra′tion** *n.* *4*

des·pi·ca·ble (des′pi·kə·bəl, di·spik′ə·bəl) *adj.* Despised; contemptible; mean; vile. [<L *despicari* despise] **—des′pi·ca·bil′i·ty, des′pi·ca·ble·ness** *n.* **—des′pi·ca·bly** *adv.* *5*

des·ul·to·ry (des′əl·tôr′ē, -tō′rē) *adj.* **1** Aimless; changeable; unmethodical. **2** Not connected or relevant; random. [<L *de-* down + *salire* to leap, jump] **—des′ul·to′ri·ly** *adv.* **—des′ul·to′ri·ness** *n.* *14*

de·ter·mi·nate (di·tûr′mə·nit) *adj.* **1** Definitely limited or fixed; specific; distinct. **2** Settled; conclusive. **3** Resolute;

decisive. **—de·ter′mi·nate·ly** *adv.* **—de·ter′mi·nate·ness** *n.* *13*

di·a·tribe (dī′ə·trīb) *n.* An abusive denunciation; invective. [<Gk. *diatribē* a wearing away] *4*

dic·tion (dik′shən) *n.* **1** The use, choice, and arrangement of words and modes of expression. **2** The manner of enunciating words in speaking or singing. [<L *dicere* say] *13*

di·dac·tic (dī·dak′tik, di-) *adj.* **1** Intended to instruct; expository. **2** Morally instructive; perceptive. **3** Overly inclined to teach; pedantic. Also **di·dac′ti·cal.** [<Gk. *didaskein* teach] **—di·dac′ti·cal·ly** *adv.* **—di·dac′ti·cism** *n.* *13*

dil·a·to·ry (dil′ə·tôr′ē, -tō′rē) *adj.* **1** Given to or characterized by delay; tardy; slow. **2** Causing delay. **—dil′a·to′ri·ly** *adv.* **—dil′a·to′ri·ness** *n.* *11*

dis·a·gree·ment (dis′ə·grē′mənt) *n.* **1** Failure to agree; disparity; variance. **2** A difference of opinion. **3** A quarrel; altercation. *4*

dis·burse (dis·bûrs′) *v.t.* **·bursed, ·burs·ing** To pay out; expend. [<OF *des-* away + *bourse* a purse] **—dis·burs′a·ble** *adj.* **—dis·burse′ment, dis·burs′er** *n.* *15*

dis·creet (dis·krēt′) *adj.* Showing consideration of the privacy or trust of others, as by suppressing curious inquiry; prudent; circumspect. [<LL *discretus* pp. of *discernere* cern] **—dis·creet′ly** *adv.* **—dis·creet′ness** *n.* *15*

dis·crete (dis·krēt′) *adj.* **1** Distinct or separate. **2** Ma up of distinct parts or separate units. [<LL *discretus.* S DISCREET.] **—dis·crete′ly** *adv.* **—dis·crete′ness** *n.*

dis·cur·sive (dis·kûr′siv) *adj.* Wandering from one subje or point to another; digressive. [<L *discursus* a running t and fro] **—dis·cur′sive·ly** *adv.* **—dis·cur′sive·ness** *n.* *3*

dis·si·dent (dis′ə·dənt) *adj.* Dissenting; differing. — One who dissents; dissenter. [<L *dis-* apart + *sedere* sit] *6*

dis·si·pate (dis′ə·pāt) *v.* **·pat·ed, ·pat·ing** *v.t.* **1** To disperse or drive away. **2** To disintegrate or dissolve utterly. **3** To squander: to *dissipate* a fortune. **—v.i.** **4** To become dispersed; scatter. **5** To engage in excessive or dissolute pleasures. [<L *dissipare*] *13*

dis·so·nance (dis′ə·nəns) *n.* **1** A discordant mingling of sounds. **2** *Music* A combination of tones that give a harsh or unpleasant effect when sounded together. **3** Harsh disagreement. Also **dis′so·nan·cy.** *6*

dis·con·cert (dis′kən·sûrt′) *v.t.* **1** To cause to lose one's composure or confidence; confuse; upset. **2** To frustrate, as a plan. [<MF *dis-* apart + *concerter* agree] **—dis′con·cert′ing** *adj.* **—dis′con·cert′ing·ly** *adv.* *6*

dis·traught (dis·trôt′) *adj.* **1** Distracted or bewildered, as by anxiety; upset. **2** Maddened; tormented. [<L *distrahere,* distract] *4*

doc·ile (dos′əl, *Brit.* dō′sīl) *adj.* **1** Easy to train; teachable. **2** Easy to manage or handle. [<L *docilis* able to be taught] **—doc′ile·ly** *adv.* **—do·cil·i·ty** (do·sil′ə·tē, dō-) *n.* **—Syn.** **2** tractable, compliant, obedient, pliant. *1*

doc·tri·naire (dok′trə·nâr′) *adj.* Theoretical; visionary. — *n.* One whose views are derived from theories rather than from facts. *11*

dol·drums (dol′drəmz) *n. pl.* **1** Those parts of the ocean near the equator where calms or fitful winds prevail. **2** A dull, depressed, or bored condition of mind; the dumps. [?] *13*

dor·mant (dôr′mənt) *adj.* **1** Sleeping. **2** Quiet; motionless. **3** Sleeping or resting, as certain animals and plants in winter.

4 Not erupting: said of a volcano. **5** Inactive; unused. [<L *dormire* to sleep] **—dor′man·cy** *n.*   15

do·tage (dō′tij) *n.* **1** Feebleness of mind, as a result of old age; senility. **2** Foolish and extravagant affection. [<DOTE + -AGE]   4

dour (dour, dŏor) *adj.* **1** Gloomy; sullen. **2** Aloof; forbidding. **3** Unyielding. [<L *durus*] **—dour′ly** *adv.* **—dour′ness** *n.*   3

duc·tile (duk′til, -tīl′) *adj.* **1** Capable of being hammered thin or drawn out, as certain metals. **2** Easily led; tractable. [<L *ducere* lead] **—duc·til′i·ty, duc′tile·ness** *n.*   11

dudg·eon (duj′ən) *n.* Sullen displeasure.[?]   8

dunce (duns) *n.* A stupid or ignorant person. [<Johannes *Duns* Scotus, 13th-century theologian]   10

du·plic·i·ty (dyōō·plis′ə·tē) *n. pl.* **·ties** Deception in speech or conduct. [<L *duplex* twofold] **—Syn.** deceitfulness, double-dealing, dissimulation, hypocrisy.   12

du·ress (dyōō·res′, dyŏor′is) *n.* **1** Compulsion by force or fear. **2** Restraint, as by confinement in prison. [<OF *duresse* hardness, constraint <L *durus* hard]   4

dy·nam·ic (dī·nam′ik) *adj.* **1** Of or pertaining to motion or unbalanced forces. **2** Of or pertaining to dynamics. **3** Mentally or spiritually energetic, forceful, or powerful: a *dynamic* leader. Also **dy·nam′i·cal.** [<Gk. *dynamis* power] **—dy·nam′i·cal·ly** *adv.*   4

e·bul·lient (i·bul′yənt) *adj.* **1** Bubbling over with enthusiasm. **2** In a boiling condition. [<L *ex-* out + *bullire* boil] **—e·bul′lient·ly** *adv.* **—e·bul′lience, e·bul′lien·cy** *n.*   12

ec·cle·si·as·tic (i·klē′zē·as′tik) *adj.* Ecclesiastical. *—n.* A cleric; churchman. [<Gk. *ekklēsia* assembly]   11

e·clipse (i·klips′) *n.* **1** *Astron.* The dimming or elimination of light reaching an observer from a heavenly body. A **lunar eclipse** is caused by the passage of the moon through the earth's shadow; a **solar eclipse** by the passage of the moon between the sun and the observer. **2** Any dimming or passing into obscurity, as of fame. *—v.t.* **e·clipsed, e·clips·ing 1** To cause an eclipse of; darken. **2** To dim or obscure: Age *eclipsed* her beauty. **3** To outshine; surpass. [<Gk. *ek-* out + *leipein* leave] **—Syn.** *v.* **1** obscure, hide, conceal. **3** overshadow.   6

ef·fete (i-fēt′) *adj.* **1** Incapable of further production; exhausted; barren. **2** Characterized by weakness, self-indulgence, decadence, etc. [<L *ex-* out + *fetus* a breeding] **—ef·fete′ness** *n.*   8

ef·front·er·y (i·frun′tər·ē) *n. pl.* **·er·ies** Insolent assurance; audacity; impudence. [<L *ex-* out + *frons, frontis* forehead, face]   15

e·gre·gious (i·grē′jəs, -jē·əs) *adj.* Unusually or conspicuously bad; flagrant. [<L *ex-* out + *grex, gregis* the herd] **—e·gre′gious·ly** *adv.* **—e·gre′gious·ness** *n.*   9

eke (ēk) *v.t.* **eked, ek·ing 1** To supplement; piece out; usu. with *out.* **2** To obtain or produce (a living) with difficulty: usu. with *out.* [<OE *ēcan*]   12

el·ee·mos·y·nar·y (el′ə·mos′ə·ner′ē, el′ē·ə-) *adj.* **1** Of or pertaining to charity or alms. **2** Charitable; nonprofit: *eleemosynary* institutions. **3** Aided by or dependent upon charity. *—n. pl.* **·nar·ies** A recipient of charity. [<Med. L *eleemosyna* alms]   8

e·lic·it (i·lis′it) *v.t.* To draw out or forth, as by some attraction or inducement; bring to light. [<L *ex-* out + *lacere* entice] **—e·lic′i·ta′tion, e·lic′i·tor** *n.*   11

el·lip·ti·cal (i·lip′ti·kəl) *adj.* **1** Of, pertaining to, or shaped like an ellipse. **2** Characterized by ellipsis; shortened by the

omission of a word or words. Also **el·lip′tic. —el·lip′ti·cal·ly** *adv.*   15

e·lu·sive (i·lōō′siv) *adj.* **1** Tending to elude. **2** Difficult to understand. **—e·lu′sive·ly** *adv.* **—e·lu′sive·ness** *n.*   8

e·ma·ci·at·ed (i·mā′shē·ā′tid) *adj.* Very thin; wasted away, as from disease or starvation.   11

e·merge (i·murj′) *v.i.* **e·merged, e·merg·ing 1** To come forth into view or existence. **2** To become noticeable or apparent: The truth *emerged.* [<L *ex-* out + *mergere* to dip] **—e·mer·gent** (i·mûr′jənt) *adj.* **—e·mer′gence** *n.*   4

e·mer·i·tus (i·mer′ə·təs) *adj.* Retired from active service but retained in an honorary position. [<L *emereri* earn, deserve]   11

e·mol·lient (i·mol′yənt, -ē·ənt) *adj.* Softening or soothing. *—n. Med.* A soothing preparation for the skin or mucous membranes. [<L *ex-* thoroughly + *mollis* soft]   15

e·mol·u·ment (i·mol′yə·mənt) *n.* The compensation, gain, or profit arising from an office or employment. [<L *ex-* out + *molere* to grind]   15

em·pir·i·cal (em·pir′i·kəl) *adj.* Relating to or based on experience and observation rather than on theory or principle. **—em·pir′i·cal·ly** *adv.*   15

en·co·mi·um (in·kō′mē·əm, en-) *n. pl.* **·mi·ums** or **·mi·a** (-mē·ə) A formal expression of praise; eulogy. [<Gk. *enkōmion* eulogy]   4

en·er·vate (en′ər·vāt) *v.t.* **·vat·ed, ·vat·ing** To deprive of energy or strength; weaken. *—adj.* (i·nûr′vit) Enervated. [<L *enervare* weaken] **—en·er·va′tion, en′er·va′tor** *n.*   15

en·gen·der (in·jen′dər, en-) *v.t.* To cause to exist; produce. [<L *ingenerare* to generate in]   4

en·hance (in·hans′, -häns′, en-) *v.t.* **·hanced, ·hanc·ing** To make higher or greater, as in reputation, cost, beauty, quality, etc. [<L *in-* in + *altus* high] **—en·hance′ment** *n.* **—Syn.** heighten, intensify, strengthen, improve.   12

en·thrall (in·thrôl′, en-) *v.t.* **·thralled, ·thral·ling 1** To keep spellbound; fascinate; charm. **2** ENSLAVE. Also **en·thral′. —en·thrall′ment, en·thral′ment** *n.*   9

e·phem·er·al (i·fem′ər·əl) *adj.* **1** Living one day only, as certain insects. **2** Short-lived; transitory. *—n.* Anything lasting for a very short time. [<Gk. *ephēmeros* < *epi-* on + *hēmera* day] **—e·phem′er·al·ly** *adv.* **—e·phem′er·al·ness** *n.* **—Syn.** *adj.* **2** transient, passing, temporal, temporary.   3

ep·i·cure (ep′ə·kyŏor) *n.* A person who enjoys and is knowledgeable about good food and drink; gourmet. [<*Epicurus,* 342?–270 B.C., Greek philosopher] **—ep′i·cu·re′an** (-kyŏo·rē′ən) *adj., n.* **—ep′i·cu·re′an·ism, ep′i·cur·ism** *n.*   10

ep·i·gram (ep′ə·gram) *n.* **1** A pithy, caustic, or thought-provoking saying. **2** A short, witty, usu. satiric poem. [<Gk. *epigramma* an inscription] **—ep′i·gram·mat′ic** or **·i·cal** *adj.* **—ep′i·gram·mat′i·cal·ly** *adv.* **—ep′i·gram′ma·tist** *n.*   6

ep·i·taph (ep′ə·taf, -täf) *n.* An inscription on a tomb or monument in honor or in memory of the dead. [<Gk. *epi-* upon, at + *taphos* a tomb] **—ep′i·taph′ic** (-taf′ik) *adj.*   6

ep·i·thet (ep′ə·thet) *n.* A word or phrase, often disparaging, used to describe or to substitute for the name of a person or thing. [<L < Gk. < *epi-* upon + *tithenai* place] **—ep′i·thet′ic** or **·i·cal** *adj.*   6

ep·och (ep′ək, *Brit.* ē′pok) *n.* **1** A point in time which marks the beginning of some new development, condition, discovery, etc. **2** An interval of time regarded in terms of extraordinary events and far-reaching results. **3** *Geol.* A time interval shorter than a period. **4** *Astron.* An arbitrarily chosen moment of time, used as a reference point. [<Gk. *epochē* a stoppage, point of time] —**ep′och·al** *adj.* *15*

e·qua·nim·i·ty (ē′kwə·nim′ə·tē, ek′wə-) *n.* Evenness of mind or temper; composure; calmness. [<L *aequus* even + *animus* mind] —**Syn.** repose, serenity, self-possession, poise, tranquility. *4*

e·quiv·o·cal (i·kwiv′ə·kəl) *adj.* **1** Having two or more meanings or interpretations. **2** Uncertain; doubtful. **3** Suspicious; questionable; dubious. [<L *aequus* equal + *vox* voice] —**e·quiv′o·cal·ly** *adv.* —**e·quiv′o·cal·ness** *n.* *14*

er·rat·ic (i·rat′ik) *adj.* **1** Not conforming to rules or standards; queer; eccentric. **2** Irregular, as in course or direction; wandering; straying. —*n.* An erratic person or thing. Also **er·rat′i·cal.** [<L *errare* wander] —**er·rat′i·cal·ly** *adv.* —**Syn.** **1** odd, peculiar, capricious, abnormal, unpredictable, whimsical, changeable. *15*

er·u·dite (er′yo͞o·dīt) *adj.* Very learned; scholarly. [<L *erudire* instruct] —**er′u·dite·ly** *adv.* —**er′u·dite·ness** *n.* *3*

es·chew (es·cho͞o′) *v.t.* To shun, as something unworthy or injurious. [<OF *eschiver*] —**es·chew′al** *n.* *1*

es·o·ter·ic (es′ə·ter′ik) *adj.* **1** Confined to a select circle; confidential. **2** Designed for or understood by an initiated and enlightened few; abstruse; profound. [<Gk. *esōterikos* inner] —**es′o·ter′i·cal·ly** *adv.* *4*

eth·ics (eth′iks) *n. pl.* (*construed as sing. in defs.* 1 & 3) **1** The study and philosophy of human conduct, with emphasis on the determination of right and wrong. **2** The basic principles of right action, esp. with reference to a particular person, profession, etc. **3** A work or treatise on morals. *13*

eth·nic (eth′nik) *adj.* **1** Of, pertaining to, or belonging to groups of mankind who are of the same race or nationality and who share a common language, culture, etc. **2** Pertaining to peoples neither Jewish nor Christian. —*n. Informal* A member of a minority ethnic group, esp., in the U.S., a non-black minority. Also **eth′ni·cal.** [<Gk. *ethnos* nation] —**eth′ni·cal·ly** *adv.* —**eth·nic′i·ty** (eth·nis′ə·te) *n.* *15*

et·y·mol·o·gy (et′ə·mol′ə·jē) *n. pl.* **·gies 1** The history of a word, prefix, suffix, etc., tracing it back to its earliest known form or root. **2** The branch of linguistics dealing with the origin and development of words, prefixes, etc. [<Gk. *etymon* original meaning + -LOGY] *2*

eu·tha·na·si·a (yo͞o′thə·nā′zhē·ə, -zhə) *n.* **1** Painless, peaceful death. **2** The deliberate putting to death of a person suffering from a painful and incurable disease; mercy killing. [<Gk. *eu-* good + *thanatos* death] *6*

ex·cul·pate (eks′kəl·pāt, ik·skul′-) *v.t.* **·pat·ed, ·pat·ing** To declare free from blame; prove innocent. [<EX-¹ + L *culpare* blame. —**ex′cul·pa′tion** *n.* —**ex·cul′pa·to′ry** *adj.* *5*

ex·e·cra·ble (ek′sə·krə·bəl) *adj.* **1** Abominable; accursed. **2** Appallingly bad. —**ex′e·cra·bly** *adv.* *14*

ex·i·gent (ek′sə·jənt) *adj.* **1** Urgent; pressing. **2** Very demanding or exacting. [<L *exigere* to demand] *13*

ex·ig·u·ous (ig·zig′yo͞o·əs, ik·sig′-) *adj.* Scanty; meager. [<L *exiguus* scanty] —**ex·i·gu·i·ty** (ek′sə·gyo͞o′ə·tē), **ex·ig′u·ous·ness** *n.* *13*

ex·or·bi·tant (ig·zôr′bə·tənt) *adj.* Going beyond usual and proper limits; excessive; extravagant. [<LL *exorbitare* go astray] —**ex·or′bi·tance, ex·or′bi·tan·cy** *n.* —**ex·or′bi·tant·ly** *adv.* *8*

ex·ot·ic (ig·zot′ik) *adj.* **1** Belonging by nature or origin to another part of the world; foreign. **2** Unusually strange or different; fascinating. —*n.* Something exotic. [<Gk. *exōtikos* foreign < *exō* outside] —**ex·ot′i·cal·ly** *adv.* —**ex·ot′i·cism** *n.* *9*

ex·pe·di·ent (ik·spē′dē·ənt) *adj.* **1** Serving to promote a desired end; suitable; useful; advisable. **2** Pertaining to or based on utility or advantage rather than what is just or right. —*n.* **1** That which furthers or promotes an end. **2** A device; shift. [<L *expedire* make ready] —**ex·pe′di·ent·ly** *adv.* *5*

ex·pi·ate (ek′spē·āt) *v.t.* **·at·ed, ·at·ing** To atone for; make amends for. [<L *ex-* completely + *piare* appease] —**ex′pi·a′tion, ex′pi·a′tor** *n.* —**ex′pi·a·to′ry** *adj.* *3*

ex·tem·po·rize (ik·stem′pə·rīz) *v.t. & v.i.* **·rized, ·riz·ing** To do, make, or compose without preparation; improvise. —**ex·tem′po·ri·za′tion, ex·tem′po·riz′er** *n.* *5*

ex·ten·u·ate (ik·sten′yo͞o·at) *v.t.* **·at·ed, ·at·ing 1** To represent as less blameworthy; make excuses for. **2** To cause to seem less serious or blameworthy: *extenuating circumstances.* [<L *extenuare* weaken <*ex-* out + *tenuis* thin] —**ex·ten′u·a′tion, ex·ten′u·a′tor** *n.* *6*

ex·trap·o·late (ik·strap′ə·lāt) *v.t. & v.i.* **·lat·ed, ·lat·ing 1** *Math.* To estimate (a function) beyond the range of known values. **2** To infer (a possibility) beyond the strict evidence of a series of facts, events, observations, etc. [<EXTRA- + (INTER)POLATE] —**ex·trap′o·la′tion** *n.* *2*

ex·tri·cate (eks′trə·kāt) *v.t.* **·cat·ed, ·cat·ing** To free from hindrance, difficulties, etc.; disentangle. [<L *ex-* out + *tricae* troubles] —**ex·tri·ca·ble** (eks′tri·kə·bəl) *adj.* —**ex′tri·ca·bly** *adv.* —**ex·tri·ca′tion** *n.* *2*

fac·tious (fak′shəs) *adj.* Given to, characterized by, or promoting faction; turbulent; partisan. —**fac′tious·ly** *adj.* —**fac′tious·ness** *n.* *15*

fal·la·cious (fə·lā′shəs) *adj.* Of, pertaining to, or involving a fallacy. —**fal·la′cious·ly** *adv.* —**fal·la′cious·ness** *n.* —**Syn.** deceptive, erroneous, illusory, misleading. *11*

fal·low (fal′ō) *adj.* Left unseeded after being plowed. —*n.* **1** Land left unseeded after plowing. **2** The act of plowing land and leaving unseeded. —*v.t. & v.i.* To make, keep, or become fallow. [<OE *fealga* fallow land] —**fal′low·ness** *n.* *14*

far·ci·cal (fär′si·kəl) *adj.* Of, pertaining to, or of the nature of a farce; absurd. —**far′ci·cal·ly** *adv.* —**far′ci·cal·ness, far′ci·cal′i·ty** *n.* —**Syn.** comical, laughable, ludicrous, ridiculous. *14*

fas·tid·i·ous (fas·tid′ē·əs) *adj.* **1** Hard to please. **2** Overly delicate or sensitive; squeamish. [<L *fastidium* disgust] —**fas·tid′i·ous·ly** *adv.* —**fas·tid′i·ous·ness** *n.* *11*

fat·u·ous (fach′o͞o·əs) *adj.* Stubbornly or complacently stupid. [<L *fatuus* foolish] —**fat′u·ous·ly** *adv.* —**fat′u·ous·ness** *n.* *3*

fea·si·ble (fē′zə·bəl) *adj.* **1** That may be done; practicable. **2** Capable of being successfully used. **3** Reasonable; probable. [<OF *faisable* < *faire* do] —**fea′si·bil′i·ty, feas′·si·ble·ness** *n.* —**fea′si·bly** *adv.* *14*

fe·cund (fē′kund, fek′und) *adj.* Fruitful; fertile. [<L *fecundus*] —**fe·cun·di·ty** (fi·kun′də·tē) *n.* —**Syn.** productive, prolific, rich, teeming. *4*

fe·do·ra (fə·dôr′ə, -dō′rə) *n.* A low hat, usu. of soft felt, with the crown creased lengthwise. [<*Fédora*, a play by V. Sardou, 1831–1908, French playwright] *11*

fe·line (fē′līn) *adj.* **1** Of or pertaining to cats or catlike animals. **2** Catlike; sly. —*n.* One of the cat family. [<L *felis* cat] —**fe′line·ly** *adv.* —**fe′line·ness, fe·lin·i·ty** (fə·lin′ə·tē) *n.* *8*

fel·o·ny (fel′ə·nē) *Law n. pl.* **·nies** One of the gravest of crimes, as treason, murder, rape, etc., and punishable by imprisonment or death. *8*

fer·ret (fer′it) *n.* A small weasel sometimes trained to hunt rodents. —*v.t.* **1** To search out by careful investigation: with *out.* **2** To drive out of hiding with a ferret. **3** To hunt with ferrets. —*v.i.* **4** To hunt by means of ferrets. To search. [<L *fur* a thief] —**fer′ret·er** *n.* *2*

fet·id (fet′id, fē′tid) *adj.* Emitting an offensive odor. [<L *fetere* stink]—**fet′id·ly** *adv.* —**fet′id·ness** *n.* *11*

fi·as·co (fē·as′kō) *n. pl.* **·cos** or **·coes** A complete or humiliating failure. [Ital.] *1*

fi·nesse (fi·nes′) *n.* **1** Subtle skill or style, as in a performance. **2** Adroit and tactful handling of a situation or person. **3** A stratagem or artifice. **4** In bridge, an attempt to take a trick with a lower card when one holds a higher card, in the hope that the opposing hand yet to play will not hold a taking card of intermediate value. —*v.* **fi·nessed, fi·ness·ing** *v.t.* **1** To change or bring about by finesse. **2** In bridge, to play as a finesse. —*v.i.* **3** To use finesse. **4** In bridge, to make a finesse. [<F *fin* fine[1]] *6*

flac·cid (flak′sid) *adj.* Lacking firmness or elasticity; flabby. [<L *flaccidus* < *flaccus* limp] —**flac′cid·ly** *adv.* —**flac·cid′i·ty, flac′cid·ness** *n.* *15*

flag·ging[1] (flag′ing) *adj.* Growing weak; becoming languid or exhausted: *flagging* spirits.

flag·ging[2] (flag′ing) *n.* **1** A pavement of flagstones; also, flagstones collectively. **2** The act of paving with flagstones. *15*

fla·grant (flā′grənt) *adj.* Openly scandalous; notorious. [<L *flagrare* to blaze, burn] —**fla′grance, fla′gran·cy** *n.* —**fla′grant·ly** *adv.* —**Syn.** glaring, outrageous, shocking. *11*

flam·boy·ant (flam·boi′ənt) *adj.* **1** Characterized by extravagance; showy; bombastic. **2** Ornate. **3** Having a wavy edge, as of flame. [F<OF *flambe* flame] —**flam·boy′ance, flam·boy′an·cy** *n.* —**flam·boy′ant·ly** *adv.* *3*

flot·sam (flot′səm) *n.* **1** *Law* Goods cast or swept from a vessel into the sea and found floating. **2** Any worthless objects. **3** Vagrants or unattached persons [<AF *floteson* < *floter* float] *13*

for·ay (fôr′ā, for′ā) *v.i.* **1** To venture out, as to raid or explore. —*v.t.* **2** *Archaic* To pillage. —*n.* **1** A raid, esp. on a military mission: a *foray* behind enemy lines. **2** A venturing out, as into unfamiliar surroundings. [<OF *feurre* forage] —**for′ay·er** *n.* *14*

for·bear·ance (fôr·bâr′əns, fər-) *n.* **1** The act of forbearing; the patient endurance of offenses. **2** A refraining from retaliation or retribution. *11*

forth·right (fôrth′rīt′, fôrth′-) *adj.* Straightforward; direct. —*adv.* **1** Straightforwardly; with directness or frankness. **2** At once. —**Syn.** candid, blunt, open, honest. *4*

for·tu·i·tous (fôr·t⁽ʸ⁾oo′ə·təs) *adj.* Occurring by chance. [<L *fortuitus* <*fors* chance] —**for·tu′i·tous·ly** *adv.* —**for·tu′i·tous·ness** *n.* —**Syn.** accidental, casual, contingent, incidental. • *Fortuitous* is not a synonym for *fortunate.* A *fortuitous* discovery is simply an accidental one, and not necessarily lucky. On the other hand, a *fortunate* discovery brings luck and good *fortune.* *6*

frac·tious (frak′shəs) *adj.* **1** Disposed to rebel; unruly. **2** Peevish; cross. —**frac′tious·ly** *adv.* —**frac′tious·ness** *n.* *4*

fres·co (fres′kō) *n. pl.* **·coes** or **·cos 1** The art of painting on a surface of plaster, esp. while the plaster is still moist.

2 A picture so painted. —*v.t.* **fres·coed, fres·co·ing** To paint in fresco. [Ital., fresh] —**fres′co·er, fres′co·ist** *n.* *7*

ful·some (fool′səm, ful′-) *adj.* Offensive and distasteful because excessive: *fulsome* praise. [<FULL, *adj.* + -SOME] —**ful′some·ly** *adv.* —**ful′some·ness** *n.* *12*

gal·va·nize (gal′və·nīz) *v.t.* **·nized, ·niz·ing 1** To stimulate to muscular action by electricity. **2** To rouse to action; startle; excite. **3** To protect (iron or steel) from rust with a coating of zinc. —**gal′va·ni·za′tion** *n.* *10*

gam·ut (gam′ət) *n.* **1** The entire range of musical tones. **2** The whole range of anything: the *gamut* of emotions. [<Med. L *gamma ut* <*gamma,* the first note of the early musical scale + *ut* (later, *do*); the names of the notes of the scale were taken from a medieval Latin hymn: *Ut queant laxis Resonare fibris, Mira gestorum Famuli tuorum, Solve polluti Labii reatum, Sancte Iohannes*] *14*

gar·gan·tu·an (gär·gan′choo·ən) *adj. Often cap.* Huge; gigantic; prodigious. [<*Gargantua,* the peace-loving giant in Rabelais' satire *Gargantua and Pantagruel*] *10*

gar·ru·lous (gar′yə·ləs) *adj.* Given to continual and tedious talking. [<L *garrulus* talkative] —**gar′ru·lous·ly** *adv.* —**gar·ru·li·ty** (gə·roo′lə·tē), **gar′ru·lous·ness** *n.* —**Syn.** talkative, loquacious, verbose, effusive, long-winded. *12*

gen·o·cide (jen′ə·sīd) *n.* The systematic extermination of a racial or national group. [<Gk. *genos* race + -CIDE] *11*

gen·re (zhän′rə) *n.* A type or category, as of art, literature, etc. [F<L *genus, -eris* race, kind] *8*

ger·ry·man·der (jer′i·man′dər, ger′-) *v.t.* To alter, as the shape of voting districts of a state or region, to the contrived advantage of a political party or other group. —*n.* A contrived or unfair redistricting of a state or region. [<E. *Gerry,* 1744–1814, + (SALA)MANDER; from the shape of a district formed in Massachusetts while Gerry was governor] *11*

ges·tate (jes′tāt) *v.t.* **·tat·ed, ·tat·ing 1** To carry in the womb during pregnancy. **2** To form in the mind. [Back formation from GESTATION] *9*

gin·ger·ly (jin′jər·lē) *adj.* Cautious or careful. —*adv.* Cautiously; carefully. [?] *3*

glos·sa·ry (glos′ə·rē, glôs′-) *n. pl.* **·ries** An explanatory list of the difficult, technical, or foreign words used in a particular work or area of knowledge. [<L *glossa* gloss[2]] —**glos·sar·i·al** (glo·sâr′ē·əl, glô-) *adj.* —**glos·sar′i·al·ly** *adv.* —**glos′sa·rist** *n.* *2*

gour·mand (goor′mənd; *Fr.* goor·män′) *n.* A person who takes great pleasure in eating and drinking, but without the knowledge or discrimination of a gourmet. [<OF, a glutton] *4*

gour·met (goor·mā′; *Fr.* goor·me′) *n.* A person who has a considerable knowledge and appreciation of fine foods and wines. [F<OF, a winetaster] *4*

graph·ic (graf′ik) *adj.* **1** Vividly effective and detailed. **2** Of, like, or represented by graphs. **3** Of, pertaining to, or expressed in handwriting. **4** Written or expressed by means of signs, symbols, etc. **5** Of or pertaining to the graphic arts. Also **graph′i·cal.** [<Gk. *graphein* write] —**graph′i·cal·ly, graph′ic·ly** *adv.* *2*

gra·tu·i·tous (grə·t⁽ʸ⁾oo′ə·təs) *adj.* **1** Given freely without charge or conditions. **2** Without cause; uncalled for; unnecessary. [<L *gratuitus* given as a favor] —**gra·tu′i·tous·ly** *adv.* —**gra·tu′i·tous·ness** *n.* *14*

grit (grit) *n.* **1** Rough, hard particles, as of sand or fine gravel. **2** A coarse compact sandstone adapted for grindstones. **3**

Resolute courage; pluck. —*v.* **grit·ted, grit·ting** *v.t.* **1** To grind or press (the teeth) together, as in anger or determination. —*v.i.* **2** To give forth a grating sound. [<OE *grēot*]   *9*

gu·ber·na·to·ri·al (gᵞōō′bər·nə·tôr′ē·əl, -tō′rē) *adj.* Of or pertaining to a governor or the office of governor. [<L *gubernare* govern]   *11*

ha·rangue (hə·rang′) *n.* An oration; esp., a loud and vehement speech. —*v.* **·rangued, ·rangu·ing** *v.t.* To address in a harangue.—*v.i.* To deliver a harangue. [<OF] **—ha·rangu′er** *n.*   *7*

har·bin·ger (här′bin·jər) *n.* A forerunner and announcer of something to come. —*v.t.* To act as a harbinger to; presage. [<OF *herbergeor* provider of shelter]   *8*

har·py (här′pē) *n. pl.* **·ples** A rapacious person; a plunderer. [<HARPY]   *10*

Har·py (här′pē) *n. pl.* **·ples** *Gk. Myth.* One of three winged monsters with the head of a woman and the legs and talons of a bird. [<Gk. *Harpyia*, lit., seizers]   *10*

hau·teur (hō·tûr′; *Fr.* ō·tœr′) *n.* Haughty manner or spirit; haughtiness. [F]   *7*

He·gi·ra (hi·jī′rə, hej′ə·rə) *n.* The flight of Mohammed from Mecca to Medina in 622, regarded as the beginning of the Mohammedan era. [<Ar. *hijrah* departure]   *7*

hei·nous (hā′nəs) *adj.* Extremely wicked; atrocious; hateful. [<OF *haine* hatred] **—hei′nous·ly** *adv.* **—hei′nous·ness** *n.*   *4*

her·met·ic (hûr·met′ik) *adj.* Impervious to liquids or gases. Also **her·met′i·cal.** [<Gk. *Hermes (Trismegistus),* god of alchemy] **—her·met′i·cal·ly** *adv.*   *10*

hi·a·tus (hī·ā′təs) *n. pl.* **·tus·es** or **-tus 1** A gap or break, with a part missing, as in a manuscript; lacuna. **2** Any interruption or break. **3** In pronunciation, a pause due to the concurrence of two separate vowels without an intervening consonant, as in *pre-eminent.* [L]   *14*

his·tri·on·ic (his′trē·on′ik) *adj.* **1** Of or pertaining to actors, acting, or to the stage. **2** Theatrical in manner, esp. if excessively so. [<L *histrio* actor] **—his′tri·on′i·cal·ly** *adv.*   *12*

hol·o·caust (hol′ə·kôst) *n.* **1** A sacrifice wholly consumed by fire. **2** Wholesale destruction or loss of life by fire, war, etc. [<Gk. *holos* whole + *kaustos* burnt] **—hol′o·caus′tal, hol′o·caus′tic** *adj.*   *5*

hom·age (hom′ij, om′-) *n.* **1** Deep regard, honor, respect, or veneration, esp. as shown by some action. **2** In feudal law, formal acknowledgment of tenure by a tenant to his lord. [<LL *homo* vassal, client, man]   *1*

ho·mo·ge·ne·ous (hō′mə·jē′nē·əs, hom′ə-) *adj.* **1** Of the same composition or character throughout. **2** Of the same kind, nature, etc., as another; similar. [<Gk. *homos* same + *genos* race] **—ho′mo·ge′ne·ous·ly** *adv.* **—ho·mo·ge·ne·i·ty** (hō′mə·jə·nē′ə·tē, hom′ə-), **ho′mo·ge′ne·ous·ness** *n.*   *5*

hu·mane (ʰyōō·mān′) *adj.* **1** Having or showing kindness, tenderness, compassion, etc. **2** Tending to refine or make civilized. **—hu·mane′ly** *adv.* **—hu·mane′ness** *n.* **—Syn. 1** charitable, merciful, sympathetic, benevolent, clement.   *11*

hy·brid (hī′brid) *n.* **1** An offering of two animals or plants of different species, varieties, breeds, etc. **2** Anything of mixed origin or unlike parts. **3** *Ling.* A word composed of elements from more than one language. —*adj.* Of, pertaining to, or like a hybrid. [<L *hybrida*] **—hy′brid·ism** *n.*   *9*

hy·per·bo·le (hī·pûr′bə·lē) *n.* Deliberate exaggeration in writing or speaking, used to create an effect, as in *He was as tall as a mountain.* [<Gk. *hyperbolē* excess]   *8*

hy·per·crit·i·cal (hī′pər·krit′i·kəl) *adj.* Excessively critical or fussy. **—hy′per·crit′i·cal·ly** *adv.*   *15*

hyp·o·crite (hip′ə·krit) *n.* One who pretends to have virtues, feelings, qualities, etc., that he does not possess. [<Gk. *hypokritēs* an actor.] **—hyp′o·crit′i·cal** *adj.* **—hyp′o·crit′i·cal·ly** *adv.* **—Syn.** deceiver, dissembler, pretender, cheat.   *15*

hy·po·thet·ical (hī′pə·thet′i·kəl) *adj.* **1** Having the nature of or based on hypothesis; assumed conditionally or tentatively as a basis for argument or investigation. **2** Given to using hypotheses. Also **hy′po·thet′ic. —hy′po·thet′·i·cal·ly** *adv.*   *14*

i·con·o·clast (ī·kon′ə·klast) *n.* **1** One who destroys religious images. **2** One who attacks traditional beliefs or institutions. [<Gk. *eikōn* image + *-klastēs* breaker] **—i·con′o·clasm** *n.* **—i·con′o·clas′tic** *adj.* **—i·con′o·clas′ti·cal·ly** *adv.*   *11*

id·i·o·syn·cra·sy (id′ē·ə·sing′krə·sē) *n. pl.* **·sies 1** Any distinctive quality, characteristic, habit, etc. peculiar to an individual; quirk. **2** The physical and mental constitution unique to an individual or group. [<Gk. *idios* peculiar + *synkrasis* a mixing together] **—id′i·o·syn·crat′ic** (-sin·krat′ik) *adj.* **—id′i·o·syn·crat′i·cal·ly** *adv.*   *11*

i·dyll (īd′l) *n.* **1** A short poem or prose piece depicting simple scenes of pastoral life. **2** Any event or scene suitable for such a work. **3** A romantic episode. Also **i′dyl.** [<Gk. *eidos* form] **—i′dyl·list, i′dyl·ist** *n.*   *12*

ig·no·min·y (ig′nə·min′ē) *n. pl.* **·min·ies 1** Disgrace or dishonor. **2** That which causes disgrace. [<L *in-* not + *nomen* name, reputation]   *11*

il·lic·it (i·lis′it) *adj.* Not permitted; unlawful. [<L *in-* not + *licitus* licit] **—il·lic′it·ly** *adv.* **—il·lic′it·ness** *n.*   *14*

il·lu·so·ry (i·lōō′sər·ē,-zər-) *adj.* Misleading; deceptive; unreal. Also **il·lu′sive** (-siv). **—il·lu′so·ri·ly** *adv.* **—il·lu′so·ri·ness** *n.*   *8*

im·bibe (im·bīb′) *v.* **·bibed, ·bib·ing** *v.t.* **1** To drink in; drink. **2** To take in (moisture); absorb. **3** To receive into the mind or character. —*v.i.* **4** To drink. [<L *in-* in + *bibere* to drink] **—im·bib′er** *n.*   *8*

im·ma·nent (im′ə·nənt) *adj.* Remaining or operating within; inherent. [<L *in-* in + *manere* stay] **—im′ma·nent·ly** *adv.*   *6*

im·passe (im′pas, im·pas′) *n.* **1** A blind passage open only at one end; blind alley. **2** Any serious and insurmountable obstacle or problem. [F]   *11*

im·pec·ca·ble (im·pek′ə·bəl) *adj.* **1** Not liable to commit sin or wrong. **2** Without fault or error; flawless. [<L *in-* not + *peccare* to sin] **—im·pec′ca·bil′i·ty** *n.* **—im·pec′ca·bly** *adv.*   *5*

im·ped·i·ment (im·ped′ə·ment) *n.* **1** That which hinders or impedes; an obstruction. **2** A speech defect, as a stammer. **3** *Law* Anything that prevents the contraction of a valid marriage. **—im·ped′i·men′tal, im·ped′i·men′ta·ry** *adj.* **—Syn. 1** barrier, encumbrance, hindrance, obstacle.   *9*

im·per·turb·a·ble (im′pər·tûr′bə·bəl) *adj.* Incapable of being agitated or perturbed; calm; impassive. **—im′per·turb′a·bil′i·ty, im′per·turb′a·ble·ness** *n.* **—im′per·turb′a·bly** *adv.*   *14*

im·pli·ca·tion (im′pli·kā′shən) *n.* **1** The act of implicating or the state of being implicated. **2** The act of implying. **3** Something implied, esp. so as to lead to a deduction.   *12*

im·por·tune (im′pôr·t^yōōn′, im·pôr′chən) *v.* **·tuned, ·tun·ing** *v.t.* **1** To annoy or trouble with persistent requests or demands. —*v.i.* **2** To make persistent requests demands. [<L *importunus* having no access, vexatious] —**im′por·tun′er** *n.*   11

im·pri·ma·tur (im′pri·mä′tər, -mā′-, im·prim′ət^yōōr) *n.* **1** An official license to print or publish a book or pamphlet. **2** Approval in general; sanction. [L, let it be printed]   14

in·ad·ver·tent (in′əd·vûr′tənt) *adj.* **1** Not careful or attentive; negligent. **2** Unintentional; not deliberate: an *inadvertent* omission of the translator's name. [<L *in-* not + *advertere* to turn toward] —**in′ad·ver′tent·ly** *adv.*   9

in·car·nate (in·kär′nāt) *v.t.* **·nat·ed, ·nat·ing** **1** To give bodily form to. **2** To give concrete shape or form to; actualize. **3** To be the embodiment of; typify. —*adj.* (-nit) **1** Invested with flesh. **2** Embodied; personified: a fiend *incarnate*. **3** Flesh-colored. [<LL *incarnare* embody in flesh]   11

in·cho·ate (in·kō′it, in′kō·āt) *adj.* Only begun or entered upon; incipient. [<L *incohare* begin] —**in·cho′ate·ly** *adv.* —**in′cho·a′tion, in·cho′ate·ness** *n.*   13

in·cip·i·ent (in·sip′ē·ənt) *adj.* Just beginning; in the first stages. [<L *incipere* begin] —**in·cip′i·ence, in·cip′i·en·cy** *n.* —**in·cip′i·ent·ly** *adv.*   11

in·ci·sive (in·sī′siv) *adj.* **1** Cutting; incising. **2** Acute; penetrating; sharp: *incisive* wit. —**in·ci′sive·ly** *adv.* —**in·ci′sive·ness** *n.*   12

in·cog·ni·to (in·kog′nə·tō, in′kəg·nē′tō) *adj. & adv.* With one's true name or identify not revealed. —*n. pl.* **·tos** (-tōz) **1** The state or disguise of being incognito. **2** One who lives, travels, etc., incognito. [<L *in-* not + *cognoscere* know]   7

in·com·men·su·rate (in′kə·men′shər·it) *adj.* **1** Incommensurable. **2** Inadequate; disproportionate. —**in′com·men′su·rate·ly** *adv.* —**in′com·men′su·rate·ness** *n.*   6

in·cor·ri·gi·ble (in·kôr′ə·jə·bəl, -kor′-) *adj.* That cannot be corrected, changed, or reformed: an *incorrigible* liar. —*n.* An incorrigible person. [<L *in-* not + *corrigere* to correct] —**in·cor′ri·gi·ble·ness, in·cor′ri·gi·bil′i·ty** *n.* —**in·cor′ri·gi·bly** *adv.*   1

in·cred·u·lous (in·krej′ə·ləs) *adj.* **1** Refusing belief; skeptical. **2** Caused by or showing doubt or disbelief. [<L *in-* not + *credulus* gullible] —**in·cred′u·lous·ly** *adv.*   11

in·cul·cate (in·kul′kāt, in′kul-) *v.t.* **·cat·ed, ·cat·ing** To impress upon the mind by frequent and emphatic repetition; instill. [<L *inculcare* tread on] —**in·cul·ca·tion** (in′kul·kā′shən), **in′cul·ca′tor** *n.*   15

in·cul·pate (in·kul′pāt, in′kul-) *v.t.* **·pat·ed, ·pat·ing** To incriminate. [<L *in-* in + *culpa* fault] —**in′cul·pa′tion** *n.* —**in·cul′pa·to·ry** (-pə·tôr′ē, -tō′rē) *adj.*   15

in·dict (in·dīt′) *v.t.* **1** *Law* To prefer an indictment against. **2** To change with a crime. [<AF *enditer* make known, inform] —**in·dict′a·ble** *adj.* —**in·dict′er, in·dict′or** *n.*   6

in·di·gent (in′də·jənt) *adj.* Needy; poor. [<L *indigere* to lack, want] —**in′di·gence, in′di·gen·cy** *n.* **in′di·gent·ly** *adv.*   6

in·ef·fa·ble (in·ef′ə·bəl) *adj.* **1** Too overwhelming for expression in words; indescribable. **2** Too lofty or sacred to be spoken. [<L *in-* not + *effabilis* utterable] —**in·ef′fa·bil′i·ty** *n.* —**in·ef′fa·bly** *adv.*   3

in·ept (in·ept′) *adj.* **1** Not suitable or fit. **2** Absurd; foolish. **3** Clumsy; awkward. [<L *in-* not + *aptus* fit] —**in·ep′ti·tude, in·ept′ness** *n.* —**in·ept′ly** *adv.*   13

in·ex·o·ra·ble (in·ek′sər·ə·bəl) *adj.* Not to be moved by entreaty; unyielding. [<L *in-* not + *exorare* move by entreaty] —**in·ex′o·ra·bil′i·ty, in·ex′o·ra·ble·ness** *n.* —**in·ex′o·ra·bly** *adv.*   12

in·fal·li·ble (in·fal′ə·bəl) *adj.* **1** Incapable of fallacy or error. **2** Not apt to fail; reliable; certain: an *infallible* cure. **3** In Roman Catholic theology, incapable of error in matters relating to faith and morals: said of the Pope speaking *ex cathedra*. —*n.* One who or that which is infallible. —**in·fal′li·bil′i·ty, in·fal′li·ble·ness** *n.* —**in·fal′li·bly** *adv.*   4

in·frac·tion (in·frak′shən) *n.* The act of breaking or violating a rule, law, agreement, etc. [<L *infringere* destroy]   4

in·gen·ious (in·jēn′yəs) *adj.* **1** Possessed of skill in making or inventing. **2** Cleverly conceived or made. [<L *ingenium* natural ability] —**in·gen′ious·ly** *adv.* —**in·gen′ious·ness** *n.* —**Syn.** **1** adroit, clever, creative, resourceful.   15

in·gen·u·ous (in·jen′yōō·əs) *adj.* **1** Free from dissimulation; frank. **2** Innocent; artless. [<L *ingenuus* inborn, natural, frank] —**in·gen′u·ous·ly** *adv.* —**in·gen′u·ous·ness** *n.*   15

in·her·ent (in·hir′ənt, -her′-) *adj.* Naturally and inseparably associated with a person or thing; innate. —**in·her′ence, in·her′en·cy** (*pl.* **·cies**) *n.* —**in·her′ent·ly** *adv.* —**Syn.** essential, natural, characteristic, instinctual, native.   13

in·junc·tion (in·jungk′shən) *n.* **1** The act of enjoining; a command. **2** *Law* A judicial order requiring the party enjoined to take or, usu., to refrain from some specified action. [<L *injungere* join to, enjoin]   12

in·noc·u·ous (i·nok′yōō·əs) *adj.* **1** Having no harmful qualities. **2** Not stimulating or controversial; banal, inoffensive, etc. [<L *in-* not + *nocuus* harmful] —**in·noc′u·ous·ly** *adv.* —**in·noc′u·ous·ness** *n.*   2

in·quis·i·tive (in·kwiz′ə·tiv) *adj.* **1** Given to questioning, esp. to satisfy curiosity. **2** Inclined to the pursuit of knowledge. —**in·quis′i·tive·ly** *adv.* —**in·quis′i·tive·ness** *n.*   12

in·sen·si·ble (in·sen′sə·bəl) *adj.* **1** Not capable of or deprived of perception or feeling. **2** Unconscious. **3** Indifferent, unaware, or apathetic. **4** Inanimate. **5** Imperceptible. —**in·sen′si·bil′i·ty, in·sen′si·ble·ness** *n.* —**in·sen′si·bly** *adv.*   9

in·sid·i·ous (in·sid′ē·əs) *adj.* **1** Designed to entrap; full of wiles. **2** Doing or contriving harm. **3** Awaiting a chance to harm. **4** Causing harm by stealthy, usu. imperceptible means: an *insidious* disease. [<L *insidere* sit in, lie in wait] —**in·sid′i·ous·ly** *adv.* —**in·sid′i·ous·ness** *n.*   14

in·sip·id (in·sip′id) *adj.* **1** Without flavor; tasteless. **2** Unexciting; dull. [<L *in-* not + *sapidus* savory] —**in·sip′id·ly** *adv.* —**in·sip′id·ness** *n.*   1

in·sou·ci·ance (in·sōō′sē·əns; *Fr.* an·sōō·syäns′) *n.* Carefree unconcern; heedlessness. [F]   12

in·tran·si·gent (in·tran′sə·jənt) *adj.* Refusing to agree or compromise; irreconcilable. —*n.* One who is intransigent; a radical or revolutionary. [<L *in-* not + *transigere* agree] —**in·tran′si·gence, in·tran′si·gen·cy** (-jən·sē) *n.*   14

in·trep·id (in·trep′id) *adj.* Unshaken in the presence of danger; dauntless. [<L *in-* not + *trepidus* agitated] —**in·tre·pid·i·ty** (in′trə·pid′ə·tē) *n.* —**in·trep′id·ly** *adv.*   13

in·ure (in·yōor′) *v.* **·ured, ·ur·ing** *v.t.* **1** To harden or toughen; habituate. —*v.i.* **2** To have or take effect; be applied. [<OF *en-* (causative) + *euvre* work, use] —**in·ure′ment** *n.*   4

i·ras·ci·ble (i·ras′ə·bəl, ī-) *adj.* **1** Easily angered; irritable. **2** Caused by anger. [<L *irasci* be angry.] **—i·ras′ci·bil′i·ty, i·ras′ci·ble·ness** *n.* **—i·ras′ci·bly** *adv.*   *9*

ir·i·des·cence (ir′ə·des′əns) *n.* The rainbowlike appearance shown by various bodies, as oil films, mother-of-pearl, etc., when they reflect light. [<Gk. *iris, iridos* rainbow + -ESCENCE]   **—ir′i·des′cent** *adj.*   **—ir·i·des′cent·ly** *adv.*   *10*

i·ro·ny (ī′rə·nē) *n. pl.* **·nies 1** The use of words to signify the opposite of what they usu. express, as: "When he lost his wallet, he said, 'This is my lucky day.' " **2** A condition of affairs or events exactly the reverse of what was expected or hoped for. [<Gk. *eirōneia* affected ignorance, pretense]   *14*

jad·ed (jā′did) *adj.* **1** Worn-out; exhausted. **2** Satiated; sated, as from overindulgence. **—jad′ed·ly** *adv.* **—jad′ed·ness** *n.*   *9*

Ja·nus (jā′nəs) *Rom. Myth.* The god of portals and beginnings, having two faces, one in front, one in back of his head.
Ja·nus-faced (jā′nəs·fāst′) *adj.* Deceitful.   *10*

jaunt·y (jôn′tē, jän′-) *adj.* **jaunt·i·er, jaunt·i·est** Sprightly; lively. [<F *gentil* elegant] **—jaunt′i·ly** *adv.* **—jaunt′i·ness** *n.*   *3*

jeop·ard·y (jep′ər·dē) *n. pl.* **·ard·ies 1** Exposure to death loss, or injury; danger; peril. **2** The peril in which a defendant is put when placed on trial for a crime. [<OF *jeu parti* even chance]   *7*

jer·e·mi·ad (jer′ə·mī′ad) *n.* A lament; tale of woe. [<F *Jérémie* Jeremiah]   *10*

jin·go (jing′gō) *n. pl.* **·goes** One who boasts of his patriotism and favors an aggressive foreign policy. *—adj.* Of or like jingoes. [?] **—jin′go·ism, jin′go·ist** *n.* **—jin′go·is′tic** *adj.*   *9*

jo·vi·al (jō′vē·əl) *adj.* Possessing or expressive of good-natured mirth or gaiety; jolly. [<LL *Jovialis* (born under the influence) of Jupiter] **—jo·vi·al·i·ty** (jō′vē·al′ə·tē) *n.* **—jo′vi·al·ly** *adv.*   *13*

ju·di·cious (jōō·dish′əs) *adj.* Having, acting on, or resulting from sound judgment; wise; prudent. [<L *judicium* judgment] **—ju·di′cious·ly** *adv.* **—ju·di′cious·ness** *n.*   *1*

jug·ger·naut (jug′ər·nôt) *n.* A massive force that destroys whatever resists it. [< JUGGERNAUT]
Jug·ger·naut (jug′ər·nôt) An incarnation of the Hindu deity Vishnu whose idol was drawn on a heavy car under the wheels of which devotees were said to have thrown themselves to be crushed. [<Hind. *jagannāth* lord of the universe]   *7*

Ju·no·esque (jōō′nō·esk′) *adj.* Resembling the stately beauty of Juno.   *10*

jun·ta (hōōn′tə, jun′-) *n.* **1** A Central or South American legislative council. **2** A group of people, often military leaders, who exercise control over a government, esp. following a coup d'état. Also **jun′to** (-tō). [<L *juncta* joined]   *7*

ki·net·ic (ki·net′ik) *adj.* **1** Producing motion; motor. **2** Consisting in or depending upon motion: *kinetic* energy. [<Gk. *kineein* to move]   *15*

la·con·ic (lə·kon′ik) *adj.* Using or consisting of few words; short and forceful. Also **la·con′i·cal.** [<Gk. *Lakōn* a Spartan, with ref. to the habitual terseness of Spartan speech] **—la·con′i·cal·ly** *adv.*   *10*

la·i·ty (lā′ə·tē) *n. pl.* **·ties 1** The people as distinguished from the clergy. **2** Those outside any specified profession. [<LAY²]   *8*

lam·bent (lam′bənt) *adj.* **1** Playing with a soft, undulatory movement; gliding. **2** Softly radiant. **3** Touching lightly but brilliantly: *lambent* wit. **—lam′bent·ly** *adv.* [<L *lambere* to lick] **—lam′ben·cy, lam′bent·ness** *n.* **—Syn. 1** dancing, flickering, licking, wavering. **2** glistening, lustrous, refulgent.   *15*

lam·poon (lam·pōōn′) *n.* A written satire designed to bring a person into ridicule or contempt. *—v.t.* To abuse or satirize in a lampoon. [<MF *lampons* let's drink] **—lam·poon′er** or **lam·poon′ist, lam·poon′er·y** *n.* **—Syn.** *v.* deride, mock, ridicule.   *3*

lan·guid (lan′gwid) *adj.* **1** Indisposed to physical exertion; affected by weakness. **2** Wanting in interest or animation. **3** Lacking in force or quickness of movement. [< *languere* languish] **—lan′guid·ly** *adv.* **—lan′guid·ness** *n.* **—Syn. 1** drooping, fatigued, languorous, listless, weary.   *1*

lar·gess (lär·jes′, -zhes′, lär′jəs) *n.* **1** A gift; gratuity. **2** Liberality; bounty. Also **lar·gesse′.** [<L *largus* abundant]   *7*

la·tent (lā′tənt) *adj.* Not visible or apparent; dormant. [<L *latere* be hidden] **—la′ten·cy, la′tent·ly** *adv.*   *2*

laud·a·ble (lô′də·bəl) *adj.* Worthy of approval; praiseworthy. **—laud′a·bil′i·ty, laud′a·ble·ness** *n.* **—laud′a·bly** *adv.*   *14*

leg·end (lej′ənd) *n.* **1** An unauthenticated story from early times, preserved by tradition and popularly thought to have a basis in fact. **2** Such stories, collectively. **3** An unusually famous or notable person, thing, or event. **4** An inscription or motto on a coin or monument **5** A key to a map or chart. **6** A title, brief explanation, etc., accompanying an illustration. [<L *legere* read]   *8*

le·thal (lē′thəl) *adj.* **1** Causing death; fatal. **2** Pertaining to death. [<L *lethum, letum* death] **—le′thal·ly** *adv.*   *6*

le·thar·gic (li·thär′jik) *adj.* Affected by lethargy. Also **le·thar′gi·cal. —le·thar′gi·cal·ly** *adv.*   *5*

lev·i·ty (lev′ə·tē) *n. pl.* **·ties 1** Lightness or humor; lack of gravity in mood, character, or behavior. **2** Fickleness [<L *levis* light]   *3*

lex·i·con (lek′sə·kon) *n.* **1** A word list or vocabulary pertaining to a specific subject, field, author, etc. **2** DICTIONARY. [< Gk. *lexikos* pertaining to words]   *2*

lim·bo (lim′bō) *n.* **1** *Often cap. Theol.* A region on the edge of hell to which are consigned the souls of the righteous who died before the coming of Jesus and the souls of infants who died before baptism. **2** A place of neglect or oblivion for unwanted persons or things. [<L *limbus* border]   *12*

lim·pid (lim′pid) *adj.* **1** Characterized by liquid clearness; transparent. **2** Clear and intelligible; lucid: a *limpid* style. [<L *limpidus* clear] **—lim·pid·i·ty** (lim·pid′ə·tē), **lim′pid·ness** *n.* **—lim·pid·ly** *adv.*   *12*

lit·er·al (lit′ər·əl) *adj.* **1** Strictly based on the exact, standard meanings of the words or expressions: a *literal* interpretation of the Bible. **2** Following the exact words or construction of the original: a *literal* translation. **3** Matter-of-fact; unimaginative: a *literal* person. **4** Exact as to fact or detail; not exaggerated. [<L *littera* letter] **—lit′er·al′i·ty, lit′er·al·ness** *n.* **—lit′er·al·ly** *adv.*   *1*

lithe (līth) *adj.* Bending easily; limber. [<OE *lithe*] **lithe′ly** *adv.* **—lithe′ness** *n.*   *9*

loath (lōth, lō<u>th</u>) *adj.* Strongly disinclined; averse: often with *to.* **—nothing loath 1** Willing. **2** Willingly [<OE *lāth* hateful]   *1*

log·ger·head (lôg'ər·hed', log'-) *n.* **1** A blockhead; fool. **2** A large sea turtle of tropical Atlantic waters: also loggerhead turtle. —**at loggerheads** Engaged in a quarrel. [<regional E *logger* log tied to a horse's leg + HEAD] *13*

lo·qua·cious (lō·kwā'shəs) *adj.* Given to continual talking. [<L *loqui* to talk] —**lo·qua'cious·ly** *adv.* —**lo·qua·cious·ness, lo·quac·i·ty** (lō·kwas'ə·tē) *n.* —**Syn.** chattering, garrulous, talkative, verbose, vociferous. *4*

low·er·ing (lou'ər·ing) *adj.* **1** Overcast with clouds; threatening. **2** Frowning or sullen. —**low'er·ing·ly** *adv.* —**low'er·ing·ness** *n.* *12*

lu·cra·tive (lōo'krə·tiv) *adj.* Productive of wealth; profitable. [<L *lucrum* wealth] —**lu'cra·tive·ly** *adv.* —**lu'cra·tive·ness** *n.* *7*

lu·gu·bri·ous (lōo·gyōo'brē·əs) *adj.* Sad, mournful, or dismal, esp. in a ludicrous way. [<L *lugere* mourn] —**lu·gu'bri·ous·ly** *adv.* —**lu·gu'bri·ous·ness** *n.* *6*

lu·nar (lōo'nər) *adj.* **1** Of or pertaining to the moon. **2** Round or shaped like a crescent. **3** Measured by revolutions of the moon. [<L *luna* the moon] *9*

Mach·i·a·vel·li·an (mak'ē·ə·vel'ē·ən) *adj.* Of or pertaining to Machiavelli, or to the unscrupulous doctrines of political opportunism associated with his name. —*n.* A follower of Machiavelli. Also **Mach'·a·vel'i·an.** —**Mach'i·a·vel'li·an·ism'** *n.* *10*

mag·na·nim·i·ty (mag'nə·nim'ə·tē) *n. pl.* **·ties** **1** The quality or condition of being magnanimous. **2** A magnanimous deed. *6*

mal·a·droit (mal'ə·droit') *adj.* Clumsy or blundering. [<MAL- + F *adroit* clever] —**mal'a·droit'ly** *adv.* —**mal'a·droit'·ness** *n.* *7*

mal·a·prop·ism (mal'ə·prop·iz'əm) *n.* **1** An absurd misuse of words that sound somewhat alike. **2** An example of this, as *Measles is highly contiguous* (instead of *contagious*). [<Mrs. *Malaprop.* See MALAPROP.] *10*

ma·lign (mə·līn') *v.t.* To speak slander of. —*adj.* **1** Having an evil disposition toward others; ill-disposed; malevolent **2** Tending to injure; pernicious. [<L *malignare* contrive maliciously] —**ma·lign'er** *n.* —**ma·lign'ly** *adv.* —**Syn.** *v.* slur, vilify, defame, depreciate, discredit, belittle, disparage. *12*

mal·le·a·ble (mal'ē·ə·bəl) *adj.* **1** Capable of being shaped by hammering, rolling, pressure, etc. **2** Capable of being disciplined, trained, changed, etc. [<L *malleus* hammer —**mal'le·a·bil'i·ty, mal'le·a·ble·ness** *n.* —**mal'le·a·bly** *adv.* *6*

ma·raud (mə·rôd') *v.i.* **1** To rove in search of booty. —*v.t.* **2** To invade for plunder; raid. —*n.* A foray. [<F *maraud* a rogue] —**ma·raud'er** *n.* —**Syn.** *v.t.* despoil, loot, pillage, ransack, ravage. *1*

mas·o·chism (mas'ə·kiz'əm) *n.* The obtaining of pleasure, esp. sexual gratification, by submitting to physical or mental cruelty. [<Leopold von Sacher-*Masoch,* 1835–95, Austrian writer] —**mas'o·chist** *n.* —**mas'o·chis'tic** *adj.* —**mas'och·is'ti·cal·ly** *adv.* *10*

ma·te·ri·al·ism (mə·tir'ē·əl·iz'əm) *n.* **1** The doctrine that facts of experience are all to be explained by reference to the reality and laws of physical or material substance. **2** Undue regard for material and worldly rather than spiritual matters. —**ma·te'ri·al·ist** *adj., n.* —**ma·te'ri·al·is·tic** *adj.* —**ma·te'ri·al·is'ti·cal·ly** *adv.* *14*

ma·tric·u·late (mə·trik'yə·lāt) *v.t. & v.i.* **·lat·ed, ·lat·ing** **1** To enroll, esp. in a college or university as a candidate for a degree. **2** *Can.* To pass final high-school examinations. —*n.* A candidate for a college or university degree. [<Med. L. *matrix* womb, origin, public roll] —**ma·tric'u·lant, ma·tric'u·la'tion, ma·tric'u·la'tor** *n.* *6*

maud·lin (môd'lin) *adj.* **1** Foolishly and tearfully sentimental. **2** Made foolish from drinking too much alcoholic liquor. [<OF *Maudelene,* (Mary) Magdalen, who was often depicted with eyes swollen from weeping] *10*

mav·er·ick (mav'ər·ik) *n.* **1** An unbranded or orphaned animal, esp. a calf. **2** A person characterized by independence or nonconformity in relation to a group with which he is affiliated, as a political party. [<S. A. *Maverick,* 1803–70, Texas lawyer, who did not brand his cattle] *11*

mawk·ish (mô'kish) *adj.* **1** Characterized by false or feeble sentimentality. **2** Provoking disgust; sickening. [<obs. *mawk* a maggot] —**mawk'ish·ly** *adv.* —**mawk'ish·ness** *n.* *2*

mel·lif·lu·ous (mə·lif'lōo·əs) *adj.* Sweetly or smoothly flowing; dulcet: a *mellifluous* voice. [<L *mel* honey + *fluere* flow] —**mel·lif'lu·ous·ly** *adv.* —**mel·lif'lu·ous·ness** *n.* *1*

mem·o·ra·bil·i·a (mem'ə·rə·bil'ē·ə) *n. pl.* Things worthy of remembrance, or an account of them. [<L *memorabilis* memorable] *5*

men·da·cious (men·dā'shəs) *adj.* **1** Addicted to lying; deceitful. **2** Untrue; false. [<L *mendax* lying] —**men·da'cious·ly** *adv.* —**men·da'cious·ness, men·dac·i·ty** (men·das'ə·tē) *n.* *3*

men·tor (men'tər, -tôr) *n.* A wise and trusted teacher, guide, and friend. [<*Mentor,* the wise guardian of Telemachus in the Odyssey.] *10*

mer·ce·nar·y (mûr'sə·ner'ē) *adj.* **1** Influenced by desire for gain or reward; greedy. **2** Serving in a foreign army for pay or profit; hired: *mercenary* soldiers. —*n. pl.* **·nar·ies** **1** A mercenary soldier. **2** Any hireling. [<L *merces* reward, pay] —**mer'ce·nar'i·ly** *adv.* —**mer'ce·nar'i·ness** *n.* *4*

mer·cu·ri·al (mər·kyŏor'ē·əl) *adj.* **1** Apt to change moods abruptly and with little cause; volatile. **2** Suggestive of the qualities associated with the god Mercury; lively, quick, and ingenious: a *mercurial* wit. **3** Of, containing, or caused by the element mercury. —*n.* A preparation containing mercury. —**mer·cu'ri·al·ly** *adv.* —**mer·cu'ri·al·ness** *n.* *10*

mes·mer·ism (mes'mə·riz'əm, mez'-) *n.* HYPNOTISM. [F. A. *Mesmer,* 1734–1815, German physician] —**mes·mer'ic** (mes·mer'ik, mez-), **mes·mer'i·cal** *adj.* —**mes·mer'i·cal·ly** *adv.* —**mes'mer·ist** *n.* *10*

met·a·mor·pho·sis (met'ə·môr'fə·sis) *n. pl.* **·pho·ses** (-fə·sēz) **1** A passing from one form or shape into another, esp. by means of sorcery, etc. **2** Complete transformation of character, purpose, circumstances, etc. **3** A person or thing metamorphosed. **4** *Biol.* A developmental change in form, structure, or function in an organism, esp. after leaving the egg and before attaining sexual maturity. [<Gk. *meta-* beyond + *morphē* form] *8*

met·a·phor (met'ə·fôr, -fər) *n.* A figure of speech in which one object is likened to another by speaking of it as if it were that other, as in *The sun was a chariot of fire.* [<Gk. *meta-* beyond, over + *pherein* to carry] —**met'a·phor'ic** (-fôr'ik, -for'ik) or **·i·cal** *adj.* —**met'a·phor'i·cal·ly** *adv.* • *Metaphors* and *similes* both make comparisons, but the metaphor is distinguished from the simile by the omission of an introductory word such as "like" or "as." For example, *The moon is a silver coin* is a metaphor; *The moon is like a silver coin* is a simile. *8*

me·ton·y·my (mə·ton′ə·mē) *n.* ·**mies** A figure of speech that employs an associated or closely connected word rather than the word itself, as "the crown prefers" for "the king prefers." [<Gk. *meta-* altered + *onyma* name **—met′o·nym·ic** (met′ə·nim′ik), **met′o·nym′i·cal** *adj.* **—met′o·nym′i·cal·ly** *adv.* 14

mi·nu·ti·ae (mi·n⁽ʸ⁾oō′shi·ē) *n.pl.* *of* **mi·nu′ti·a** (-shē·ə, -shə) Small or unimportant details. [L] 9

mis·con·strue (mis′kən·stroō′) *v.t.* **strued,** **·stru·ing** To interpret erroneously; misunderstood. **—mis′con·struc′tion** (-struk′shən) *n.* 8

mis·no·mer (mis·nō′mər) *n.* 1 A name wrongly applied. 2 The giving of a wrong name to a person in a legal document. [<OF *mes-* wrongly + *nomer* name] 2

mne·mon·ic (ni·mon′ik) *adj.* Pertaining to, aiding, or designed to aid the memory. Also **mne·mon′i·cal.** [<Gk. *mnē·mōn* mindful] 13

mode (mōd) *n.* 1 Manner, way, or method of acting, being, doing, etc. 2 Prevailing style or fashion of dress, behavior, etc. 3 *Gram.* MOOD. 4 *Music* Any of the seven possible permutations of the tones of a major scale in which the original order is preserved. 5 *Stat.* That value, magnitude, or score which occurs the greatest number of times in a given series of observations; norm. [<L *modus* means, manner] 3

mo·dus op·er·an·di (mō′dəs op′ə·ran′dē, -dī) A manner of operation or procedure. [L] 1

mo·nog·a·my (mə·nog′ə·mē) *n.* 1 The principle or practice of marriage with but one person at a time. 2 *Zool.* The habit of having but one mate. [<Gk. *monos* single + *gamos* marriage] **—mo·nog′a·mous** *adj.* **—mo·nog′a·mist** *n.* 9

moot (moōt) *adj.* 1 Still open to discussion; debatable: a *moot* point. 2 Altogether academic; having no practical significance. **—***n.* 1 Discussion or argument. 2 In Anglo-Saxon times, a meeting of freemen for the discussion of local affairs. **—***v.t.* 1 To debate; discuss. 2 To argue (a case) in a moot court. [<OE *mōt* assembly] 13

mor·i·bund (môr′ə·bund, -bənd, mor′-) *adj.* Dying; at the point of death. [<L *mori* die] **—mor′i·bun′di·ty** *n.* 5

mo·rose (mə·rōs′) *adj.* Sullen; gloomy. [<L *mos, moris* manner, habit] **—mo·rose′ly** *adv.* **—mo·rose′ness** *n.* **—Syn.** sad, melancholy, surly, ill-tempered. 12

muse (myoōz) *n.* A source of inspiration for artists, poets, etc. [<MUSE] 12

mys·tic (mis′tik) *adj.* 1 Of or pertaining to mystics or mysticism. 2 Of or designating an occult or esoteric rite, practice, belief, etc. 3 Mysterious; enigmatic. **—***n.* One who practices mysticism or has mystical experiences. [<Gk. *mystikos* pertaining to secret rites] 12

na·bob (nā′bob) *n.* 1 A native governor in India under the Mogul empire. 2 A very rich and prominent man. [<Ar. *nuwwab*] **—na′bob·er·y, na′bob·ism** *n.* **—na′bob·ish** *adj.* 7

na·dir (nā′dər, -dir) *n.* 1 The point of the celestial sphere intersected by a diameter extending from the zenith. 2 The lowest possible point. [<Ar. *naḍir (es·semt)* opposite (the zenith)] 7

nar·cis·sism (när′sə·siz′əm) *n.* Excessive interest in or admiration for oneself; self-love. Also **nar·cism** (när′siz·əm). [<NARCISSUS] **—nar′cis·sist** *n.* **—nar′cis·sis′tic** *adv.* 10

neb·u·lous (neb′yə·ləs) *adj.* 1 Having its parts confused or mixed; indistinct: a *nebulous* idea. 2 Like a nebula. **—neb′u·lous·ly** *adv.* **—neb′u·lous·ness** *n.* 3

nem·e·sis (nem′ə·sis) *n.* Retributive justice; retribution. [<Gk. *nemein* distribute] 10

ne·ol·o·gism (nē·ol′ə·jiz′əm) *n.* 1 A new word or phrase. 2 The use of new words or new meanings for old words. Also **ne·ol′o·gy** (*pl.* ·**gies**). [<NEO- + Gk. *logos* word] **—ne·ol′o·gist** *n.* **—ne·ol′o·gis′tic, ne·ol′o·gis′ti·cal** *adj.* 12

ne·o·phyte (nē′ə·fīt) *n.* 1 A recent convert. 2 Any novice or beginner. [<Gk. *neophytos* novice] 1

nig·gard·ly (nig′ərd·lē) *adj.* 1 Avaricious; stingy. 2 Scanty or measly: a *niggardly* portion. **—***adv.* Stingily. **—nig′gard·li·ness** *n.* **—Syn.** *adj.* 1 miserly, parsimonious, tightfisted. 4

ni·hil·ism (nī′əl·iz′əm, nī′hil-) *n.* 1 *Philos.* The doctrine that nothing exists or can be known. 2 The rejection of religious and moral creeds. 3 A political doctrine holding that the existing structure of society should be destroyed. [<L *nihil* nothing + -ISM] **—ni′hil·ist** *n.* **—ni′hil·is′tic** *adj.* 6

nos·trum (nos′trəm) *n.* 1 A patent medicine; quack recipe. 2 Anything savoring of quackery: political *nostrums.* [<L *noster* our own; because prepared by those selling it] 1

nox·ious (nok′shəs) *adj.* Causing, or tending to cause, injury to health or morals; poisonous. [<L *nocere* to hurt] **—nox′ious·ly** *adv.* **—nox′ious·ness** *n.* **—Syn.** deadly, hurtful, pernicious. 5

nu·ance (n⁽ʸ⁾oō′äns, n⁽ʸ⁾oō·äns′) *n.* 1 A shade of difference in tone or color. 2 A slight degree of difference in anything perceptible to the mind. [<OF *nuer* to shade] 2

ob·du·rate (ob′d⁽ʸ⁾ə·rit) *adj.* 1 Unmoved by feelings of humanity or pity; hard. 2 Perversely impenitent. 3 Unyielding; stubborn. [<L *ob-* completely + *durare* harden] **—ob′du·ra·cy** (-rə·sē), **ob′du·rate·ness** *n.* **—ob′du·rate·ly** *adv.* 3

ob·lo·quy (ob′lə·kwē) *n. pl.* ·**quies** 1 An expression of severe censure or denunciation. 2 The state of one who is so censured; disgrace. **—Syn.** 1 reprobation, vilification, defamation, calumny, opprobrium. 2 ignominy. [<L *ob-* against + *loqui* speak] 15

ob·se·qui·ous (ob·sē′kwē·əs, əb-) *adj.* Too eager to please; fawning; servile. [<L *ob-* towards + *sequi* follow] **—ob·se′qui·ous·ly** *adv.* **—ob·se′qui·ous·ness** *n.* 12

ob·so·lete (ob′sə·lēt) *adj.* Being out of use or out of fashion, as a word or style. [<L *obsolescere* grow old] **—ob′so·lete′ly** *adv.* **—ob′so·lete′ness** *n.* 2

ob·tuse (əb·t⁽ʸ⁾oōs′) *adj.* 1 Blunt or rounded. 2 Lacking alertness or sensitivity; intellectually sluggish or slow. 3 Heavy, dull, and indistinct, as a sound. 4 Having a measure between 90° and 180°: an *obtuse* angle. • See ANGLE. [<L *obtusus* blunt] **—ob·tuse′ly** *adv.* **—ob·tuse′ness** *n.* 11

of·fi·cious (ə·fish′əs) *adj.* Volunteering unwanted service or advice, esp. in an unduly forward manner. [<L *officium* service] **—of·fi′cious·ly** *adv.* **—of·fi′cious·ness** *n.* **—Syn.** meddlesome, interfering, obtrusive, nosy. 12

om·i·nous (om′ə·nəs) *adj.* Like or marked by an evil omen; sinister; threatening. [<L *omen, ominis* an omen] **—om′i·nous·ly** *adv.* **—om′i·nous·ness** *n.* 4

om·nip·o·tent (om·nip′ə·tənt) *adj.* Unlimited in authority or power. **—the Omnipotent** God. **—om·nip′o·tent·ly** *adv.* **—Syn.** mighty, almighty, powerful, authoritative. 1

om·ni·scient (om·nish′ənt) *adj.* Having infinite knowledge; knowing everything. —the Omniscient God. *omni-* all + *sciens* knowing] —**om·ni·science** (om·nish'əns) *n.* —**om·ni'scient·ly** *adv.*   5

on·er·ous (on'ər·əs) *adj.* Imposing or characterized by difficulty, labor, responsibility, etc. [<L *onus, oneris* a burden] —**on'er·ous·ly** *adv.* —**on'er·ous·ness** *n.* —**Syn.** arduous, burdensome, exacting, oppressive.   3

on·o·mat·o·poe·ia (on'ə·mat'ə·pē'ə) *n.* 1 The formation of words in imitation of natural sounds, as *crack, splash,* or *bow-wow.* 2 The use of such words, as in poetry. Also **on'o·mat·o·po·e'sis** (-pō·ē'sis), **on'o·mat·o·py** (-mat'ə·pē). [<Gk. *onoma* name + *poieein* make] —**on'o·mat·o·poe'ic** or **·i·cal, on'o·mat·o·po·et'ic** (-pō·et'ik) *adj.* —**on'o·mat·o·po·et'i·cal·ly** *adv.*   14

o·paque (ō·pāk') *adj.* 1 Impervious to light or other radiation. 2 Loosely, imperfectly transparent. 3 Impervious to reason; unintelligent. 4 Having no luster; dull. 5 Unintelligible; obscure: an *opaque* style. —*n.* Something opaque. [<L *opacus* shaded, darkened] —**o·paque'ly** *adv.* —**o·paque'ness** *n.*   2

op·por·tune (op'ər·t^yōōn') *adj.* Meeting some requirement, esp. at the right time; timely. [<L *opportunus* suitable, lit., at the port.] —**op'por·tune'ly** *adv.* —**op'por·tune'·ness** *n.* —**Syn.** auspicious, convenient, favorable, fortunate, well-chosen.   6

os·si·fy (os'ə·fī) *v.t.* & *v.i.* **·fied, ·fy·ing** 1 To convert or be converted into bone. 2 To make or become set, conventional, etc. [<L *os, ossis* a bone + FY] —**os·sif·ic** (o·sif'ik) *adj.* —**os'si·fi·ca'tion** *n.*   8

os·ten·si·ble (os·ten'sə·bəl) *adj.* Offered as real or having the character represented; seeming; professed or pretended. [<L *ostendere* to show] —**os·ten'si·bly** *adv.*   1

os·tra·cize (os'trə·sīz) *v.t.* **·cized, ·ciz·ing** To exclude, banish, etc. by ostracism. [<Gk. *ostrakon* a potsherd, shell, voting tablet] —**Syn.** exclude, reject, banish, expatriate, expel, oust.   9

o·vert (ō'vûrt, ō·vûrt') *adj.* Open to view; outwardly manifest. [<OF, pp. of *ovrir* to open] —**o·vert'ly** *adv.* —**Syn.** apparent, evident, obvious, clear, patent.   4

pa·gan (pā'gən) *n.* 1 One who is neither a Christian, a Jew, nor a Muslim; a heathen. 2 An irreligious person. —*adj.* Pertaining to pagans; heathenish. [<L *paganus* a rural villager] —**pa'gan·dom, pa'gan·ism** *n.*   6

pan·de·mo·ni·um (pan'də·mō'nē·əm) *n.* A tumultuous uproar; wild disorder. —**Syn.** riot, chaos, tumult. [<Gk. *pan,* neut. of *pas* all + *daimōn* an evil spirit]   1

pan·der (pan'dər) *v.i.* To seek to satisfy another's immoral, vulgar, or uninformed tastes or desires: to *pander* to the mob. —*n.* One who panders; esp., a go-between in sexual intrigues; procurer; pimp. [<*Pandarus,* a character in the Iliad] —**pan'der·er** *n.*   10

pan·o·ram·a (pan'ə·ram'ə, -rä'mə) *n.* 1 A complete view in every direction. 2 A complete or comprehensive view of a subject or of constantly passing events. 3 A picture unrolled before the spectator and representing a continuous scene. 4 CYCLORAMA. [<PAN- + Gk. *horama* sight] —**pan'o·ram'ic** *adj.* —**pan'o·ram'i·cal·ly** *adv.*   2

par·a·ble (par'ə·bəl) *n.* A short, simple tale based on familiar things, meant to convey a moral or religious lesson. [<Gk. *parabolē* a placing side by side, a comparison]   3

par·a·dox (par'ə·doks) *n.* 1 A statement that seems to contradict common belief but may nevertheless be true. 2

A self-contradictory statement or proposition. 3 A person or thing that seems to possess contradictory qualities and is thus inexplicable or inscrutable; enigma. [<Gk. *para-* contrary to + *doxa* opinion] —**par'a·dox'i·cal** *adj.* —**par'a·dox'i·cal·ly** *adv.* —**par'a·dox'i·cal·ness** *n.*   8

par·a·phrase (par'ə·frāz) *n.* A restatement of the meaning of a passage, work, etc. —*v.t.* & *v.i.* **·phrased, ·phras·ing** To express in or make a paraphrase. [<Gk. <*paraphrazein* tell the same thing in other words] —**par'a·phras'er** *n.* —**par'a·phras'tic** (-fras'tik) *adj.* —**par'a·phras'ti·cal·ly** *adv.*   2

par·a·site (par'ə·sīt) *n.* 1 *Biol.* An animal or plant that lives on or in another living organism from which it takes nourishment, usu. with harm to the host. 2 A person or thing that lives or survives by dependence on and at the expense of another. [<Gk. *parasitos,* lit., one who eats at another's table] —**par'a·sit'ic** (-sit'ik) or **·i·cal** *adj.* —**par'a·sit'i·cal·ly** *adv.* —**par·a·sit·ism** (par'ə·sī'tiz·əm, -sə·tiz'əm) *n.*   2

pa·ri·ah (pə·rī'ə) *n.* 1 One of a people of low caste in s India and Burma. 2 A social outcast. [<Tamil *paraiyar* drummer, because drummers at festivals came from this caste]   7

par·si·mo·ny (pär'sə·mō'nē) *n.* Undue reluctance to spend money; stinginess. [<L *parcere* spare]   5

par·ti·san (pär'tə·zən, -sən) *n.* 1 One who supports or endorses a party or cause with great devotion or zeal; esp., an overzealous or fanatical devotee. 2 A member of a body of irregular troops; a guerrilla. —*adj.* Pertaining to or characteristic of a partisan. Also **par'ti·zan.** [<Ital. *parte* a part] —**par'ti·san·ship** *n.*   1

pat·ent (pat'nt, *Brit.* pāt'nt; *for adj. defs. 2 & 3, usu.* pāt'nt) *n.* 1 A government protection to an inventor, securing to him for a specific time exclusive rights to his invention. 2 The rights so granted. 3 Any official document securing a right. —*v.t.* To obtain a patent on (an invention). —*adj.* 1 Protected or conferred by a patent. 2 Manifest or apparent to everybody. 3 Open, unobstructed, as a duct in the body. [<L *patens* pr.p. of *patere* lie open]   14

pa·ter·nal·ism (pə·tûr'nəl·iz'əm) *n.* The control of a country, community, or group in a manner suggestive of a father looking after his children. —**pa·ter'nal·is'tic** *adj.* —**pa·ter'nal·is'ti·cal·ly** *adv.*   6

pa·thos (pā'thos) *n.* The quality, attribute, or element, in events, speech, or art, that rouses the tender emotions, as compassion or sympathy. [Gk., suffering]   15

pen·sive (pen'siv) *adj.* 1 Engaged in or accustomed to serious or quiet reflection. 2 Expressive of, suggesting, or causing sad thoughtfulness. [<OF *penser* think] —**pen'sive·ly** *adv.* —**pen'sive·ness** *n.* —**Syn.** 1 meditative, reflective. 2 grave, melancholy, sad, sober.   5

per·e·gri·nate (per'ə·gri·nāt') **·nat·ed, ·nat·ing** *v.i.* 1 To travel from place to place. —*v.t.* 2 To travel through or along. [<L *peregrinari* travel abroad] —**per'e·gri·na'tion** *n.*   12

per·fid·i·ous (pər·fid'ē·əs) *adj.* Of or characterized by perfidy. —**per·fid'i·ous·ly** *adv.* —**per·fid'i·ous·ness** *n.*   11

per·func·to·ry (pər·fungk'tər·ē) *adj.* 1 Done mechanically or routinely; superficial. 2 Without interest or concern; apathetic. [<L *per-* through + *fungi* perform] —**per·func'to·ri·ly** *adv.* —**per·func'to·ri·ness** *n.*   13

pe·riph·er·y (pə·rif'ər·ē) *n. pl.* **·er·ies** 1 The outer bounds of any surface or area. **2** The surface of the body. **3** PERIMETER (def. 1). **4** A surrounding region, country, or area. [<Gk. *periphereia* circumference] *12*

per·son·i·fi·ca·tion (pər·son′ə·fə·kā′shən) *n.* **1** The endowment of inanimate objects or qualities with human attributes. **2** Striking or typical exemplification of a quality in one's person; embodiment: She was the *personification* of joy. **3** The representation of an abstract quality or idea by a human figure. *8*

per·spi·ca·cious (pûr′spə·kā′shəs) *adj.* Keenly discerning or understanding. [<L *perspicax* sharp-sighted] —**per′spi·ca′cious·ly** *adv.* —**per′spi·ca′cious·ness, per′spi·cac′i·ty** (-kas′ə·tē) *n.* *1*

pet·u·lant (pech′oo·lənt) *adj.* Displaying or characterized by bad humor, esp. over a minor irritation. [<L *petulans* forward] —**pet′u·lance, pet′u·lan·cy** *n.* —**pet′u·lant·ly** *adv.* —**Syn.** fretful, peevish, grumpy, complaining. *12*

phi·lip·pic (fi·lip′ik) *n.* An impassioned speech characterized by invective. —**the Philippics** A series of twelve speeches in which Demosthenes denounced Philip of Macedon. *10*

phi·lis·tine (fil′ə·stin, -stēn, fə·lis′tən, -tēn′) *Sometimes cap. n.* An ignorant, narrow-minded person, devoid of culture and indifferent to art. —*adj.* Smugly indifferent to culture and art. —**phi·lis·tin·ism** (fil′ə·stin·iz′əm, fə·lis′tə·niz′əm, -tē′-) *n.* *13*

phleg·mat·ic (fleg·mat′ik) *adj.* Having a sluggish or stolid temperament; not easily moved or excited. Also **phleg·mat′i·cal.** —**phleg·mat′i·cal·ly** *adv.* —**Syn.** indifferent, calm, dull, undemonstrative. *9*

pic·a·yune (pik′i·yōōn′) *adj.* **1** Little; worthless. **2** Concerned with unimportant or petty matters. —*n.* **1** A former small Spanish-American coin; a half-real. **2** *U.S.* A person or thing of trifling value. [<Prov. *picaioun,* dim. of *picalo* money] —**pic′a·yun′ish** *adj.* —**Syn.** *adj.* **1** paltry, worthless, measly. **2** trivial, mean, narrow-minded. *1*

pil·lage (pil′ij) *n.* **1** The act of pillaging; open robbery in war. **2** Spoil; booty. —*v.* ·**laged,** ·**lag·ing** *v.t.* **1** To strip money or property by violence, esp. in war; loot. **2** To take as loot. —*v.i.* **3** To take plunder. [<OF *piller* to plunder] —**pil′lag·er** *n.* *12*

pi·quant (pē′kənt, -känt′) *adj.* **1** Having an agreeably pungent or tart taste. **2** Interesting; tart; racy; also charmingly lively. [<F *piquer* sting] —**pi′quan·cy** *n.* —**pi′quant·ly** *adv.* *13*

Pla·ton·ic (plə·ton′ik) *adj.* **1** Of, pertaining to Plato or Platonism. **2** Designating love (Platonic love) that is spiritual rather than sensual. Also **pla·ton′ic.** —**Pla·ton′i·cal·ly, pla·ton′i·cal·ly** *adv.* *10*

plau·si·ble (plô′zə·bəl) *adj.* **1** Seeming likely to be true, but open to doubt. **2** Superficially endeavoring or calculated to gain trust: a *plausible* witness. [<L *plausibilis* deserving applause] —**plau′si·bil′i·ty, plau′si·ble·ness** *n.* —**plau′si·bly** *adv.* *3*

po·grom (pō′grəm, pō·grom′) *n.* An officially instigated massacre, esp. one directed against Jews. [Russ., destruction] *7*

poign·ant (poin′yənt, poi′nənt) *adj.* **1** Severely painful or acute to the feelings: *poignant* grief. **2** Keenly piercing: *poignant* wit. **3** Sharp or stimulating to the taste; pungent. [<L *pungere* to prick] —**poign′an·cy** *n.* —**poign′ant·ly** *adv.* —**Syn.** **1** agonizing, excruciating, piercing, sharp. *13*

pol·y·glot (pol′i·glot) *adj.* **1** Expressed in several tongues. **2** Speaking several languages. —*n.* A person or book that is polyglot. [<Gk. *polyglōttos*] —**pol·y·glot′tal, pol·y·glot′tic** *adj.* *7*

por·ten·tous (pôr·ten′təs, pōr-) *adj.* **1** Full of portents of ill; ominous. **2** Amazing; extraordinary. **3** Pretentiously solemn. —**por·ten′tous·ly** *adv.* —**por·ten′tous·ness** *n.* *14*

post·hu·mous (pos′choo·məs) *adj.* **1** Born after the father's death: said of a child. **2** Published after the author's death, as a book. **3** Arising after a person's death: a *posthumous* reputation. [<L *postumus* latest, last] —**post′hu·mous·ly** *adv.* *5*

po·ten·tial (pə·ten′shəl) *adj.* **1** Possible but not actual. **2** Having capacity for existence, but not yet existing. **3** *Physics* Existing by virtue of position: said of energy. **4** *Gram.* Indicating possibility or capability by the use of *can, could, may,* etc. **5** Having force or power. —*n.* **1** Anything that may be possible. **2** *Gram.* The potential mood. **3** *Physics* The work required to move a body from a point infinitely distant to a given point in a field of force. **4** *Electr.* A difference of electric potential; voltage. [<L *potens* potent] —**po·ten·ti·al·i·ty** (pə·ten′shē·al′ə·tē) (*pl.* ·**ties**) *n.* —**po·ten′tial·ly** *adv.* *8*

pot·pour·ri (pō·pōō·rē′) *n.* **1** A mixture of dried sweet smelling flower petals used to perfume a room. **2** A medley of musical airs or a literary miscellany. [<F, lit., rotten] *7*

pre·cip·i·tate (pri·sip′ə·tit) *adj.* **1** Rushing down headlong. **2** Lacking due deliberation; hasty. **3** Sudden and brief. —*v.* (pri·sip′ə·tāt) ·**tat·ed,** ·**tat·ing** *v.t.* **1** To hasten the occurrence of. **2** To hurl from or as from a height. **3** *Meteorol.* To cause (water vapor) to condense and fall as a liquid or solid. **4** *Chem.* To separate (a constituent) in solid form, as from a solution. —*v.i.* **5** *Meteorol.* To fall as water or ice. **6** *Chem.* To separate out of solution as a solid. **7** To fall headlong; rush. —*n.* (pri·sip′ə·tit, -tāt) A solid precipitated from a solution. [<L *praeceps* headlong] —**pre·cip′i·tate·ly** *adv.* —**pre·cip′i·tate·ness, pre·cip′i·ta′tor** *n.* —**pre·cip′i·ta′tive** *adj.* *15*

pre·cip·i·tous (pri·sip′ə·təs) *adj.* **1** Very steep. **2** Headlong and downward in motion. **3** Headlong in disposition. [<L *praeceps* headlong] —**pre·cip′i·tous·ly** *adv.* —**pre·cip′i·tous·ness** *n.* *15*

pre·co·cious (pri·kō′shəs) *adj.* **1** Developing before the natural season. **2** Unusually forward or advanced, as a child. [<L *praecox*] —**pre·co′cious·ly** *adv.* —**pre·co′cious·ness, pre·coc′i·ty** (-kos′ə·tē) *n.* *9*

pred·a·to·ry (pred′ə·tôr′ē, -tō′rē) *adj.* **1** Living by preying upon other animals: a *predatory* animal. **2** Characterized by plundering or stealing. [<L *praeda* prey] —**pred′a·tor, pred′a·to′ri·ness** *n.* —**pred′a·to′ri·ly** *adv.* *2*

pre·empt (prē·empt′) *v.t.* **1** To seize or appropriate beforehand. **2** To occupy (public land) so as to acquire by preemption. —**pre·emp′tor** *n.* *11*

pre·pos·ter·ous (pri·pos′tər·əs) *adj.* Contrary to nature, reason, or common sense; ridiculous. [<L *praeposterus* the last first, inverted] —**pre·pos′ter·ous·ly** *adv.* —**pre·pos′ter·ous·ness** *n.* —**Syn.** absurd, foolish, idiotic, irrational, silly. *14*

pri·mal (prī′məl) *adj.* **1** First; original. **2** Most important; chief. [<L *primus* first] *9*

pro·cliv·i·ty (prō·kliv′ə·tē) *n. pl.* ·**ties** Natural disposition or tendency, esp. toward something not desirable. [<L *proclivus* downward] *13*

Pro·crus·te·an (prō·krus'tē·ən) *adj.* **1** Of Procrustes. **2** Ruthlessly or violently forcing to conform. *10*

prod·i·gy (prod'ə·jē) *n. pl.* **·gies 1** Something extraordinary or awe-inspiring. **2** An exceptionally gifted child. **3** A monstrosity of nature. [<L *prodigium*] *9*

pro·fane (prō·fān', prə-) *v.t.* **·faned, ·fan·ing 1** To treat (something sacred) with irreverence or abuse; desecrate. **2** To put to an unworthy or degrading use; debase. —*adj.* **1** Manifesting irreverence or disrespect toward sacred things. **2** Not sacred or religious in theme, content, use, etc.; secular. **3** Not esoteric; ordinary. **4** Vulgar. [<L *pro-* before + *fanum* temple] —**pro·fan·a·to·ry** (prō·fan'ə·tôr'ē, -tō'rē, prə-) *adj.* —**pro·fane'ly** *adv.* —**pro·fan'er** *n.* *4*

prog·e·ny (proj'ə·nē) *n. pl.* **·nies** Offspring; descendants. [<L *progignere* beget] *13*

pro·lif·er·ate (prō·lif'ə·rāt, prə-) *v.t. & v.i.* **·at·ed, ·at·ing** To create or reproduce in rapid succession. [<L *proles* offspring + *ferre* bear] —**pro·lif·er·a'tion** *n.* —**pro·lif·er·a'tive, pro·lif'er·ous** *adj.* *12*

pro·lif·ic (prō·lif'ik, prə-) *adj.* **1** Producing abundantly, as offspring or fruit. **2** Producing creative or intellectual products abundantly: a *prolific* writer. [<L *proles* offspring + *facere* make] —**pro·lif'i·ca·cy** (-i·kə·sē), **pro·lif'ic·ness** *n.* —**pro·lif'i·cal·ly** *adv.* *9*

pro·lix (prō'liks, prō·liks') *adj.* **1** Unduly long and wordy. **2** Indulging in long and wordy discourse. [<L *prolixus* extended] —**pro·lix·i·ty** (prō·lik'sə·tē), **pro'lix·ness** *n.* —**pro'lix·ly** *adv.* *3*

pro·mis·cu·ous (prə·mis'kyōō·əs) *adj.* **1** Composed of persons or things confusedly mingled. **2** Indiscriminate; esp., having sexual relations indiscriminately or casually with various persons. **3** Casual; irregular. [<L *promiscuus* mixed] —**pro·mis'cu·ous·ly** *adv.* —**pro·mis'cu·ous·ness** *n.* *4*

prom·ul·gate (prom'əl·gāt, prō·mul'gāt) *v.t.* **·gat·ed, ·gat·ing 1** To make known or announce officially, as a law, dogma, etc. **2** To make known or effective over a wide area or extent. [<L *promulgare* make known] —**prom·ul·ga'tion** (prom'əl·gā'shən, prō'mul-), **prom'ul·gat·or** *n.* *3*

pro·pi·ti·ate (prō·pish'ē·āt) *v.t.* **·at·ed, ·at·ing** To cause to be favorably disposed; appease; conciliate. [<L *propitiare* render favorable, appease] —**pro·pi·ti·a·ble** (prō·pish'ē·ə·bəl), **pro·pi'ti·a·tive, pro·pi'ti·a·to'ry** *adj.* —**pro·pi·ti·a·tion** (prō·pish'ē·ā'shən), **pro·pi'ti·a'tor** *n.* —**Syn.** pacify, placate, mollify, reconcile. *1*

pro·po·nent (prə·pō'nənt) *n.* **1** One who makes a proposal or puts forward a proposition. **2** *Law* One who presents a will for probate. **3** One who advocates or supports a cause or doctrine. [<L *pro-* forth + *ponere* put] *14*

pro·scribe (prō·skrīb') *v.t.* **·scribed, ·scrib·ing 1** To denounce or condemn; prohibit; interdict. **2** To outlaw or banish. **3** In ancient Rome, to publish the name of (one condemned or exiled). [<L *pro-* before + *scribere* write] —**pro·scrib'er, pro·scrip'tion** (-skrip'shən) *n.* —**pro·scrip'tive** *adj.* —**pro·scrip'tive·ly** *adv.* *5*

pros·e·lyte (pros'ə·līt) *n.* One who has been converted to any opinion, belief, sect, or party. —*v.t. & v.i.* **·lyt·ed, ·lyt·ing** PROSELYTIZE. [<Gk. *proselytos* a convert to Judaism] —**pros'e·lyt·ism** (-līt'iz·əm, -lə·tiz'əm), **pros'e·lyt·ist** *n.* *14*

pro·spec·tus (prə·spek'təs) *n.* **1** A paper containing information of a proposed literary or business undertaking. **2** A summary; outline. [L, a look-out, prospect] *5*

pro·tag·o·nist (prō·tag'ə·nist) *n.* **1** The actor who played

the chief part in a Greek drama. **2** A leader in any enterprise or contest. [<Gk. *prōtos* first + *agōnistēs* a contestant, an actor] *6*

pro·te·an (prō'tē·ən, prō·tē'ən) *adj.* Readily assuming different forms or aspects; changeable. [<PROTEUS] *10*

pro·to·col (prō'tə·kol) *n.* **1** The preliminary draft of an official document, as a treaty. **2** The preliminary draft or report of the negotiations and conclusions arrived at by a diplomatic conference, having the force of a treaty when ratified. **3** The rules of diplomatic and state etiquette and ceremony. —*v.i.* To write or form protocols. [<LGk. *prōtokollon* the first glued sheet of a papyrus roll] *9*

pro·vin·cial (prə·vin'shəl) *adj.* **1** Of or characteristic of a province. **2** Confined to a province; rustic. **3** Narrow; unsophisticated; uninformed. —*n.* **1** A native or inhabitant of a province. **2** One who is provincial. —**pro·vin·ci·al·i·ty** (-shē·al'ə·tē) *n.* —**pro·vin'cial·ly** *adv.* *8*

psy·chot·ic (sī·kot'ik) *n.* One suffering from a psychosis —*adj.* Of or characterized by a psychosis. —**psy·chot'i·cal·ly** *adv.* *5*

punc·til·i·ous (pungk·til'ē·əs) *adj.* Very exacting in observing rules or conventions. [<Ital. *puntiglio* small point] —**punc·til'i·ous·ly** *adv.* —**punc·til'i·ous·ness** *n.* *14*

pun·dit (pun'dit) *n.* **1** One who is or assumes the part of an expert in making pronouncements, criticisms, predictions, etc. **2** In India, a Brahmin versed in Sanskrit lore, Hindu religion, etc. [<Skt. *pandita* learned] —**pun'dit·ry** (-rē) *n.* *7*

Pyr·rhic victory (pir'ik) A victory gained at a ruinous cost, such as that of Pyrrhus over the Romans in 279 B.C. *10*

quat·rain (kwot'rān, kwot·rān') *n.* A stanza of four lines. [<F *quatre* four] *8*

quell (kwel) *v.t.* **1** To put down or suppress by force; extinguish. **2** To quiet; allay, as pain. [<OE *cwellan* kill] **quell'er** *n.* *9*

quer·u·lous (kwer'ə·ləs, -yə·ləs) *adj.* **1** Disposed to complain or be fretful; faultfinding. **2** Indicating or expressing a complaint. [<L *queri* complain] —**quer'u·lous·ly** *adv.* —**quer'u·lous·ness** *n.* —**Syn.** 1 carping, captious, disparaging, critical, censorious. *3*

qui·es·cent (kwī·es'ənt, kwē-) *adj.* Being in a state of repose or inaction; quiet; still. [<L *quiescere* be quiet] —**qui·es'cence** *n.* —**qui·es'cent·ly** *adv.* *12*

quix·ot·ic (kwik·sot'ik) *adj.* **1** Pertaining to or like Don Quixote, the hero of a Spanish romance ridiculing knight errantry. **2** Ridiculously chivalrous or romantic; having high but impractical sentiments, aims, etc. —**quix·ot'i·cal·ly** *adv.* —**quix·ot·ism** (kwik'sə·tiz'əm) *n.* *10*

quiz·zi·cal (kwiz'i·kəl) *adj.* **1** Mocking; teasing. **2** Perplexed; puzzled. **3** Queer; odd. —**quiz'zi·cal·ly** *adv.* *12*

rai·son d'ê·tre (re·zôn' de'tr') *French* A reason or excuse for existing. *7*

rau·cous (rô'kəs) *adj.* **1** Rough in sound; hoarse; harsh. **2** Noisy and rowdy. [<L *raucus*] —**rau'cous·ly** *adv.* —**rau'cous·ness** *n.* *13*

re·cal·ci·trant (ri·kal'sə·trənt) *adj.* Not complying; obstinate; rebellious; refractory. —*n.* One who is recalcitrant. [<L *re-* back + *calcitrare* to kick] —**re·cal'ci·trance, re·cal'ci·tran·cy** *n.* *9*

re·course (rē'kôrs, -kōrs, ri·kôrs', -kōrs') *n.* **1** Resort to or application for help or security in trouble. **2** The person or thing resorted to. [<L *recursus* a running back] *1*

re·cur (ri·kûr') *v.i.* **·curred, ·cur·ring 1** To happen again or repeatedly. **2** To come back or return, as to the memory, in conversation, etc. [<L *re-* back + *currere* run] *13*

ref·er·ent (ref′ər·ənt) *n.* Something referred to, esp. the thing to which reference is made in any verbal statement. *14*

re·frac·to·ry (ri·frak′tər·ē) *adj.* **1** Hard to control; stubborn; obstinate. **2** Resisting heat. **3** Resisting treatment, as a disease. —*n. pl.* **·ries 1** A refractory or obstinate person or thing. **2** Any of various highly heat-resistant materials. [<L *refractarius*] —**re·frac′to·ri·ly** *adv.* —**re·frac′to·ri·ness** *n.* *5*

re·ga·li·a (ri·gā′lē·ə, -gāl′yə) *n. pl.* **1** The insignia and emblems of royalty, as the crown, scepter, etc. **2** The distinctive symbols, insignia, etc., of any society, order, or rank. **3** Fine clothes; fancy trappings. *5*

re·gime (ri·zhēm′) *n.* **1** System of government or administration. **2** A particular government or its duration of rule. **3** A social system. **4** REGIMEN. Also **ré·gime** (rā·zhēm′). [<F <L *regimen*] *5*

reg·i·men (rej′ə·mən) *n.* A system of diet, exercise, etc., used for therapeutic purposes. [<L *regimen* <*regere* to rule] *5*

re·gress (ri·gres′) *v.i.* To go back; move backward; return. —*n.* (rē′gres) **1** A going back; return. **2** A return to a less perfect or lower state; retrogression. [<L *regressus,* pp. of *regredi* go back] —**re·gres′sive** *adj.* —**re·gres′sive·ly** *adv.* —**re·gres′sor** *n.* *5*

re·mon·strate (ri·mon′strāt) *v.* **·strat·ed, ·strat·ing** *v.t.* **1** To say or plead in protest or opposition. —*v.i.* **2** To protest; object. [<L *re-* again + *monstrare* show] —**re·mon·stra·tion** (rē′mon·strā′shən, rem′ən-), **re·mon′stra·tor** *n.* —**re·mon′stra·tive** (-strə′tiv) *adj.* *3*

re·morse (ri·môrs′) *n.* The keen or hopeless anguish caused by a sense of guilt; distressing self-reproach. [<LL *remorsus* a biting back] —**re·morse′ful** *adj.* —**re·morse′ful·ly** *adv.* —**re·morse′ful·ness** *n.* *2*

rep·er·toire (rep′ər·twär) *n.* **1** A list of works, as of music or drama, that a company or person is prepared to perform. **2** Such works collectively. **3** The aggregate of devices, methods, etc., used in a particular line of activity: the teacher's *repertoire* of visual aids. [<LL *repertorium* inventory] *12*

re·pine (ri·pīn′) *v.i.* **·pined, ·pin·ing** To be discontented or fretful. [<RE- + PINE²] —**re·pin′er** *n.* *13*

re·sil·ient (ri·zil′yənt) *adj.* **1** Springing back to a former shape or position after being bent, compressed, etc. **2** to recover quickly; buoyant. [<L *resilire* to rebound] —**re·sil′ient·ly** *adv.* *5*

res·pite (res′pit) *n.* **1** Postponement; delay. **2** Temporary relief from labor or effort; an interval of rest. [<Med. L *respectus* delay] *5*

res·tive (res′tiv) *adj.* **1** Restless; fidgety: *The audience grew restive.* **2** Unwilling to submit to control; unruly; balky. [<F *rester* remain, balk] —**res′tive·ly** *adv.* —**res′tive·ness** *n.* *13*

ret·i·cent (ret′ə·sənt) *adj.* **1** Reluctant to speak or speak freely; habitually silent; reserved. **2** Subdued or restrained; shunning bold statement: *reticent* prose. [<L *re-* again + *tacere* be silent] —**ret′i·cence, ret′i·cen·cy** *n.* —**ret′i·cent·ly** *adv.* *4*

ret·ro·gress (ret′rə·gres) *v.i.* **1** To go back to a more primitive or worse condition. [<L *retro-* backward + *gradi* walk] —**ret′ro·gres′sion** *n.* —**ret′ro·gres′sive** *adj.* —**ret′ro·gres′sive·ly** *adv.* *1*

re·ver·ber·ate (ri·vûr′bə·rāt) *v.* **·at·ed, ·at·ing** *v.i.* **1** To resound or reecho. **2** To be reflected or repelled. **3** To rebound or recoil. —*v.t.* **4** To echo back (a sound); reecho. **5** To reflect. [<L *reverberare* strike back, cause to rebound <*re-* back + *verberare* to beat] —**re·ver′ber·ant** *adj.* —**re·ver′ber·a′tor** *n.* *5*

rhet·o·ric (ret′ə·rik) *n.* **1** Skill in the use of language, as in writing or speech. **2** The pretentious use of language. [<Gk. *rhētorikē (technē)* rhetorical (art)] *14*

rib·ald (rib′əld) *adj.* Of or indulging in coarse, vulgar language or jokes. —*n.* A ribald person. [<OF *ribauld*] —**Syn.** *adj.* improper, unseemly, gross, obscene, impure. *2*

ris·i·ble (riz′ə·bəl) *adj.* **1** Having the power of laughing. **2** Of a nature to excite laughter. **3** Pertaining to laughter. [<L *risus,* p.p. of *ridere* to laugh] —**ris′i·bly** *adv.* *13*

sad·ism (sā′diz·əm, sad′iz·əm) *n.* **1** The obtaining of sexual gratification by inflicting pain. **2** A morbid delight in cruelty. [<Comte Donatien de *Sade,* 1740–1814, French writer] —**sad·ist** (sā′dist, sad′ist) *n., adj.* —**sa·dis·tic** (sə·dis′tik, sā-) *adj.* —**sa·dis′ti·cal·ly** *adv.* *10*

sa·ga·cious (sə·gā′shəs) *adj.* **1** Ready and apt to apprehend and to decide on a course; intelligent. **2** Shrewd and practical. [<L *sagax* wise] —**sa·ga′cious·ly** *adv.* —**sa·ga′cious·ness** *n.* —**Syn.** **1** acute, discerning, clear-sighted, keen, perspicacious. *3*

sa·li·ent (sā′lē·ənt) *adj.* **1** Standing out prominently: a *salient* feature. **2** Extending outward; projecting: a *salient* angle. **3** Leaping; springing. —*n.* An extension, as of a fortification or a military line protruding toward the enemy. [<L *salire* to leap] —**sa′li·ence, sa′li·en·cy** *n.* —**sa′li·ent·ly** *adv.* —**Syn.** **1** conspicuous, noticeable, significant. **2** jutting. *13*

sanc·ti·mo·ni·ous (sangk′tə·mō′nē·əs) *adj.* Making ostentatious display or a hypocritical pretense of sanctity. —**sanc′ti·mo′ni·ous·ly** *adv.* —**sanc′ti·mo′ni·ous·ness** *n.* *11*

san·gui·nar·y (sang′gwə·ner′ē) *adj.* **1** Attended with bloodshed. **2** Prone to shed blood; bloodthirsty. [<L *sanguis* blood] —**san′gui·nar′i·ly** *adv.* —**san′gui·nar′i·ness** *n.* *8*

san·guine (sang′gwin) *adj.* **1** Of buoyant disposition; hopeful. **2** Having the color of blood; ruddy: a sanguine complexion. **3** *Obs.* Bloodthirsty; sanguinary. Also **san·guin·e·ous** (sang·gwin′ē·əs). [<L *sanguis* blood] —**san′guine·ly** *adv.* —**san′guine·ness** *n.* —**Syn.** **1** ardent, enthusiastic, optimistic. **2** rubicund. *8*

sar·don·ic (sär·don′ik) *adj.* Scornful or derisive; sneering; mocking; cynical. [<Gk. *sardanios* bitter, scornful] —**sar·don′i·cal·ly** *adv.* —**sar·don′i·cism** *n.* *13*

sat·ur·nine (sat′ər·nīn) *adj.* **1** Having a grave, gloomy, or morose disposition or character. **2** In astrology, born under the supposed dominance of Saturn. [<L *Saturnus* Saturn] —**sat′ur·nine·ly** *adv.* —**sat′ur·nine′ness** *n.* *10*

sa·voir faire (sà·vwàr fâr′) Ability to see and to do the right thing; esp., sophisticated social poise. [F, lit., to know how to act] *7*

schism (siz′əm, skiz′əm) *n.* **1** A division of a church into factions because of differences in doctrine. **2** A splitting into antagonistic groups. [<Gk. *schizein* to split] *12*

sci·on (sī′ən) *n.* **1** A child or descendant. **2** A bud or shoot from a plant or tree, used in grafting. [<OF *cion*] *4*

scrim·shaw (skrim′shô) *n.* **1** The carving and engraving of usu. whalebone or whale ivory, as by American sailors. **2** An article so made. —*v.t.* **1** To make into scrimshaw by carving or engraving. —*v.i.* **2** To create scrimshaw. [?] *11*

scru·pu·lous (skrōo′pyə·ləs) *adj.* **1** Cautious in action for fear of doing wrong; conscientious. **2** Resulting from the exercise of scruples; careful. —**scru′pu·lous·ly** *adv.* —**scru′pu·los′i·ty** (-los′ə·tē), **scru′pu·lous·ness** *n.* — **Syn. 1** ethical, honest, upright. **2** exact, precise.   *1*

sec·u·lar (sek′yə·lər) *adj.* **1** Of or pertaining to this world; temporal; worldly. **2** Not controlled by the church; civil; not ecclesiastical. **3** Not concerned with religion; not sacred: *secular* art. **4** Not bound by monastic vows, and not living in a religious community. **5** Of or describing a trend or process continuing for a long, indefinite period of time. —*n.* **1** A member of the clergy who is not bound by monastic vows and who does not live in a religious community. **2** A layman as distinguished from a member of the clergy. [<L *saeculum* generation, age]   *9*

sen·su·ous (sen′shōo·əs) *adj.* **1** Of, pertaining or appealing to, or perceived or caused by the senses. **2** Keenly appreciative of or susceptible to the pleasures of sensation. —**sen′su·ous·ly** *adv.* —**sen′su·ous·ness** *n.*   *5*

sen·ten·tious (sen·ten′shəs) *adj.* **1** Saying much in few words; terse; pithy. **2** Habitually using or full of aphoristic language. **3** Habitually using or full of moralistic language. [<L *sententia* opinion] —**sen·ten′tious·ly** *adv.* —**sen·ten′tious·ness** *n.*   *6*

se·ques·ter (si·kwes′tər) *v.t.* **1** To place apart; separate. **2** To seclude; withdraw: often used reflexively. **3** *Law* To take (property) into custody until a controversy, claim, etc., is settled. **4** In international law, to confiscate and control (enemy property) by preemption. [<LL *sequestrare* remove, lay aside] —**se·ques′tered** *adj.*   *9*

se·ra·glio (si·ral′yō, -räl′-) *n. pl.* **·glios** **1** That part of a sultan's palace where his harem lives. **2** The palace of a sultan. Also **se·rail** (se·rāl′). [<Ital. *serraglio* an enclosure]   *7*

ser·aph (ser′əf) *n. pl.* **ser·aphs** or **ser·a·phim** (ser′ə·fim) An angel of the highest order, usu. represented as having six wings. [<Heb. *serāphīm*, pl.] —**se·raph·ic** (si·raf′ik) *adj.* —**se·raph′i·cal·ly** *adv.*   *7*

shib·bo·leth (shib′ə·leth) *n.* A test word or pet phrase of a party; a watchword. [<Heb. *shibbōleth*, a word mispronounced by certain Hebrew spies, betraying them as aliens. *Judges* 12:4–6]   *7*

sig·ni·fi·ca·tion (sig′nə·fə·kā′shən) *n.* **1** That which is signified; meaning; sense; import. **2** The act of signifying; communication.   *8*

sil·hou·ette (sil′ōo·et′) *n.* **1** A profile drawing or portrait having its outline filled in with uniform color, usu. black. **2** The outline of a solid figure. —*v.t.* **·et·ted**, **·et·ting** To cause to appear in silhouette; outline. [<Étienne de *Silhouette*, 1709–1767, French minister]   *10*

sim·i·le (sim′ə·lē) *n.* A figure of speech expressing comparison or likeness by the use of such terms as *like* or *as.* [<L *similis* similar] • See METAPHOR.   *8*

si·mo·ny (sī′mə·nē, sim′ə-) *n.* The purchase or sale of sacred things, as ecclesiastical preferment. [<*Simon* (Magus), who offered Peter money for the gift of the Holy Spirit *Acts* 8:9–24]   *10*

si·ne·cure (sī′nə·kyŏor, sin′ə-) *n.* A position or office providing compensation or other benefits but requiring little or no responsibility or effort. [<L *sine* without + *cura* care]   *2*

sin·u·ous (sin′yŏo·əs) *adj..* **1** Characterized by turns or curves; winding; undulating; tortuous: a *sinuous* path. **2** Devious; indirect; not straightforward. [<L *sinus* bend] —**sin′u·**

ous·ly *adv.* —**sin·u·os·i·ty** (sin′yŏo·os′ə·tē), **sin′u·ous·ness** *n.*   *9*

So·crat·ic method (sə·krat′ik, sō-) The method of instruction by questions and answers, as adopted by Socrates in his disputations, leading the pupil either to a foreseen conclusion or to contradict himself.   *10*

sol·e·cism (sol′ə·siz′əm) *n.* **1** A grammatical error or a violation of approved idiomatic usage. **2** Any impropriety or incongruity. [<Gk *soloikos* speaking incorrectly] —**sol′e·cist** *n.* —**sol′e·cis′tic** or **·ti·cal** *adj.*   *10*

spe·cious (spē′shəs) *adj.* Apparently good, right, logical, etc., but actually without merit or foundation: *specious* reasoning. [<L *speciosus* fair] —**spe′cious·ly** *adv.* —**spe′cious·ness** *n.*   *5*

spec·trum (spek′trəm) *n. pl.* **·tra** (-trə) or **·trums** **1** The continuous band of colors observed when a beam of white light is diffracted, as by a prism, according to wavelength, ranging from red, the longest visible rays, to violet, the shortest. **2** Any array of radiant energy ordered according to a varying characteristic, as frequency, wavelength, etc. **3** A band of wave frequencies: the radio *spectrum.* **4** A series or range within limits: a wide *spectrum* of activities. [L, a vision]   *5*

spec·u·late (spek′yə·lāt) *v.i.* **·lat·ed**, **·lat·ing** **1** To weigh mentally or conjecture; ponder; theorize. **2** To make a risky investment with hope of gain. [<L *speculari* look at, examine] —**spec′u·la·tor** *n.* —**spec′u·la·to·ry** (-lə·tôr′ē, -tō′rē) *adj.* —**Syn. 1** guess, presume, surmise, venture, hazard.   *5*

spo·rad·ic (spə·rad′ik) *adj.* **1** Occurring infrequently; occasional. **2** Not widely diffused; occurring in isolated cases: a *sporadic* infection. Also **spo·rad′i·cal.** [<Gk. *sporas* scattered] —**spo·rad′i·cal·ly** *adv.* —**spo·rad′i·cal·ness** *n.* —**Syn. 1** irregular, fitful, spasmodic, intermittent.   *14*

spu·ri·ous (spyŏor′ē·əs) *adj.* **1** Seemingly real or genuine, but actually not; false; counterfeit. **2** Illegitimate, as of birth. [<L *spurius*] —**spu′ri·ous·ly** *adv.* —**spu′ri·ous·ness** *n.*   *8*

stac·ca·to (stə·kä′tō) *adj.* **1** *Music* Played, or to be played, with brief pauses between each note. **2** Marked by abrupt, sharp sounds or emphasis: a *staccato* style of speaking. —*adv.* So as to be staccato. —*n.* Something staccato. [<Ital. *staccare* detach]   *6*

stat·u·to·ry (stach′ə·tôr′ē, -tō′rē) *adj.* **1** Pertaining to a statute. **2** Created by or dependent upon legislative enactment. —**stat′u·tor′i·ly** *adv.*   *2*

sten·to·ri·an (sten·tôr′ē·ən, -tō′rē-) *adj.* Extremely loud. [<*Stentor*, a herald in the *Iliad*, famous for his loud voice] —**sten·to′ri·an·ly** *adv.*   *10*

stig·ma (stig′mə) *n. pl.* **stig·ma·ta** (stig·mä′tə, stig′mə·tə) or (*esp. for def. 2*) **stig·mas** **1** A mark of disgrace. **2** *Bot.* That part of a pistil which receives the pollen. **3** *Biol.* Any spot or small opening. **4** A spot or scar on the skin. **5** *Med.* Any physical sign of diagnostic value. **6** *pl.* The wounds that Christ received at the Crucifixion. [L, mark, brand] — **stig·mat·ic** (-mat′ik), **·ic·al** *adj.* —**Syn. 1** blemish, blot, spot, taint, stain.   *9*

sto·ic (stō′ik) *n.* A person apparently unaffected by pleasure or pain. —*adj.* Indifferent to pleasure or pain; impassive: also **sto′i·cal.** [<STOIC] —**sto′i·cal·ly** *adv.* —**sto′i·cal·ness** *n.*   *10*

stol·id (stol′id) *adj.* Expressing no feeling; impassive. [<L *stolidus* dull] —**sto·lid·i·ty** (stə·lid′ə·tē), **stol′id·ness** *n.* —**stol′id·ly** *adv.*   *12*

stri·dent (strīd′nt) *adj.* Having a loud and harsh sound; grating. [<L *stridere* to creak] **—stri′dence, stri′den·cy** *n.* **—stri′dent·ly** *adv.* 3

sub·jec·tive (səb·jek′tiv) *adj.* 1 Of or belonging to that which is within the mind and not subject to independent verification. 2 Expressing very personal feelings or opinions: a *subjective* piece of writing. 3 Highly influenced by the emotions or by prejudice. 4 *Med.* Of the kind of which only the patient is aware: said of symptoms. 5 *Gram.* Designating the case and function of the subject of a sentence. **—sub·jec′tive·ly** *adv.* **—sub·jec′tive·ness, sub·jec·tiv·i·ty** (sub′jek·tiv′ə·tē) *n.* 14

sub·ser·vi·ent (səb·sûr′vē·ənt) *adj.* 1 Servile; obsequious; truckling. 2 Adapted to promote some end or purpose, esp. in a subordinate capacity. **—n.** One who or that which subserves. **—sub·ser′vi·ent·ly** *adv.* **—sub·ser′vi·ent·ness, sub·ser′vi·ence, sub·ser′vi·en·cy** *n.* 1

sub·tle (sut′l) *adj.* **sub·tler** (sut′lər, sut′l·ər), **sub·tlest** 1 Not easily detected; elusive; delicate: a *subtle* aroma. 2 Characterized by or requiring keenness of mind, vision, hearing, etc.: *subtle* humor; *subtle* variations in sound. 3 Very skillful or ingenious: a *subtle* craftsman. 4 Not direct or obvious: a *subtle* hint. [<L *subtilis* fine] **—sub′tle·ness** *n.* **—sub′tly** *adv.* 2

sul·len (sul′ən) *adj.* 1 Showing ill-humor, as from dwelling upon a grievance; morose; glum. 2 Depressing; somber: *sullen* clouds. 3 Slow; sluggish. 4 Melancholy; mournful. [<AF *solein* sullen, alone] **—sul′len·ly** *adv.* **—sul′len·ness** *n.* **—Syn.** 1 gloomy, sad, sulky, moody. 14

su·per·cil·i·ous (sōō′pər·sil′ē·əs) *adj.* Haughtily contemptuous; arrogant. [<L *supercilium* eyebrow, pride] **—su′per·cil′i·ous·ly** *adv.* **—su′per·cil′i·ous·ness** *n.* 9

su·pine (sōō·pīn′, sə-) *adj.* 1 Lying on the back, or with the face turned upward. 2 Having no interest or care; listless. [<L *supinus*] **—su·pine′ly** *adv.* **—su·pine′ness** *n.* 13

syb·a·rite (sib′ə·rīt) *n.* A person devoted to luxury or sensuality; voluptuary. [<*Sybaris* an ancient Greek city in southern Italy] **—syb·a·rit·ic** (sib′ə·rit′ik), **syb′a·rit′i·cal** *adj.* **—syb′a·rit′i·cal·ly** *adv.* 10

syl·lo·gism (sil′ə·jiz′əm) *n.* 1 *Logic* A form of reasoning consisting of three propositions. The first two propositions, called *premises*, have one term in common furnishing a relation between the two other terms, which are linked in the third, called the *conclusion*. Example: All men are mortal *(major premise)*; kings are men *(minor premise)*; therefore, kings are mortal *(conclusion)*. 2 Reasoning that makes use of this form; deduction. [<Gk. *syn-* together + *logizesthai* infer] **—syl′lo·gis′tic, syl′lo·gis′ti·cal** *adj.* **—syl′lo·gis′ti·cal·ly** *adv.* 8

sy·nec·do·che (si·nek′də·kē) *n.* A figure of speech in which a part stands for a whole or a whole for a part, a material for the thing made of it, etc., as *bronze* for a *statue*. [<Gk. *syn-* together + *ekdechesthai* take from] **—syn·ec·doch·ic** (sin′ek·dok′ik), **syn′ec·doch′i·cal** *adj.* 14

ta·boo (tə·bōō′, ta-) *n. pl.* **·boos** 1 A religious or social prohibition against touching or mentioning someone or something or doing something because such persons or things are considered sacred, dangerous, etc. 2 The system or practice of such prohibitions. 3 Any restriction or ban based on custom or convention. **—adj.** Restricted, prohibited, or excluded by taboo, custom, or convention. **—v.t.** 1 To place under taboo. 2 To avoid; ostracize as taboo. Also **ta·bu′.** [<Tongan] 7

tac·it (tas′it) *adj.* 1 Existing, inferred, or implied without being directly stated. 2 Not spoken; silent. 3 Emitting no sound. [<L *tacitus*, pp. of *tacere* be silent] **—tac′it·ly** *adv.* **—tac′it·ness** *n.* 3

tac·i·turn (tas′ə·tûrn) *adj.* Habitually silent or reserved. [<L *tacitus*. See TACIT.] **—tac·i·tur·ni·ty** (tas′ə·tûr′nə·tē) *n.* **—tac′i·turn·ly** *adv.* **—Syn.** uncommunicative, reticent. 2

te·mer·i·ty (tə·mer′ə·tē) *n.* Foolish boldness; rashness; foolhardiness. [<L *temeritas*] **—Syn.** audacity, heedlessness, recklessness, presumption, venturesomeness. 5

tem·po·ral[1] (tem′pər·əl) *adj.* 1 Of or pertaining to the present as opposed to a future life. 2 Worldly; material, as opposed to spiritual. 3 Ephemeral; transitory, as opposed to eternal. 4 Of or relating to time. 5 *Gram.* Of, pertaining to, or denoting time: *temporal* conjunctions. [<L *tempus, temporis* time] **—tem·po·ral·i·ty** (tem′pə·ral′ə·tē), **tem′po·ral·ness** *n.* **—tem′po·ral·ly** *adv.*

tem·po·ral[2] (tem′pər·əl) *adj.* Of, pertaining to, or situated at the temple or temples of the head. 4

ten·ta·tive (ten′tə·tiv) *adj.* 1 Not definite or final; subject to change. 2 Somewhat uncertain or timid: a *tentative* glance. [<L *tentatus*, pp. of *tentare* to try, probe] **—ten′ta·tive·ly** *adv.* **—ten′ta·tive·ness** *n.* 4

ten·u·ous (ten′yōō·əs) *adj.* 1 Without much substance; slight; weak: *tenuous* arguments. 2 Thin; slender. 3 Having slight density; rare. [<L *tenuis* thin] **—ten′u·ous·ly** *adv.* **—ten′u·ous·ness, ten·u·i·ty** (te·n°yōō′ə·tē, tə-) *n.* 2

thes·pi·an (thes′pē·ən) *adj.* Often cap. Of or relating to drama; dramatic. **—n.** An actor or actress. [<*Thespis*, 6th-c. B.C. Gk. poet] 10

thwart (thwôrt) *v.t.* To obstruct (a plan, a person, etc.) as by interposing an obstacle; frustrate. **—n.** 1 An oarsman's seat extending athwart a boat. 2 A brace athwart a canoe. **—adj.** Lying, moving, or extending across something; transverse. **—adv. & prep.** Athwart. [<ON *thvert*, neut. of *thverr* transverse] **—thwart′er** *n.* 3

ti·rade (tī′rād, tī·rād′) *n.* A prolonged declamatory outpouring, as of censure. [<Ital. *tirata* a volley] 4

tor·pid (tôr′pid) *adj.* 1 Having lost sensibility or power of motion, partially or wholly, as a hibernating animal; dormant; numb. 2 Slow to act or respond; sluggish. 3 Apathetic; spiritless; dull. [<L *torpidus* < *torpere* be numb] **—tor·pid·i·ty** (tôr·pid′ə·tē), **tor′pid·ness** *n.* **—tor′pid·ly** *adv.* 5

to·tal·i·tar·i·an (tō·tal′ə·târ′ē·ən) *adj.* 1 Designating or characteristic of a government controlled exclusively by one party or faction that suppresses political dissent by force or intimidation and whose power to control the economic, social, and intellectual life of the individual is virtually unlimited. 2 Tyrannical; despotic. **—n.** An adherent of totalitarian government. **—to·tal′i·tar′i·an·ism** *n.* 5

to·tem (tō′təm) *n.* 1 An animal, plant, or other natural object believed to be ancestrally related to a tribe, clan, or family group, and serving as its emblem, as among the North American Indians. 2 A representation of such an emblem. [<Algon.] **—to·tem·ic** (tō·tem′ik) *adj.* **—to′tem·ism** *n.* 5

tox·ic (tok′sik) *adj.* 1 Poisonous. 2 Due to or caused by poison or a toxin. [<Gk. *toxicon (pharmakon)* (a poison) for arrows <*toxon* a bow] **—tox′i·cal·ly** *adv.* **—tox·ic′i·ty** (-sis′ə·tē) *n.* 8

tran·scend (tran·send′) *v.t.* 1 To go or pass beyond the limits of: knowledge that *transcends* reason. 2 To rise above in excellence or degree. —*v.i.* **3** To be surpassing; excel. [<L *trans-* beyond, over + *scandere* to climb] *9*

trav·es·ty (trav′is·tē) *n. pl.* **-ties 1** A grotesque imitation, as of a lofty subject; burlesque. **2** A distorted or absurd rendering or example, as if in mockery: a *travesty* of justice. —*v.t.* **·tied, ·ty·ing** To make a travesty of; burlesque; parody. [<Ital. *travestire* to disguise] *13*

truc·u·lent (truk′yə·lənt) *adj.* Of savage character; cruel; ferocious. [<L *trux, trucis* fierce] —**truc·u·lence** (truk′yə·ləns), **truc′u·len·cy** *n.* —**truc′u·lent·ly** *adv.* —**Syn.** barbarous, brutal, fierce, ruthless, vicious. *13*

tryst (trist, trīst) *n.* **1** An appointment to meet at a specified time or place. **2** The meeting place agreed upon. **3** The meeting so agreed upon. [<OF *triste, tristre* an appointed station in hunting] *1*

tu·mid (t′ōō′mid) *adj.* **1** Swollen; enlarged; protuberant. **2** Inflated or pompous. [<L *tumidus* <*tumere* swell] —**tu·mid′i·ty, tu′mid·ness** *n.* *3*

tur·bid (tûr′bid) *adj.* **1** Muddy or opaque: a *turbid* stream. **2** Dense; heavy: *turbid* clouds of smoke. **3** Confused; disturbed. [<L *turbidus* <*turbare* to trouble] —**tur′bid·ly** *adv.* —**tur′bid·ness, tur·bid·i·ty** (tûr·bid′ə·tē) *n.* • **turbid, turgid** Because these words sound alike, they are often confused: *Turbid* usu. refers to water, smoke, etc., so filled with sediment or particles as to be opaque. *Turgid* means abnormally swollen or inflated. *15*

tur·gid (tûr′jid) *adj.* **1** Unnaturally distended; swollen. **2** Using high-flown language; bombastic: *turgid* prose. [<L *turgere* swell] —**tur·gid·i·ty** (tər·jid′ə·tē), **tur′gid·ness** *n.* —**tur′gid·ly** *adv.* • See TURBID. *15*

ty·coon (tī·kōōn′) *n.* **1** *Informal* A wealthy and powerful business leader. **2** A Japanese shogun. [<Japanese *taikun* a mighty lord] *7*

u·biq·ui·tous (yōō·bik′wə·təs) *adj.* Existing, or seeming to exist, everywhere at once; omnipresent. —**u·biq′ui·tous·ly** *adv.* —**u·biq′ui·tous·ness** *n.* *1*

ul·te·ri·or (ul·tir′ē·ər) *adj.* **1** Not so pertinent as something else: *ulterior* considerations. **2** Intentionally unrevealed; hidden: *ulterior* motives. **3** Later in time, or secondary in importance; following; succeeding. **4** Lying beyond or on the farther side of a certain bounding line. [<L, compar. of *ulter* beyond] —**ul·te′ri·or·ly** *adv.* *1*

un·con·scion·a·ble (un·kon′shən·ə·bəl) *adj.* **1** Unbelievably bad, wrong, inequitable, etc.: an *unconscionable* error. **2** Wholly unscrupulous. —**un·con′scion·a·ble·ness** *n.* —**un·con′scion·a·bly** *adv.* *12*

un·couth (un·kōōth′) *adj.* **1** Marked by awkwardness or oddity; outlandish. **2** Coarse, boorish, or unrefined, as in manner or speech. [<OE *uncūth* unknown] —**un·couth′ly** *adv.* —**un·couth′ness** *n.* *3*

unc·tu·ous (ungk′chōō·əs) *adj.* **1** Like an unguent; greasy. **2** Greasy or soapy to the touch, as certain minerals. **3** Characterized by excessive or affected sincerity, sympathy, concern, etc. **4** Unduly smooth or suave in speech or manner. **5** Having plasticity, as clay. [<L *unctum* ointment, orig. neut. p.p. of *ungere* anoint] —**unc′tu·ous·ly** *adv.* —**unc′tu·ous·ness, unc·tu·os′i·ty** (-chōō·os′ə·tē) *n.* *2*

un·du·late (un′dyə·lāt, -jə-) *v.* **·lat·ed, ·lat·ing** *v.t.* **1** To cause to move like a wave or in waves. **2** To give a wavy appearance or surface to. —*v.i.* **3** To move like a wave or waves. **4** To have a wavy form or appearance. —*adj.* (-lit, -lāt) Having a wavelike appearance, surface, or markings: also **un′du·lat′ed.** [<L *unda* wave] *5*

un·gain·ly (un·gān′lē) *adj.* **1** Awkward; clumsy. **2** Not attractive. —**un·gain′li·ness** *n.* *3*

u·nique (yōō·nēk′) *adj.* **1** Being the only one of its kind; single; sole. **2** Being without equal; unparalleled. **3** Very unusual or remarkable; exceptional, extraordinary, etc. [<L *unicus* < *unus* one] —**u·nique′ly** *adv.* —**u·nique′ness** *n.* *2*

u·til·i·tar·i·an (yōō·til′ə·târ′ē·ən) *adj.* **1** Of or pertaining to utility; esp., placing utility above beauty, the amenities of life, etc. **2** Of, pertaining.to, or advocating utilitarianism. —*n.* An advocate of utilitarianism. *3*

ux·o·ri·ous (uk·sôr′ē·əs, -sō′rē-, ug·zôr′ē-, -zō′rē-) *adj.* Excessively devoted to or dominated by one's wife. [<L *uxor* wife] —**ux·o′ri·ous·ly** *adv.* —**ux·o′ri·ous·ness** *n.* *9*

vac·u·ous (vak′yōō·əs) *adj.* **1** Having no contents; empty. **2** Lacking intelligence; blank. [<L *vacuus*] —**vac′u·ous·ly** *adv.* —**vac′u·ous·ness** *n.* *2*

va·gar·y (və̄′gə·rē, və·gâr′ē) *n. pl.* **·gar·ies** A wild fancy; extravagant notion. [<L *vagari* wander] *3*

val·id (val′id) *adj.* **1** Based on facts or evidence; sound: a *valid* argument. **2** Legally binding: a *valid* will. [<L *validus* powerful] —**val′id·ly** *adv.* —**va·lid·i·ty** (və·lid′ə·tē), **val′id·ness** *n.* *3*

vap·id (vap′id, vā′pəd) *adj.* **1** Having lost sparkle and flavor. **2** Flat; insipid. [<L *vapidus* insipid] —**va·pid·i·ty** (və·pid′ə·tē), **vap′id·ness** *n.* —**vap′id·ly** *adv.* *3*

var·i·ant (vâr′ē·ənt) *adj.* **1** Varying; differing, esp. differing from a standard or type. **2** *Archaic* Variable; changeable. —*n.* **1** A person or thing that differs from another in form only. **2** A different spelling, pronunciation, or form of the same word. *8*

ve·he·ment (vē′ə·mənt) *adj.* **1** Arising from or marked by strong feeling or passion. **2** Acting with great force; violent. [<L *vehemens, -entis* impetuous, rash] —**ve′he·mence, ve′he·men·cy** *n.* —**ve′he·ment·ly** *adv.* —**Syn. 1** ardent, fervent, zealous, fierce. **2** energetic, forceful, intense, powerful. *9*

ve·nal (vē′nəl) *adj.* **1** Capable of being corrupted or bribed. **2** Characterized by corruption or bribery. [<L *venum* sale] —**ve·nal·i·ty** (vē·nal′ə·tē) *n.* —**ve′nal·ly** *adv.* *15*

ven·det·ta (ven·det′ə) *n.* Private warfare or feud, as in revenge for a murder, injury, etc. [<L *vindicta* vengeance] *7*

ve·ni·al (vē′nē·əl, vēn′yəl) *adj.* So slight or trivial as to be overlooked, as a fault. [<L *venia* forgiveness, mercy] —**ve′ni·al′i·ty** (-al′ə·tē), **ve′ni·al·ness** *n.* —**ve′ni·al·ly** *adv.* —**Syn.** excusable, forgivable, pardonable. *15*

ver·ti·go (vûr′tə·gō) *n. pl.* **·goes** or **ver·tig·i·nes** (vər·tij′ə·nēz) A disorder in which a person or his surroundings seem to whirl about in such a way as to make the person dizzy and usu. sick. [L, lit., a turning around] *3*

ves·tige (ves′tij) *n.* **1** A trace of something absent, lost, or gone. **2** *Biol.* A remnant of an organ that is no longer functional. [<F <L *vestigium* a footprint] —**Syn. 1** hint, remnant, tinge, touch. *5*

vir·tu·o·so (vûr′chōō·ō′sō) *n. pl.* **·si** (-sē) or **·sos 1** A master of technique in some fine art, esp. in musical performance. **2** A knowledgeable collector or lover of curios or works of art. —*adj.* Of or characteristic of a virtuoso. [<LL *virtuosus* full of excellence] *7*

vo·ra·cious (vô·rā′shəs, vō-, və-) *adj.* **1** Eating with greediness; ravenous. **2** Very eager, as in some desire; insatiable. **3** Immoderate: a *voracious* appetite. [<L *vorax* < *vorare* devour] —**vo·ra′cious·ly** *adv.* —**vo·rac·i·ty** (-ras′ə·tē), **vo·ra′cious·ness** *n.* *1*

war·y (wâr′ē) *adj.* **war·i·er, war·i·est 1** Carefully watching and guarding. **2** Shrewd; wily. [<OE *wær*] **—war′i·ly** *adv.* **—war′i·ness** *n.*   *4*

whim·si·cal (ʰwim′zi·kəl) *adj.* **1** Capricious; fanciful; unpredictable. **2** Odd; fantastic; quaint. **—whim·si·cal′i·ty** (-kal′ə·tē) (*pl.* ·**ties**), **whim′si·cal·ness** *n.* **—whim′si·cal·ly** *adv.*   *2*

wind·fall (wind′fôl′) *n.* **1** Something, as ripening fruit, brought down by the wind. **2** A piece of unexpected good fortune.   *2*

wry (rī) *adj.* **wri·er, wri·est 1** Bent to one side or out of position; contorted; askew. **2** Made by twisting or distorting the features: a *wry* smile. **3** Distorted or warped, as in interpretation or meaning. **4** Somewhat perverse or ironic: *wry* humor. —*v.t.* **wried, wry·ing** To twist; contort. [<OE *wrīgian* move, tend] **—wry′ly** *adv.* **—wry′ness** *n.*   *2*

xen·o·pho·bi·a (zen′ə·fō′bē·ə, zē′nə-) *n.* Dislike or fear of strangers or foreigners. [<Gk. *xenos* a stranger + -PHOBIA] **—xen′o·phob′ic** *adj.*   *1*

zeal·ot (zel′ət) *n.* One who is zealous, esp. to an immoderate degree; partisan, fanatic, etc. **—zeal′ot·ry** *n.*   *1*

Index